The Youth Unemployment Crisis

Recent Titles in the

CONTEMPORARY WORLD ISSUES
Series

Books in the **Contemporary World Issues** series address vital issues in today's society such as genetic engineering, pollution, and biodiversity. Written by professional writers, scholars, and nonacademic experts, these books are authoritative, clearly written, up-to-date, and objective. They provide a good starting point for research by high school and college students, scholars, and general readers as well as by legislators, businesspeople, activists, and others.

Each book, carefully organized and easy to use, contains an overview of the subject, a detailed chronology, biographical sketches, facts and data and/or documents and other primary source material, a forum of authoritative perspective essays, annotated lists of print and nonprint resources, and an index.

Readers of books in the Contemporary World Issues series will find the information they need in order to have a better understanding of the social, political, environmental, and economic issues facing the world today.

The Youth Unemployment Crisis

A REFERENCE HANDBOOK

Christina G. Villegas

An Imprint of ABC-CLIO, LLC
Santa Barbara, California • Denver, Colorado

Library of Congress Cataloging-in-Publication Data

Names: Villegas, Christina G., author.

Title: The youth unemployment crisis : a reference handbook / Christina G. Villegas.

Description: Santa Barbara, California : ABC-CLIO, [2019] | Series: Contemporary world issues | Includes bibliographical references and index.

Identifiers: LCCN 2018035506 (print) | LCCN 2018037823 (ebook) | ISBN 9781440859755 (ebook) | ISBN 9781440859748 (alk. paper)

Subjects: LCSH: Unemployed youth—United States. | Youth—United States—Social conditions.

Classification: LCC HD6273 (ebook) | LCC HD6273 .V55 2019 (print) | DDC 331.3/413793—dc23

LC record available at https://lccn.loc.gov/2018035506

ISBN: 978-1-4408-5974-8 (print)
      978-1-4408-5975-5 (ebook)

23 22 21 20 19   1 2 3 4 5

This book is also available as an eBook.

ABC-CLIO
An Imprint of ABC-CLIO, LLC

ABC-CLIO, LLC
130 Cremona Drive, P.O. Box 1911
Santa Barbara, California 93116–1911
www.abc-clio.com

This book is printed on acid-free paper ∞

Manufactured in the United States of America

Contents

Youth unemployment has become one of the most pressing issues in contemporary American life. Even prior to the housing collapse and subsequent economic downturn in the latter part of the first decade of the 2000s, youth unemployment rates were on the rise. The Great Recession, following the financial crisis of 2007–2008, led to skyrocketing unemployment rates in every demographic, but youth were among the hardest hit. Jobs once considered "starter jobs" because they did not require experience and paid lower wages became more attractive to older workers with more skills and experience. As teenagers and young adults found it increasingly hard to gain a foothold in the job market, the unemployment rate among youth, aged 16 to 24, grew to nearly three times the national average of prime-age workers. As a result, many youth resorted to moving back in with their parents, living in poverty, or giving up on the job search altogether.

In spite of the economic recovery of recent years, the youth unemployment rate continues to hover at or more than double the general rate. Moreover, the unemployment rate for youth does not even included the large numbers of young workers who have stopped looking for work altogether and are not engaged in education or training to improve their chance of employment in the future. This should cause great concern. Long-term youth unemployment and disconnection from the workforce present substantial immediate and long-term fiscal and social challenges. Young people who are unemployed or disconnected from the workforce will spend years trying to catch up financially and will miss out on the valuable work experience, job training, and social connections obtained by the employed. The untapped employment potential of young people additionally results in billions of dollars of uncollected taxes and increased social safety net spending. Research additionally shows that unemployed and disconnected youth are more likely to suffer from a range of pathologies, to participate in harmful, risky, or delinquent behaviors and to generally disengage from their communities.

The Youth Unemployment Crisis: A Reference Handbook is a valuable resource for students and general readers seeking to identify the key issues of the crisis. The book examines the scope and nature of youth unemployment in America and presents a balanced discussion of various aspects of the crisis, including its evolution, contributing factors, consequences, and proposed responses from the public and private sectors. It also provides a listing of key actors and resources as a foundation for further research and engagement of the topic.

The Youth Unemployment Crisis is organized into seven chapters. Chapter 1, "Background and History," highlights the importance of the topic by reviewing the scope and nature of youth unemployment in America. It introduces key concepts and explores the history of youth in the labor force, focusing on key moments along the youth unemployment timeline. It then examines the social and economic contexts in which youth unemployment is high and discusses various factors that may be contributing to the crisis.

Chapter 2, "Problems, Controversies, and Solutions," outlines the most problematic immediate and long-term consequences of high rates of youth unemployment and disconnection. It further addresses efforts taken by government and private sector leaders to combat these problems and discusses proposed solutions to the crisis of youth unemployment and disconnection.

Chapter 3, "Perspectives," includes nine essays written by authors from a variety of viewpoints and professional backgrounds on a range of topics related to the issue of youth employment. These essays are intended to supplement and enrich the presentation of the crisis laid out in Chapters 1 and 2.

Chapter 4, "Profiles," lists and describes key governmental and nongovernmental organizations involved in a wide array of efforts to combat youth unemployment and disconnectedness.

Chapter 5, "Data and Documents," offers data and primary source documents to provide readers with firsthand information on the following: Who is unemployed, and what patterns are emerging? Who or what is responsible, and what can be learned from this crisis? And, how can such a crisis be solved, and in the future, prevented?

Chapter 6, "Resources," provides an annotated list of selected books, articles, and reports on a variety of topics related to youth employment and unemployment, which offers readers a starting point for further research. A few nonprint sources are listed and annotated as well.

Chapter 7, "Chronology," offers a concise timeline of defining moments and major events affecting youth employment in the United States.

The book concludes with a glossary of key terms relating to the youth unemployment crisis.

I would like to thank Catherine Lafuente and Robin Tutt of ABC-CLIO who assisted me in various stages of this project and Martha Elwell, who reviewed drafts of several of the chapters. I am additionally grateful to Marilyn Gareis, the administrative support coordinator for the political science department at California State University, San Bernardino, for her assistance in various administrative tasks and to the Institute for Child Development and Family Relations and the Faculty Center for Excellence for supporting the publication of this manuscript with funded writing time.

The Youth Unemployment Crisis

Introduction: The Nature and Scope of Youth Unemployment

America has long been referred to as the land of opportunity based on the possibility for economic and social upward mobility. A generation ago, it was generally assumed that by the time children reached adulthood they would exceed their parents' standard of living at any given age in terms of income and net worth. Unfortunately, for many of today's youth the likelihood of such upward mobility is becoming rarer. As millennials (the generation that includes individuals born after 1980 and before 2000) have come of age over the past decade, a growing body of evidence suggests that they are less financially secure than their parents were at the same age (Allison 2017). Additionally troublesome, the gap in economic well-being between the young and the old is greater than ever before, with older generations enjoying greater home value appreciation, higher incomes, and lower unemployment rates (Fry et al. 2011). Moreover, a growing body of research shows that today's youth

---

An unemployed college student protests as a part of the Occupy Wall Street demonstration in New York City on September 27, 2011. Although a strong correlation still exists between educational attainment and success, large numbers of college graduates—saddled with debt—find themselves unemployed, underemployed, or employed in jobs that do not require a degree. (Roberta Munoz/Dreamstime.com)

are taking much longer than past generations to leave home and gain financial independence.

The decline in upward mobility and economic independence among America's youth is driven by several factors, but a primary element is most certainly the failure of many youth to establish and maintain a consistent presence in the workforce. Over the past two decades, youth in America have encountered greatly diminished employment prospects. In spite of the economic growth and job creation of the past several years, young Americans between the ages of 16 to 24 continue to experience unemployment at nearly twice the national average (Bureau of Labor Statistics 2018a). Additionally, although a strong correlation still exists between educational attainment and success, large numbers of college graduates—saddled with debt—are underemployed or choosing to work in occupations that do not require a degree or are below their skill level (Kroger and Gould 2017). This unfortunate state of affairs has significant implications for the nation's future economic and social well-being—as even short bouts of unemployment or under-productivity can negatively impact an individual's future economic stability and potential for upward mobility.

To better understand the nature and scope of the employment crisis facing the nation's youth it is useful to clarify a few terms. The employment-to-population ratio signifies the proportion of individuals in the population at large who are currently employed. A high employment-to-population ratio is generally a good indicator that jobs are readily available to those seeking work. The unemployment rate refers to those who are not currently employed but are participating in the labor force by actively seeking a job—sending out resumes, filling out applications, interviewing for positions, and so on. Although the unemployment rate is customarily used to signify whether or not people who desire employment are able to find it, the rate is not always an accurate indicator since it does not include the percentage of people who have become discouraged and have stopped looking for work and/or have decided to pursue other options, such as education or full-time parenthood.

The labor force participation rate includes both those individuals who are employed and those who are unemployed but are actively looking for work. The labor force participation rate, which excludes those who have stopped looking for employment, is one means of identifying the level of interest that individuals have in working. As with the unemployment rate, however, labor force participation rates might decline not from a lack of interest in work, but because those who desire to work have become discouraged and have given up the search for employment. Furthermore, a high labor force participation rate masks the number of youth who fall into the category of underemployed or "involuntary" part-time workers, meaning they have secured part-time employment, but desire to work full time. Consequently, unemployment numbers alone often understate the employment problem facing today's youth. An accurate study of youth unemployment should examine not only the unemployment and underemployment rate, but also the number of youth who have left the labor force altogether and are therefore not counted in the number of either the employed or the unemployed.

Over the past decade the labor force participation rate for younger workers has undergone a steady decline, while at the same time older people have started to remain in the workforce longer than ever before. Older workers who have officially "retired" from their career are increasingly taking on part-time or lower-wage jobs to supplement their retirement and social security benefits. In 2009, the labor force participation rate for individuals over the age of 55 surpassed the labor force participation rate of teens, and by 2015 the number of employed persons over the age of 55 was seven times greater than the number of employed teens (Bureau of Labor 2017). In 2014, the youth labor force participation rate dropped to the lowest level since the government started keeping track in 1948 (Furchtgott-Roth and Meyer 2015).

A decrease in the youth labor participation rate is not always a bad sign. For example, it could result from youth exiting the workforce to participate in activities that will develop their human capital such as enrollment in summer school, college, or other educational options. As educators, parents, and policy makers emphasize the value of education, increased enrollment may incidentally cause a decrease in labor force participation. Several indicators suggest, however, that many young people are dropping out of the labor market for reasons other than augmented school enrollment. One problem with using higher enrollment rates to explain a decrease in labor force participation is that students and workers are not always separate and distinct groups. Many young people who enroll in education continue to participate in the workforce to support themselves, to finance their education, and to gain work experience. Secondly, even if there were no overlap between individuals attending school and participating in the workforce, the decline in the labor market participation rate among youth has been greater than the increase in educational enrollment rates. In the first two years of the Great Recession, for instance, youth enrollment in high school and college increased by 861,000, but youth labor force participation decreased by 1.5 million (Edwards and Hertel-Fernandez 2010). This suggests that a large number of youth have become disconnected. That is, they have not only given up looking for work, but they are also failing to participate in education or training programs that might improve their opportunity to reconnect in the future.

Disconnected youth are a primary concern of those studying youth unemployment. Without attachment to school or work, disconnected youth risk missing out long-term on the educational and employment experiences necessary to transition into successful adulthood. Disconnected youth are also more likely than their peers to lack familial and community support systems that provide potential connections for employment and housing and financial assistance. They are, consequently, at the greatest risk of suffering negative outcomes associated with bouts of unemployment, including poverty, substance abuse, and criminal behavior. Although the numbers fluctuate from year to year, a broad reading of the numbers reveals that an average of one in seven American youth have become disconnected or disengaged from education and the workforce. Even based on a more narrowly defined interpretation of disconnection—which includes only those who have not worked or attended school at any time during the previous year and who are not parenting while married to a connected spouse—over 6 percent of noninstitutionalized youth are disconnected and many more are at risk of disconnection (Fernandes-Alcantara 2015).

In effort to provide a foundation for further understanding the nature, scope, and implications of the youth unemployment crisis in the United States, this chapter will examine key moments in the crisis and the socioeconomic contexts in which it is most prevalent. The chapter will conclude with an analysis of various factors that may be contributing to youth unemployment, underemployment, and disconnection in the United States.

Key Moments

Over the past two centuries, the United States has experienced major structural shifts in the way people have lived and worked that have directly impacted youth. Prior to the mid-1800s, careers were almost entirely inherited callings. Children were expected to follow in their parents' footsteps. They would, therefore, receive firsthand parental training from a young age in the line of work they would engage in throughout their lifetime. By the turn of the 20th century, it was becoming more and more customary for individuals to choose their own vocation. Once young people had established a career, however, that career would more than likely define their life until retirement. From the post–World War II era through the late 1970s, when the United States began to experience a rapid decline in manufacturing accompanied by a wave of technological change, it was typical even for those with only a high school diploma to find stable, long-term employment and to work their way into a middle-class lifestyle.

This is no longer the case for many of America's youth. The upward trajectory of youth participation in the labor force, employment, and wages following World War II began a decades' long decline in the 1980s. By the early 2000s, it was clear that the job market was becoming less accessible to young workers as the employment-to-population ratio of young people steadily eroded in spite of economic growth. By 2007, the youth labor force participation rate had fallen to 59.4 percent, down from 68.8 percent in 2000 (Congressional Research Service [CRS] 2015).

The Great Recession, following the financial crisis of 2007–2008, exacerbated negative youth employment trends. While lawmakers largely focused policy making on assisting retirees and prime-age workers, young workers were the most adversely affected in terms of declining employment and labor force participation rates. Although the recession officially ended in June 2009, young people continued to fare poorly in the labor market. By April 2010, the unemployment rate of youth had soared to an all-time high, peaking at 19.6 percent. In 2014 the labor force participation rate was 47.6 percent for youth compared to a rate of 76.7 percent for prime-age workers and the youth unemployment rate was 13.4 percent compared to a rate of 5.2 percent for prime-age workers (CRS 2015). The employment situation for teenagers, aged 16 to 19, was even worse. In October 2009, teenagers experienced an unemployment rate of 27.6 percent, the highest number on record since 1948 (Edwards and Hertel-Fernandez 2010). In addition, between 2000 and 2011 the nation experienced a great reversal in employment rates based on age group. Whereas the teen employment rate decreased dramatically during this time period, the employment rate of those aged 55 to 74 increased fairly substantially, as older workers with higher levels of education and more competitive job experience delayed retirement (Sum et al. 2014).

From 2015 to 2018, the nation experienced significant growth in gross domestic production and a parallel increase in the number of available payroll jobs. Correspondingly, labor force participation and employment rates have improved for youth. Despite signs of recovery, however, several factors indicate that it is too soon to celebrate. Improvement in the youth unemployment rate continues to lag, remaining twice as high as the national average. Teens, in particular, are continuing to experience extraordinary difficulty finding part-time work during the school year and full-time work during the summer. In a study on teen unemployment Harrington and Khatiwada (2016) conclude that the numbers of teens who are unemployed, underemployed, or have given up looking for work altogether clearly indicate that low rates of teen employment do not stem from a lower desire among teens to work, but rather from a deterioration in their ability to find work. Even older youth, who have obtained a four-year degree, continue to struggle finding full-time employment that meets their skill level. Although unemployment rates for recent college graduates have receded to pre-recession levels, their underemployment rates remain elevated—and, in spite of high levels of debt, many are resorting to low-wage, part-time work (Abel et al. 2014). Particularly disturbing are the millions of youth who remain disconnected and are, therefore, neither improving their human capital nor earning an income. Those who continue to be unemployed or disconnected in spite of the nationwide economic recovery are more likely to have higher barriers to reconnection. In fact, numbers demonstrating an overall reduction in youth unemployment and disconnection mask the great variation of that decline in terms of demographic groups and geographic regions. This variation reveals that a healthy economy alone is not enough to prevent many young people from unemployment, marginalization, and disconnection from the workforce.

Socioeconomic Contexts

Every demographic and socioeconomic group has been affected by the problem of youth unemployment. Nevertheless, employment, unemployment, and disconnection rates have varied greatly based on race and ethnicity, gender, educational attainment, family income, geographic location, and involvement in the juvenile justice system. Often those who need work experience the most are receiving its benefits the least. Across demographics there are certain common trends or major risk factors, including teen pregnancy and failure to complete high school, that contribute to high rates of unemployment and disconnection. The fact that these risk factors are higher in certain demographic subgroups than in others exacerbates the problem of youth unemployment and disconnection within those groups.

Race and Ethnicity

Labor force participation, employment, and disconnection rates differ greatly based on race and ethnicity. Among teens and young adults, whites have the highest labor force participation rate and employment-to-population ratio relative to youth of color. Asian youth have the lowest labor force participation rate and employment-to-population ratio followed by blacks and Hispanics. Although the lower employment-to-population ratio among minority youth typically correlates to higher unemployment rates as well, Asian youth are the exception. Asian teenagers and young adults who participate in the labor force typically have an even lower unemployment rate than whites (Bureau of Labor Statistics 2018b). This can be attributed to the fact that the lower labor force participation rates among Asian youth compared to that of other demographics is driven by their high rates of school enrollment. Asian teens and young adults are more than 20 percent more likely to be enrolled in school and are much more likely to obtain a bachelor's degree than the national average (Ross and

Svajlenka 2016). By 2015, more than half of Asians over the age of 25 had completed a bachelor's degree or above, giving them an even higher advanced-degree completion rate than non-Hispanic whites (Ryan and Bauman 2016). Furthermore, the high levels of educational attainment among Asian youth eventually contribute to a comparatively higher employment-to-population ratio once they reach prime working age. On the opposite end of the spectrum, African American and Hispanic youth have low labor force participation rates and are less likely than both Asians and whites to be enrolled in school or to have completed high school and college (U.S. Census Bureau 2017). Consequently, the lower labor force participation rates and higher unemployment rates of non-Asian minority youth are less likely to improve with age.

Gender

For much of the 20th century the labor force participation rate of females was much lower than that of males. Dramatic changes in social norms concerning marriage, childrearing, and female labor force participation over the past 50 years drastically increased the employment opportunities available to females. As a consequence, the female employment-to-population ratio, particularly among young women, has been trending upward since the mid-1960s. Recent shifts in the labor market, however, have affected the prospects of young men and women alike. Between 2000 and 2014, the employment-to-population ratio of both male and female youth underwent decline, albeit males experienced a greater share of that decline (CRS 2015). Several additional trends developed during that same period. While males are less likely to be enrolled in high school or college and are more vulnerable to job loss than females, females are slightly more likely to be absent from both school and the workplace (Fernandes-Alcantara 2015). This is attributable to the fact that female youth are more liable to be parenting. Early parenthood is a key factor contributing to youth disconnection rates among young women, particularly when they are teens.

Teen mothers are much more likely than their peers to drop out of high school, to live in poverty, and to rely on the welfare system. Among the five major ethnic groups, young Latinas have highest rate of early motherhood and are the only demographic to have a disproportionately higher rate of disconnection than their male counterparts (Burd-Sharps and Lewis 2017). Among females of all ethnic groups, Native American women, who have the second highest youth pregnancy rate combined with second highest high school dropout rate, are the most likely to experience disconnection (Burd-Sharps and Lewis 2017). In comparison, females who do not have children at a young age are less disposed to disconnection than their male counterparts. Among males, young African American men face a considerably higher disconnection rate than any other demographic. The disconnection rate of black male youth is more than twice the rate of nonwhite Hispanic males and nearly three times the rate of white males (Fernandes-Alcantara 2015). Furthermore, regardless of parenting status, black males are more than twice as likely to be disconnected as black females, who themselves have a higher disconnection rate than that of whites and Hispanics of both genders.

Education and Work Experience

A generation ago career success was less dependent on secondary and postsecondary education. Workers with postsecondary education held only a small percentage of jobs. Youth, particularly males, who did not complete high school were able to find jobs in agriculture, manufacturing, the military, and so on that frequently led to a lucrative career. Over the past several decades, changes in the labor market have progressively diminished such opportunities for young people with limited education. Today, more than 60 percent of jobs require postsecondary education or training (Carnevale et al. 2013). Consequently, there are few opportunities for those with a high school diploma or less to find a job that serves as a stepping stone to a well-paying profession. The completion of high school and at least some level of postsecondary education or training has become more and more crucial for stable employment and for higher earnings and job advancement. Even when those who have dropped out of high school or who only possess a high school degree are able to secure employment, they are more liable to be employed in short-term jobs long after they have left school, compared to college graduates who have a much easier time finding stable, long-term employment following graduation (CRS 2015). While completing high school is no longer sufficient for ensuring reasonable prospects in the job market, failure to complete high school all but guarantees a life of poverty. High school dropouts are almost three times as likely to be unemployed as those who graduate from college (Bureau of Labor Statistics 2018c).

Individuals' level of education not only affects their likelihood of employment stability, but it also contributes to their lifetime earning potential. According to data from the U.S. Bureau of Labor Statistics, the earnings and employment rate of individuals over the age of 25 increase exponentially based on level of education (Vilorio 2016). Interestingly, while workers with master's and doctoral degrees out-earn on average those with lower-level degrees, the same data shows that workers with a professional degree have an even higher earning average and lower unemployment rate than those with academic degrees. Such workers earn on average more than three times the earnings of those with less than a high school diploma and are much less prone to experience bouts of unemployment. Furthermore, distinctions in earnings based on education attainment have substantially increased over the past three decades, as those engaged in higher education experienced a significant increase in earnings, while the real wages of those with only a high school degree dramatically declined (Autor 2015).

In addition to level of education, a history of past work experience is strongly correlated to better employment outcomes in the job market. Employers are much more inclined to hire workers with experience. Research shows that a history of employment is a strong predictor of current employment. Teens and young adults with work experience in the previous year are more likely to be currently employed (Sum et al. 2014). Moreover, the benefits of part-time teen employment and full-time employment as a young adult extend to improved employment and earning outcomes later in life, as early employment often provides young people the opportunity to develop occupational skills and transferable soft skills such as the ability to communicate well, problem solve, and work as part of a team. Young people with work experience additionally have an easier time securing professional references and are more aware of available employment opportunities.

While those with more education in addition to work experience perform much better in the job market statistically, it is unclear whether increasing access to traditional four-year college degrees is the best means of ensuring higher levels of employment and intergenerational income mobility. In recent years, a wide array of voices have challenged the "college for all" mantra, arguing that it is inhibiting the expansion of valuable postsecondary education and training alternatives, particularly those tailored to meet the needs of disadvantaged youth. The subsequent chapter will thus explore the benefits of nontraditional constructive approaches to postsecondary education in addition to conventional four-year degrees.

Family Income

In an eye-opening exposé of the growing class-based opportunity gap among America's youth, Harvard professor and policy expert Robert Putnam (2015) provides evidence that youth born into poverty-stricken backgrounds today are far less likely than their counterparts in previous generations to experience upward mobility. Putnam demonstrates that while gender and racial bias are less of a barrier to upward mobility in modern America than they were in the 1950s, class origin has become a greater barrier. In fact, disparities in both education attainment and family income are now stronger indicators of the probability of youth employment and disconnection than disparities by race. Harrington and Khatiwada (2016) found, for example, that teens from affluent families with an annual income above $100,000 were more than twice as likely as teens from low-income families with an annual income under $20,000 to be employed during the summer months.

Affluent youth of both genders from all racial and ethnic groups are less likely to be disconnected than their counterparts in poor households, but the effect of family income on employment is especially pronounced for young males. A recent study by the National Bureau of Economic Research found that although overall employment rates increased for both genders in connection with increases in parental income, males raised in families in the top 80 percent of income earners are employed at higher rates than their female counterparts. In contrast, males raised in the lowest-income quintile, especially those raised by a single parent, are less likely to be employed than females raised in the same financial environment (Karageorge 2016). This may be due in part to the fact that female youth who have lived in poverty—especially those who have no premarital teen births—have better educational outcomes and are less likely to be involved with the juvenile justice system than male youth who have lived in poverty (Ratcliffe 2015).

The length of time that youth have spent in poverty also affects the degree to which they are connected through education and employment. Youth who have experienced persistent poverty, having lived below the federal poverty line for at least half of their childhood, are 13 percent less likely to complete high school and 43 percent less likely to complete college than children who experienced poverty but were not persistently poor. Persistently poor youth are also nearly 40 percent less likely than those who have not experienced persistent poverty to be consistently employed as young adults (Ratcliffe 2015).

There are many reasons why family income is a strong predictor of the future employment success of youth. One of the most prominent is that parents themselves have a major impact on youth employment outcomes. Parents in middle-to-upper-class homes are far more inclined to have achieved high levels of education and are therefore frequently well suited to foster the same success in their children by deliberately cultivating their children's cognitive, social, and cultural skills and exposing them to an array of valuable educational and extracurricular activities. In addition to high educational attainment, affluent parents tend to have friends from a variety of professional backgrounds and connections to a broad social network. The social ties of lower-class parents, on the other hand, are typically limited to members of their extended family and immediate neighbors (Putnam 2015). This means that children from more affluent backgrounds are more disposed than children from working class or poverty-stricken homes to come in contact on a daily basis with a wide range of organizations, professionals, and informal advisors from whom they can derive employment and educational opportunities or guidance.

Location and Neighborhood

Unemployment and disconnection rates among teens and young adults vary substantially by geographic location—with many of the best-performing metropolitan areas in regions with highly educated residents, including state capitals and university towns, and many of the worst concentrated in the South, Southwest, and California (Ross and Svajlenka 2016). Among cities that have been most affected by the problem of youth unemployment and disconnection are those that have suffered a decline in manufacturing and other major industries, combined with stringent labor laws, poor education performance, neighborhood segregation, and high rates of violence. Chicago, for instance, has become a national leader in joblessness among young people, particularly young black people. Citing a report published by the Great Cities Institute, Alexia Elejalde-Ruiz (2017) observes that in addition to high youth unemployment, the city has one of the largest race disparities in terms of early 20-somethings who are both out of school and out of work. In 2015, among the city's population of 20 to 24-year-olds, 40 percent of blacks and 7 percent of whites fell into this category compared to the national average disconnection rate for this age group of 25 percent for blacks and 13 percent for whites, respectively.

One of the most significant geographical factors affecting youth employment outcomes is a phenomenon known as spatial mismatch that occurs when potential employees are geographically isolated from job-rich areas. Spatial mismatch affects labor market involvement both for youth living in rural areas with few employment opportunities and for youth living in urban areas with minimal access to transportation. As more and more industries have relocated to the suburbs in recent decades, youth living in urban areas, in particular, are not only less aware of job opportunities but are also less able to take advantage of them.

The particular neighborhood characteristics in which youth are raised can also have a major impact on their long-term labor status. Youth who grow up in neighborhoods with relatively high poverty rates are much less likely to participate in the labor force or serve in the armed forces than those from more affluent areas (Holloway and Mulherin 2004). This trend is particularly disturbing considering neighborhoods are becoming increasingly segregated along class lines. Citing data from the U.S. Census Bureau, Robert Putnam (2015) demonstrates that compared to the 1970s, fewer families today live in mixed or moderate income neighborhoods and more families live in either uniformly affluent or uniformly poor neighborhoods. In fact, neighborhood segregation has affected each major racial group. Today, affluent and impoverished minority groups are less likely to live next to each other than they were in previous decades.

As neighborhoods become more segregated by income level, fewer and fewer youth—whether rich or poor—interact in their daily lives with people outside of their socioeconomic circle. This effect has extended to a decline in cross-class marriage, further reducing the bridge between classes. The growing class-based residential and familial segregation typically means that children born into poverty have little access to the stepping-stones necessary for gainful employment and upward mobility, including access to good schools, educated family members, neighborhood mentors or role models, social and economic connections, and job referral networks (Putnam 2015). The neighborhood characteristics of poverty-stricken youth are often compounded by the fact that children born into poverty are more disposed to move and switch schools frequently. Such residential instability is directly connected to lower academic achievement and diminished employment prospects later in life (Ratcliffe 2015).

Involvement with the Juvenile Justice System

Youth involvement in the criminal justice system has proven to be an additional major impediment to both educational and employment achievement. Even children raised in persistent poverty are far more likely to remain in school and have successful employment outcomes if they have never been arrested by the time they reach the age of 20 (Ratcliffe 2015). The connection between incarceration and unemployment is often cyclical, with unemployed youth more likely to resort to criminal behavior and youth who engage in criminal behavior less likely to find employment. A lack of employment is one of the biggest predictors both of involvement in the criminal justice system and of a failure to successfully reenter society upon release. This is particularly troubling considering that more than a quarter million youth under the age of 18 are placed in juvenile and adult correction facilities each year and hundreds of thousands more are on probation (Opportunity Nation 2018). In addition to their record of incarceration, many of these teenagers and young adults are contending with multiple life challenges, including poverty, learning disabilities, a history of family instability and abuse, and involvement in the foster care system, that place them at high risk for unemployment and disconnection. Incarceration further aggravates these obstacles to educational and labor market success for several reasons. One of the main reasons is that few incarcerated youth are released with adequate educational attainment or marketable skills. Nearly half of all inmates in the nation's state and federal prisons and local jails have not completed high school or its equivalent at the time of sentencing, and more than one-third of youth who enter the system are illiterate or only marginally literate with less than a fourth-grade reading level (Wolf 2003; Coalition for Juvenile Justice 2001). While many inmates take advantage of educational resources while incarcerated, few complete their high school degree or go on to pursue higher education, and few leave the system with soft skills or an understanding of the importance of punctuality and a positive work ethic.

Youth who are released from prison also face bleak employment prospects due to the stigma associated with their record, as many employers fear hiring those who have previous involvement with the criminal justice system. This stigma is even more pronounced for young black males who make up a disproportionate percentage of incarcerated youth. In a study of the hiring disadvantage experienced by young males with a criminal record, sociologists Devah Pager, Bruce Western, and Naomi Sugie (2009) conducted a large-scale field experiment tracking the effects of race and prison record on employment. The experiment consisted in teams of black and white men who were sent to apply for low-wage jobs throughout New York City. Participants were furnished with equivalent resumes and differed only in their race and criminal background. The experiment revealed that, while employers exhibited a strong reluctance to hire applicants with criminal records generally, the employment prospects of ex-offender applicants improved significantly if they were able to interact personally with a hiring manager. This personal contact served to alleviate fears the prospective employer might have concerning the reliability and performance of ex-offenders. Unfortunately, however, black ex-offenders were far less likely to be invited to interview, giving them fewer opportunities to establish a good rapport with a prospective employer necessary to combat negative stereotypes. Without a viable pathway to reintegrate into society through gainful employment, these young offenders face a heightened risk of permanent disconnection and are increasingly likely to re-offend.

Other Factors Influencing Youth Unemployment and Disconnection

Besides individual risk factors—such as teen pregnancy, low educational attainment, and incarceration—there are several supply and demand factors that contribute to the crisis of youth unemployment in the United States. First and foremost, the performance of the labor market as a whole and the current supply of available jobs clearly impacts employment prospects for youth. Reduced demand for goods and services during recessions and periods of anemic growth cause dismal employment opportunities for the workforce generally, but are particularly detrimental to youth. Given that young people are disproportionately represented among those searching for a job, they are also disproportionately affected in times of economic downturn when employers halt or scale back the hiring of new employees. Thus, the lingering weakness of the job market between 2001 and 2015 clearly contributed to youth's struggle to find stable, gainful employment. The crisis of youth unemployment over the past couple of decades, however, can also be attributed in part to dramatic changes in the labor market, failures in the country's secondary and postsecondary educational systems, and public policies that discourage young people from pursuing jobs and employers from creating them.

Disruptive Technologies

The rapid technological change and increased global competition of the past few decades has improved the quality of life for many around the world and has increased the production and affordability of superior goods and services, but such changes have also made it more difficult for many workers, particularly those who are young, unskilled, and inexperienced, to secure jobs previously available to them. As the emergence of new technologies improves efficiency in the workplace, more and more untrained workers—most of whom are teenagers and young adults—have become vulnerable to wage decline and joblessness. While many blame the outsourcing of entry-level jobs to laborers in developing countries like China, India, and Bangladesh for displacing low-skilled workers in the United States, a recent study by researchers at Ball State University revealed that nearly nine in ten jobs that have been eliminated since 2000 were lost to automation, not to workers in other countries (Selingo 2017). Although the expanded use of robots and computing advancements has reduced the available jobs that require routine manual operations, technological development, however, generally leads to an increase in employment and wage-growth opportunity for those with specialized technical training and cognitive skills. For example, companies like John Deere and the German engineering company Siemens—previously known for supplying large numbers of entry-level, blue-collar jobs—now only recruit employees with advanced math and problem-solving skills (Selingo 2017). In light of the transformation of opportunity created by technological advancement, the youth unemployment crisis can be attributed in part to the inefficacy of primary, secondary, and tertiary education systems in the United States to adequately prepare and train up-and-coming generations for a successful transition into 21st-century jobs.

Inadequacy of Primary and Secondary Education

Once the envy of the world, America's primary and secondary education systems have fallen behind much of the developed world in preparing students for employment success in an increasingly automated, globalized economy. Firstly, although the on-time high school completion rate has reached a record high in recent years, at least 15 percent of students nationally fail to graduate in four years (National Center for Education Statistics 2016). That number is much higher for low-income, disadvantaged, and minority youth—and, in many urban areas, as few as 50 percent of students complete their degree (Guryan and Ludwig 2014). Furthermore, in contrast with many advanced democracies like the UK, France, and Germany that measure completion of secondary education based on the passage of skill assessment exams, high school graduation in the United States is based on hours of attendance and credits completed. Thus, some districts are able to use questionable methods to increase graduation rates, such as relaxing grading requirements and allowing students to participate in abbreviated credit recovery programs for courses they have failed (Dynarski 2018). Consequently, even those who do graduate often lack proficiency in basic skills. Data from the National Assessment of Educational Progress reveals that less than 40 percent of graduating seniors are proficient in reading and math (Fields 2014). In addition to failing to ensure the achievement of basic academic skills, a large percentage of high schools have eliminated programs and courses focused on developing career-oriented or vocational skills. In contrast to Europe's most economically competitive nations, in which nearly half of high school students are enrolled in vocational education programs, only 2 percent of U.S. high school students attend schools that concentrate on vocational training (Wyman 2015). As a result, a large majority of U.S. students are leaving high school tremendously ill-prepared for the workforce.

Mismatch in Skills and Expectations

At the same time that a large percentage of youth struggle to attain gainful employment, many U.S. employers report that their greatest impediment to growth is the inability to find qualified workers. Consequently, thousands of U.S. jobs go unfilled each year because applicants lack the requisite credentials. Part of this can be attributed to the fact that—although education and training is essential for stable employment, wage growth, and social mobility—investments in education are not always well integrated with the requirements of the labor market. In recent decades, for instance, the push for higher education has almost entirely focused on making it possible for more young Americans to go to college and earn a bachelor's degree. High school guidance counselors encourage four-year degrees even if students might benefit from alternatives such as community college or vocational schools. Jeffrey Selingo (2017), for example, points out that U.S. high school students are presented with few feasible routes to middle-skill careers in computer technology, high-skill manufacturing, construction, and other fields. Although such jobs are often stigmatized as being filled by those who "are not college material," many of these jobs pay more than the median annual salary earned by those with a bachelor's degree. Furthermore, while such middle-skill jobs account for more than half of the labor market, less than 45 percent of workers are sufficiently trained to fill them (Selingo 2017). Nevertheless, in response to growing emphasis on "college-for-all," large percentages of high school graduates scurry to attend a four-year college, even as many of them are not ready for the academic requirements or sure of what kind of work they want to pursue. As the university system in the United States has expanded in response to increased enrollment demand, it has not, however, adequately developed in alignment with the job market and global economy. A disconnection commonly exists between institutions of higher learning and the labor market, and evidence suggests that today's higher education system is preparing large numbers of students for jobs that no longer exist or are in short supply (Coates and Morrison 2016). This is compounded by the fact that young people who enter college with little to no work experience routinely have misconstrued impressions of the world of work. As psychologist Jean Twenge (2014) points out, young people who are told that they can be anything and to pursue their "dream" career tend to lack realistic expectations of the career choices available to them. To illustrate this point, Twenge highlights national findings that one-fifth of college freshmen expect to make a living as an actor, musician, or artist—a higher percentage than those who want to be lawyers, accountants, businesses owners, scientific researchers, or teachers. Consequently, many young people are assuming large sums of debt that will burden them for years to come for degrees that they may never complete or that may not improve their job prospects.

The pressure for young adults to go directly into a bachelor's degree program, even as they lack a realistic vision of employment possibilities related to their chosen degree, is further aggravated by the evolving expectations of employers who expect young people to be better educated than previous generations. As employers require additional qualifications as a basis for hiring, more and more young people strive toward higher levels of academic education, leaving the labor market with a surplus of theoretically oriented graduates. Entrepreneur and educator Peter Vogel observes in his book on youth joblessness that "despite the fact that there is an awareness of the misalignment between the education system and the labor market, employers use credentials—such as diplomas and grades—as the primary way to evaluate applicants." "As a result of this rather limited approach to evaluating young people," Vogel continues, "young people are forced to remain in education longer in order to meet employers' expectations. This decreases the time that young people can spend on gaining important work experience and increases the average age of job entrants" (Vogel 2015, 22–23).

Detrimental Policies

Public policies that inhibit young people from pursuing jobs and discourage employers from creating them present a final barrier to youth employment in the United States. Over time, federal, state, and local policy makers from both major parties have proposed and adopted well-intentioned labor policies that have actually thwarted young people's entry into the job market. Often such polices are adopted to benefit older, established workers with little regard for the negative effect they may have on youth employment prospects. One example is the dramatic increase in recent decades of state and local occupational licensing requirements—laws that require workers to meet specific standards and obtain a government license before they are legally permitted to perform certain jobs. Once viewed as a means of protecting the public from injury at the hands of unskilled practitioners in fields like law and medicine, state licensing mandates have extended far beyond the realm of public health and safety. Today they govern countless harmless practitioners such as interior designers, florists, beauticians, general repair contractors, pet sitters, landscapers, and tour guides. In fact, four out of every ten workers in America today must obtain a government license to work compared to fewer than one in twenty workers in the 1950s (Hershbein et al. 2015). Many of these requirements are expensive and time-intensive, making it virtually all but impossible for new workers to break into certain fields. For instance, an individual seeking to become a travel guide in Nevada must pay at least $1,500 for the license and undergo 733 days of training (Hershbein et al. 2015). Furthermore, in some fields a complete disconnect exists between the threat posed to public safety and the strictness of licensing regulations. In many states, licensing requirements for seemingly harmless practices such as interior design require more training than do emergency medical technicians (Furchtgott-Roth and Meyer 2015).

Occupational licensing laws are generally supported by established tradespeople and businesses as a means of protecting themselves from potential competition, but such protection comes at the expense of low-income, low-skilled, and younger workers. Onerous licensing requirements that are not essential for protecting public health and safety not only harm consumers by driving up the costs of basic goods and services, but they also deny many promising work options to those who need them most by making them prohibitively time-consuming or expensive to enter. In addition to cutting off certain vocations, job avenues, and entrepreneurial ideas from would-be-workers, stringent licensing regimes cause unlicensed workers—many of whom are young—to bear the burden of unemployment. Ryan Nunn (2016) explains, "Licensing creates 'crowding' in unlicensed occupations and labor occupations and labor scarcity in licensed occupations, driving a wedge between the unemployment rates in the two sectors" (7). In fact, the variation of licensing requirements might be one of the triggers for the disparity in youth unemployment rates across the nation. As Diana Furchtgott-Roth and Jared Meyer (2015) point out, the states with the most burdensome licensing requirements have much higher youth unemployment rates than those with the least burdensome requirements.

In addition to onerous licensing requirements, the widespread adoption of minimum-wage increases at the state and local levels over the past several years has affected youth employment prospects. Higher minimum-wage mandates, often referred to as living wages, are adopted by states and localities with the intention of lifting minimum-wage workers out of poverty. Improvement of some workers' incomes, however, often comes at the expense of young, inexperienced workers. Although the effect of high-wage mandates on overall employment is still a matter of debate, the bulk of economic research now confirms that mandated wage increases negatively affect the employment opportunities of teenagers and young adults, who make up more than half of all minimum-wage workers (Kalenkoski 2016).

Employers, faced with additional labor costs imposed by mandated wage increases, have limited options. They can accept lower profits, increase their prices, reduce the number of current and future employees (or the number of hours employees work), or close their doors. For many businesses the first line of defense against rising labor costs is to offset those costs by increasing prices. The relationship between mandated wage increases and higher consumer costs has already been demonstrated in the cities and states that have recently implemented such mandates. Raising the costs of goods and services, however, is not always feasible, as many businesses do not have a consumer base that is willing or able to pay increased costs. While large, national corporations may have the resources to adjust to higher employment costs by lowering profits, most low-wage workers are employed in industries with narrow profit margins, such as retailers, restaurants, or other small businesses (Saltsman 2013). Thus, these entry-level employers tend to respond to forced wage hikes by eliminating jobs or reducing work hours. Moreover, when employers are forced to pay more for their employees, they generally replace those with the lowest level of skill with labor-saving technology, such as digital ordering systems in fast-food restaurants. Employers then focus their hiring on older, more-experienced workers whose skills create value worth the higher wages. By removing the incentive for companies to hire workers with few skills and little experience who are expensive to train, minimum-wage increases have the unintended effect of pushing the least-skilled employees, usually teenagers, out of the labor market altogether.

Even without mandated minimum-wage increases, wages generally increase over time as workers develop skills and gain experience. This is supported by the reality that the number of hourly workers working at or below the federal minimum-wage in 2017 was a mere 2.3 percent of all hourly workers in the United States (Bureau of Labor Statistics 2018d). In fact, a majority of minimum-wage workers move on to higher-paying jobs within a year (Furchtgoth-Roth 2016). Consequently, when low-skilled and inexperienced workers—a large percentage of whom are teenagers or minorities—are priced out of jobs through minimum-wage laws, they lose not only current compensation but also valuable job training opportunities that will allow them to demand higher wages in the future. In short, forcing wages upward by political mandate effectively restricts the ability of many young people to prepare themselves for more lucrative work in the future and consequently reduces their lifetime earning potential (Kalenkoski 2016).

Conclusion

Besides allowing young people to contribute to their own support, participation in the labor force also permits them to gain valuable experience and to develop habits and skills that will facilitate their transitioning to adulthood and enable them to achieve the American dream of economic self-sufficiency and advancement. Unfortunately, the opportunity for productive citizenship and upward mobility is at risk for a sizeable percentage of American youth. Large numbers of youth are not reaping the benefits of gainful employment. Among those who are employed, many are working far below their level of ability or training. Others have become entirely disconnected from the workforce and are not improving their human and social capital through education or training. Because these negative trends in employment are particularly concentrated in already-disadvantaged populations, the social and economic implications for individuals and for the country at large may be severe and lasting. These implications along with proposed and potential solutions to address the root causes of youth unemployment and disconnection will be explored in the next chapter.

References

Abel, Jaison R., Richard Dietz, and Yaqin Su. 2014. "Are Recent College Graduates Finding Good Jobs?" *Current Issues in Economics and Finance* 20(1): 1–8. Federal Reserve Bank of New York. Accessed April 25, 2018. https://www .newyorkfed.org/medialibrary/media/research/current_ issues/ci20-1.pdf

Allison, Tom. 2017. *Financial Health of Young America: Measuring Generational Declines between Baby Boomers and Millennials*. Washington, DC: Young Invincibles. Accessed March 20, 2018. http://younginvincibles.org/wp-content/uploads/2017/04/FHYA-Final2017-1-1.pdf

Autor, David H. 2014. "Skills, Education, and the Rise of Earnings Inequality among the 'Other 99 Percent." *Science Magazine*, 344(6186). May 23.

Burd-Sharps, Sarah, and Kirsten Lewis. 2017. *Promising Gains, Persistent Gaps: Youth Disconnection in America*. Brooklyn, NY: Measure of America, of the Social Science Research Council. Accessed March 20, 2018. https://ssrc-static.s3.amazonaws.com/moa/Promising%20Gains%20Final.pdf

Bureau of Labor Statistics. 2017. "Teen Labor Force Participation before and after the Great Recession and Beyond." *Monthly Labor Review*. February. Accessed March 20, 2018. https://www.bls.gov/opub/mlr/2017/article/teen-labor-force-participation-before-and-after-the-great-recession.htm

Bureau of Labor Statistics. 2018a. *Employment Rates by Age, Sex, and Marital Status, Seasonally Adjusted*. April.8. Accessed May 5, 2018. https://www.bls.gov/web/empsit/cpseea10.htm

Bureau of Labor Statistics. 2018b. *Employment Status of the Civilian Non-Institutional Population by Sex, Age, and Race*. Accessed May 15, 2018. https://www.bls.gov/cps/aa2008/cpsaat5.pdf

Bureau of Labor Statistics. 2018c. *Employment Status of the Civilian Population 25 Years and Older by Educational Attainment*. Accessed May 15, 2018. https://www.bls.gov/news.release/empsit.t04.htm

Bureau of Labor Statistics. 2018d. *Characteristics of Minimum Wage Workers, 2017*. Accessed May 28, 2018. https://www.bls.gov/opub/reports/minimum-wage/2017/home.htm

Carnevale, Anthony, Nicole Smith, and Jeff Strohl. 2013. *Recovery: Job Growth and Education Requirements through 2020*. Georgetown University. Georgetown Public Policy Institute: Center on Education and the Work Force. Accessed March 20, 2018. https://cew-7632.kxcdn.com/wp-content/uploads/2014/11/Recovery2020.FR_.Web_.pdf

Coalition for Juvenile Justice. 2001. *Abandoned in the Back Row: New Lessons in Education and Delinquency Prevention*. Accessed May 15, 2018. Annual Report. Washington, DC: Coalition for Juvenile Justice. https://www.juvjustice.org/sites/default/files/resource-files/resource_122_0.pdf

Coates, Ken S., and Bill Morrison. 2016. *Dream Factories. Why Universities Won't Solve the Youth Jobs Crisis*. Toronto: TAP Books.

Congressional Research Service (CRS). 2015. *Youth and the Labor Force: Background and Trends*. Washington, DC: Congressional Research Service. May 7. Accessed March 20, 2018. https://www.everycrsreport.com/files/20150507_R42519_cdbd15b74b793435591108932ae518e95e86a1ae.pdf

Dynarski, Mark. 2018. *Is the High School Graduation Rate Really Going Up?* Washington, DC: Brookings Institution. Accessed May 28, 2018. https://www.brookings.edu/research/is-the-high-school-graduation-rate-really-going-up/

Edwards, Kathryn Ann, and Alexander Hertel-Fernandez. 2010. *The Kids Aren't Alright: A Labor Market Analysis of Young Workers*. EPI Briefing Paper #258. Washington, DC: Economic Policy Institute. April 7. Accessed March 20, 2018. https://www.epi.org/publication/bp258/

Elejalde-Ruiz, Alexia. 2017. "Report Says Youth Unemployment Chronic, Concentrated and Deeply Rooted." *Chicago Tribune*. January 2017. Accessed March 20, 2018. http://www.chicagotribune.com/business/ct-youth-unemployment-data-0129-biz-20170127-story.html

Fernarndes-Alcantara, Adrienne L. 2015. *Disconnected Youth: A Look at 16 to 24 Year Olds Who Are Not Working or in School.* Congressional Research Service. October 1. Accessed March 20, 2018. https://fas.org/sgp/crs/misc/R40535.pdf

Fields, Ray. 2014. *Towards the National Assessment of Educational Progress (NAEP) as an Indicator of Academic Preparedness for College and Job Training.* Washington, DC: National Assessment Governing Board. Accessed May 28, 2018. https://www.nagb.gov/content/nagb/assets/documents/what-we-do/preparedness-research/NAGB-indicator-of-preparedness-report.pdf

Fry, Richard, D'Vera Cohn, Gretchen Livingston, and Paul Taylor. 2011. "The Rising Age Gap in Economic Well-Being: The Old Prosper Relative to the Young." *Pew Research Center.* November 7. Accessed March 20, 2018. http://www.pewsocialtrends.org/2011/11/07/the-rising-age-gap-in-economic-well-being/

Furchtgott-Roth, Diana. 2016. "Raising the Minimum Wage Lowers Employment for Teens and Low Skill Workers." *PBS.* December 16. Accessed May 28, 2018. https://www.pbs.org/newshour/economy/column-minimum-wage-lowers-employment-teens-low-skill-workers

Furchtgott-Roth, Diana, and Jared Meyer. 2015. *Disinherited: How Washington Is Betraying America's Youth.* New York: Encounter Books.

Guryan, Johnathan, and Jens Ludwig. 2014. "Why Half of Urban Kids Drop Out." *CNN.* March 12. Accessed May 28, 2018. https://www.cnn.com/2014/03/12/opinion/ludwig-guryan-chicago-education/index.html

Harrington, Paul, and Ishwar Khatiwada. 2016. *U.S. Teens Want to Work.* Federal Reserve Bank of Boston. Accessed March 20, 2018. https://www.bostonfed.org/publications/communities-and-banking/2016/spring/us-teens-want-to-work.aspx

Hershbein, Brad, David Boddy, and Melissa S. Kearney. 2015. "Nearly 30 Percent of Workers in the US Need a License to Perform Their Job: It Is Time to Examine Occupational Licensing Practices." *Up Front*. January 27. Washington, DC: Brookings Institute. Accessed May 1, 2018. https://www.brookings.edu/blog/up-front/2015/01/27/ nearly-30-percent-of-workers-in-the-u-s-need-a-license- to-perform-their-job-it-is-time-to-examine-occupational- licensing-practices/

Holloway, Steven R., and Stephen Mulherin. 2004. "The Effect of Adolescent Neighborhood Poverty on Adult Employment." *Journal of Urban Affairs* 26, no. 4. June.

Kalenkosi, Charlene Marie. 2016. *The Effects of Minimum Wages on Youth Employment and Income*. IZA World of Labor. Accessed March 20, 2018. https://wol.iza.org/ articles/effects-of-minimum-wages-on-youth- employment-and-income/long

Karageorge, Eleni. 2016. "Growing Up in High-Poverty Areas Can Affect Your Employment." *Monthly Labor Review*. Bureau of Labor Statistics. March. Accessed May 15, 2018. https://www.bls.gov/opub/mlr/2016/beyond-bls/growing- up-in-high-poverty-areas-can-affect-your-employment.htm

Kroger, Teresa, and Elise Gould. 2017. *The Class of 2017*. Washington, DC: Economic Policy Institute. May 4. Accessed March 20, 2018. http://www.epi.org/publication/ the-class-of-2017/

National Center for Education Statistics. 2016. "Public High School 4-Year Adjusted Cohort Graduation Rate (ACGR), by Race/Ethnicity and Selected Demographic Characteristics for the United States, the 50 States, and the District of Columbia: School Year 2015–16." Accessed May 28, 2018. https://nces.ed.gov/ccd/tables/ACGR_RE_ and_characteristics_2015-16.asp

Nunn, Ryan. 2016. *Occupational Licensing and the American Worker*. The Hamilton Project. Washington, DC: Brookings Institution. Accessed May 15, 2018. https://www.brookings.edu/wp-content/uploads/2016/07/occupational_licensing_and_the_american_worker.pdf

Opportunity Nation. 2018. "Youth Justice." Accessed March 20, 2018. https://opportunitynation.org/youth-justice/

Pager, Devah, Bruce Western, and Naomi Sugie. 2009. "Sequencing Disadvantage: Barriers to Employment Facing Young Black and White Men with Criminal Records." *The Annals of the American Academy of Political and Social Science* 623: 195–213. Accessed March 20, 2018. https://www.ncbi.nlm.nih.gov/pmc/articles/PMC3583356/pdf/nihms-439026.pdf

Putnam, Robert D. 2015. *Our Kids: The American Dream in Crisis*. New York: Simon and Schuster.

Ratcliffe, Caroline. 2015. *Childhood Poverty and Adult Success*. Low-Income Families Working Initiative. Washington, DC: The Urban Institute. Accessed March 20, 2018. https://www.urban.org/sites/default/files/publication/65766/2000369-Child-Poverty-and-Adult-Success.pdf

Ross, Martha, and Nicole Prchal Svajlenka. 2016. "Employment and Disconnection among Teens and Young Adults: The Role of Place, Race, and Education." Washington, DC: Brookings Institution. Accessed March 20, 2018. https://www.brookings.edu/research/employment-and-disconnection-among-teens-and-young-adults-the-role-of-place-race-and-education/

Ryan, Camille L., and Kurt Bauman. 2016. "Educational Attainment in the United States: 2015: Population Characteristics." *Current Population Reports*. United States

Census Bureau. Accessed April 7, 2018. https://www
.census.gov/content/dam/Census/library/
publications/2016/demo/p20-578.pdf

Saltsman, Michael. 2013. "Who Really Employs Minimum-
Wage Workers?" *Wall Street Journal.* October 28. Accessed
May 28, 2018. https://www.wsj.com/articles/who-really-
employs-minimumwage-workers-1383001775?tesla=y

Selingo, Jeffrey J. 2017. "Wanted: Factory Workers, Degree
Required." *New York Times.* January 30. Accessed April 7,
2018. https://www.nytimes.com/2017/01/30/education/
edlife/factory-workers-college-degree-apprenticeships.html

Sum, Andrew. 2011. "Ignore the Teen Employment Problem
to Your Peril." *Huffington Post.* May 25. Accessed April 7,
2018. https://www.huffingtonpost.com/andrew-sum/
double-vision-the-move-to_b_825089.html.

Sum, Andrew, et al. 2014. *The Plummeting Labor Market
Fortune of Teens and Young Adults.* Washington, DC:
Metropolitan Policy Program Brookings Institution.
Accessed March 20, 2018. https://www.brookings.edu/
wp-content/uploads/2014/03/Youth_Workforce_Report_
FINAL-2.pdf

Twenge, Jean M. 2014. *Generation Me: Why Today's Young
Americans Are More Confident, Assertive, Entitled—And
More Miserable Than Ever Before.* New York: Simon and
Schuster.

U.S. Census Bureau. 2017. *Percent of People 25 Years and
Over Who Have Completed High School or College, by Race,
Hispanic Origin and Sex: Selected Years 1940 to 2017.*
Accessed May 15, 2018. https://www.census.gov/data/
tables/time-series/demo/educational-attainment/cps-
historical-time-series.html

Vilorio, Dennis. 2016. "Education Matters." *Career Outlook.*
U.S. Bureau of Labor Statistics. March. Accessed May 15,
2018. https://www.bls.gov/careeroutlook/2016/data-on-
display/pdf/education-matters.pdf

Vogel, Peter. 2015. *Generation Jobless? Turning the Youth Unemployment Crisis into Opportunity.* New York: Palgrave Macmillan.

Wolf, Caroline Harlow. 2003. "Education and Correctional Populations." Bureau of Justice Statistics Special Report. U.S. Department of Justice. January. Accessed May 15, 2018. https://www.bjs.gov/content/pub/pdf/ecp.pdf

Wyman, Nicholas. 2015. *Job U: How to Find Wealth and Success by Developing the Skills Companies Actually Need.* New York: Crown Business.

2   Problems, Controversies, and Solutions

Introduction

From one vantage point, the employment prospects for workers in the United States look bright. Over the past couple of years, for the first time since the Great Recession, the country has experienced substantial economic growth, high levels of job creation, and significantly lower levels of unemployment. As the previous chapter demonstrated, however, a closer look reveals that a crisis in youth unemployment and disconnection persists below the surface. The country continues to experience a disproportionately high rate of youth unemployment in comparison to the employment levels of those at prime working age, and millions of youth are completely absent from the labor force and not enrolled in further schooling. Consequently, a large percentage of the county's youth are stuck in a sort of unemployment limbo in the prime of their lives and are missing out on the essential benefits that early employment provides. To make matters worse, many of those who are receiving

---

A student repairs a car with his instructor as a part of an apprenticeship program. Apprenticeships are programs, lasting anywhere from one to six years, in which participants are paid by a sponsoring employer to engage in hands-on training under the direct supervision of a skilled expert. In response to ever-growing levels of college debt and mounting evidence of a skills gap between graduates seeking work and available job opportunities, state and national policy makers have begun to consider how to expand the availability of apprenticeship opportunities to a wider variety of fields. (Auremar/Dreamstime.com)

an education are not being properly prepared and trained for remunerative employment in the 21st century.

While high unemployment rates in general are associated with a range of negative individual and social consequences, elevated levels of youth unemployment are especially pernicious. Prolonged periods of unemployment and disconnection have short- and long-term debilitating effects that can impact individuals throughout their lifetime and the country for generations to come. This chapter examines the most problematic immediate and long-term economic, psychological, physical, and social consequences of high rates of youth unemployment and disconnection. It then outlines and discusses proposals by government and private sector leaders to alleviate the crisis and to respond to its most destructive effects.

Economic Consequences

High rates of youth unemployment and disconnection rates not only produce personal economic harm, but they also generate significant negative economic consequences for the nation and society as a whole. The most detrimental economic effects include individual scarring (e.g., lost earnings and employment potential) and the more widespread societal consequences (slower economic growth, fewer tax revenues, and increased government spending on social welfare and entitlement programs).

While unemployment causes economic harm at any age, it is particularly detrimental early in a person's professional career. Early periods of unemployment can stunt youths' transition into self-sufficiency and adulthood and are ultimately associated with long-term earning losses and joblessness. The situation is even worse for youth who have undergone simultaneous gaps in labor force participation and education. Even when youth who have experienced such gaps eventually secure a job, they often suffer enduring harmful effects in comparison to others who have maintained continuous education and work histories. A large body of research now demonstrates that unemployment during the early years of an individual's professional life causes a pay and employment handicap for years to come. The longer the period of early unemployment, the bigger the negative scarring effect on potential lifetime earnings and employment potential. Although youth who face early bouts of involuntary unemployment are more likely to engage in short-term human capital development, such as work-related training as a catch-up response to mitigate possible setbacks, they still, on average, suffer a long-term negative impact on their earnings (Mroz and Savage 2006). According to a Brookings Institution memo, "A six-month bout of unemployment at age 22 would reduce wages by 8% in the following year, and would reduce future earnings by about $22,000 over the next decade" (Sawhill and Karpilow 2014). Some economists have projected that the earnings deficit of early periods of unemployment can persist for up to 20 years (Morsy 2012). Although youth with higher levels of education are less at risk of joblessness, their potential earning loss is further magnified by the debt they may have acquired to finance their education if they do experience unemployment.

The long-term earning loss trend for those who have faced early bouts of unemployment can be attributed in part to the fact that they are at greater risk of subsequent periods of unemployment than those who have remained steadily employed (Morsy 2012). This increased risk of future unemployment may result in part from negative stereotypes held by employers that previously unemployed workers will not be as productive as those who have been continuously employed. Because of such perceptions, employers are frequently more apt to hire and promote those with a consistent employment record. The most significant reason why those who have been unemployed lag behind their peers in terms of future earning and employment prospects, however, is that they have lost valuable time that could have been spent developing marketable skills, acquiring work experience, and building professional networks that are essential to advancing a career. To illustrate the scarring effect of youth unemployment on the development of human and social capital, entrepreneur Peter Vogel (2015) contends, "An individual's stock of knowledge and experience depreciates over time if it is not used regularly. Likewise, social connections get lost, leading to a long-term loss of important networks. Unemployed individuals are at a disadvantage when it comes to building the necessary industry ties, which are known to be a prime source of employment opportunities" (42). Youth who are neither working nor engaged in schooling are in an even worse situation as they become completely stagnant in terms of professional development and human capital growth.

Youth unemployment also has economic implications for the caretakers of the unemployed. The unsteady employment prospects, earning losses, and growing level of student debt in recent decades have led a sizeable percentage of young people to remain in their parents' home well into adulthood. This delay in self-sufficiency imposes a significant financial burden on today's parents who are expected to care for their children much longer than in previous generations. Having to support their adult children forces many parents to delay their own retirement. As a result, they continue to occupy positions that could potentially be held by younger workers, further contributing to the crisis of youth unemployment.

The economic impact caused by historically high levels of youth unemployment and disconnection extends beyond the fiscal well-being of individuals and families to the states and the nation as a whole. To start with, the reduced earning power and productivity of those who are not working to their full potential inhibits economic growth. As Sarah Ayres (2013), a former economic policy analyst for the Center for American Progress points out, "When workers earn less because they were once unemployed, they spend less money at supermarkets, bookstores, cafes, and other businesses. The effect of taking this spending out of the economy adds up, resulting in fewer jobs and slower economic growth" (7).

Economic growth is additionally inhibited when youth aren't employed to their full capacity by the inefficient use of the nation's human resources and a loss of human talent. Faced with minimal employment opportunities, either because of a general shortage of remunerative employment or because of an existing mismatch between education or training and employment demand, many young people become less selective about the type of work they pursue. Some will accept part-time or temporary employment, while others will take jobs for which they are overeducated or over-skilled. In actuality, unemployment numbers alone mask the large number of workers who are employed in jobs for which they are overqualified and underpaid. Using data from the Department of Labor, Vedder et al. (2013) point out that "barely half of college graduates are in occupations requiring bachelor's degrees or more. Some 37 percent, in fact, are in jobs requiring a high school diploma or less, and about 11 percent are in jobs typically requiring some postsecondary education, usually an associate's degree" (11). Thus, it seems that an enormous amount of financial and educational resources are being inadequately used in the attempt to prepare individuals for work for which they will ultimately be overeducated. This inefficient use of human resources also exists on the opposite side of the equation. When employers cannot find applicants with the talents and qualifications they are seeking, they may be forced to hire those who are under-skilled and, therefore, unable to work at maximum capacity in a particular field.

Chronically high youth unemployment and disconnection further threaten the nation's immediate and long-term fiscal health by contributing to a heavy cost burden for taxpayers of all generations. When youth are unemployed, intermittently employed, or not employed to their full potential, they contribute much less in tax revenues and are more likely to rely on taxpayer-funded government services for support. Unemployed and disconnected youth who turn to crime and other socially harmful behaviors impose further fiscal costs in terms of expenditures on police and sentencing, incarceration, and crime prevention. While public assistance programs, including cash welfare payments and food and housing assistance, are designed to prevent youth from falling into poverty or turning to crime, they can further aggravate youth unemployment and disconnection by creating a lingering pattern of dependency. Harvey Golub (2013), former CEO of American Express, illustrates this danger by pointing out that if the wage premium from working is less than, equal to, or only slightly greater than the financial benefits provided by public assistance programs, the fear of losing benefits may create disincentives to work among youth—which further delays their entry into the labor market and achievement of employment potential.

Psychological and Physical Consequences

Prolonged periods of unemployment and disconnection additionally threaten the psychological and physical well-being of the nation's youth. Research has shown that engaging in productive work, particularly work that serves and benefits others, contributes to long-term happiness and physical and mental well-being. On the other hand, long-term unemployment and a lack of productive work are strongly correlated to decreased happiness and mental and physical health issues. After accounting for prior drinking behavior and psychological history, sociologist Krysia Mossakowski (2009) found that long periods of unemployment among young people were directly correlated to an increase in depressive symptoms. This correlation is particularly strong for youth who are neither working nor in education and training. Such youth are much more likely to have spent time in a mental hospital and to have received drug or alcohol treatment than their connected peers (Belfield, Levin, and Rosen 2012). They are also at increased risk of having suicidal thoughts and engaging in self-harm (Vogel 2015). A recent analysis of the health effects of youth unemployment conducted by the Gallup-Healthways Global Well-Being Index found that unemployed youth and young adults between the ages of 15 to 29 in the United States have worse physical well-being, in terms of having consistently good health and enough energy to get things done each day, than employed people aged 50 and older (Busteed and Mourshed 2016). Even more surprising, the same analysis revealed that in high-income economies, like the United States, unemployed youth with higher levels of education had worse physical well-being than unemployed youth with less education.

The deterioration of physical and mental well-being correlated with early bouts of unemployment and disconnection may be due in part to the financial stress and feeling of failure that frequently accompany joblessness, but it may also be a consequence of the prolonged idleness and social alienation associated with disconnection from education and the workforce. Compared to their peers who are working or in school or both, unemployed and disconnected youth have hundreds of additional hours of disposable time each year. As Nicholas Eberstadt (2016) observes in his book, *Men without Work*, this free time "can be devoted to recreation, reflection, and self-improvement as well as the pursuit of spirituality, and the arts, . . . [but it] can also be wasted or expended in ways that diminish the individual and his bonds to family and community" (78). A growing body of evidence suggests that the expendable time of those who are disconnected from education and the workforce in the United States is being spent in the latter way, particularly among disconnected males. A recent study by the National Bureau of Economic Research, for example, reveals that as the percentage of joblessness has increased among young males, most are not spending their free time in purposeful pursuits such as improving their social capital, volunteering, or building meaningful relationships, instead they are increasingly allocating their time to playing video games and other computer-related activities (Aguiar et al. 2017). Based on data from the Bureau of Labor Statistics annual American Time Use Survey, Eberstadt (2016) likewise reports that—whereas a large percentage of women who are not in education or in school are likely to be caring for children or other family members—only a small percentage of nonworking, disconnected men report that they are engaged in caring for children or other family members. Moreover, these men have very low levels of volunteer activity, community involvement, or religious attendance. Instead, they self-reported spending most of their day pursuing immediate sources of gratification, such as attending gambling establishments, using tobacco or illegal drugs, and watching movies or television. Even more troubling, many disconnected youth spend their expendable time in pursuit of criminal activities that are not only personally harmful but socially harmful as well.

Social Consequences

Among the most significant social costs imposed by chronic youth unemployment is that it delays the transition to adulthood and the achievement of key milestones, such as marriage and homeownership, for a large portion of the country's population. Establishing a household independent from one's parents is a chief indicator of the successful conversion to adulthood in the United States, yet today's youth are increasingly remaining in or returning to their family home. Many are waiting to establish their own households and families until they are well into their 30s or even 40s, while some never do. According to analysis of census data by the PEW Research Center, "In 2014, for the first time in more than 130 years, adults ages from eighteen to thirty-four were slightly more likely to be living in their parents' home than they were to be living with a spouse or partner in their own household" (Fry 2016). A large percentage of young adults reported that they had moved back in with their parents as a result of the Great Recession, but the trend was under way well before the recession's onset. In 1960, only 20 percent of 18- to 34-year-olds lived with their parents; by 2007—a year before the recession began—that number had increased to 28 percent. Following the recession in 2014, the number had increased once again to 32 percent (Fry 2016).

The overall trend of children remaining in or returning to their parents' home well into adulthood has become more and more common for every demographic but has been much higher than average in certain demographics, particularly those that suffer from high levels of youth unemployment and disconnection. Among black millennials, for instance, only 17 percent live with a spouse or partner, while 36 percent live with one or both of their parents (Fry 2016). The direct correlation between employment and failure to launch has been notably evident among young men of all races. As the employment numbers and inflation-adjusted wages of men have fallen significantly in recent decades, the dominant living arrangement for males between the ages of 18 and 34 is at home with one or both of their parents. One of the most significant side effects of this trend in living arrangements has been the postponement and decline of marriage for both sexes. As growing numbers of young men are remaining in their parents' home or living alone well into adulthood, young women are increasingly likely to be heading a household without a partner. According to the PEW Research Center, by 2016, "millennials surpassed all other generations in the number of household heads who were single mothers" (Fry 2017). This has significant societal implications since unmarried households in general are associated with higher rates of poverty. In fact, according to data from the Census Bureau's Current Population Survey, more millennial-headed households are in poverty than households headed by any other generation (Fry 2017).

One of the strongest predictors of the likelihood that individuals will establish their own household and raise children with a long-term spouse or partner is graduation from college. Young adults who do not enroll in or complete postsecondary education are far more likely to be living alone or with a parent than to be living with a spouse or partner. In contrast, nearly half of college graduates under the age of 34 are married or living with a partner, while less than 1 in 5 live with a parent (Fry 2016). These numbers do not discount the fact that many college graduates, who find themselves facing poor job prospects and a heavy load of student debt, are also likely to delay the establishment of their own household. In fact, high levels of student debt are certainly a leading factor influencing the growing number of young people who move back in with their parents after attending college. Nevertheless, sociologists Jason Houle and Cody Warner (2017) recently discovered that among those who acquire student debt, those with lower levels of debt have a significantly higher risk of returning home than those with higher levels of debt. The reason for this seeming anomaly is that those with lower levels of student debt are more likely to have attended nonselective colleges or to have failed to complete their degree. Those who attend college but fail to earn a degree also generally acquire debt, but, unlike those who graduate, they do not improve their job prospects. Therefore, they are often worse off financially than before they began attending school and are even less likely than their peers to successfully transition into self-sufficient adulthood.

Another social consequence of high levels of youth unemployment and disconnection is the disintegrative effect they have on the probability of social mobility. Harvey Golub (2013) explains that three factors determine whether individuals who are born into poverty are likely to rise out of poverty: finishing high school, avoiding becoming a teenage parent, and getting a full-time job. According to Golub, "Those who do all three have only a 2 percent chance of living in poverty and a 75 percent chance of joining the middle class" (2). On the other hand, when large percentages of young people experience a weak start in the labor market and struggle to achieve economic sufficiency, the prospects of social mobility, both for themselves and for their children, are diminished (Mitnik and Grusky 2015). Faced with intergenerational dependency and an inability to engage productively in the marketplace, youth risk becoming socially disconnected as well. The longer disconnection from the labor force persists, the more suscep-tible youth become to feelings of cynicism, disenfranchise-ment, and a lack of confidence in their own agency. Don Peck (2011) reports, for example, that following the rise in youth unemployment resulting from the Great Recession, millennials began to express high levels of distrust in their government and a growing sense that their financial well-being depended not on their own actions but on circumstances outside of their control. The anger and frustration that accompanies prolonged periods of unemployment and disconnection may further undermine youths' respect for their society; its governing structure; and its general values such as freedom, democracy, and capitalism. As has been demonstrated elsewhere in the world, these atti-tudes can fuel an already-growing propensity toward antisocial behavior, including substance abuse, vandalism, gang involve-ment, and other criminal activity. In fact, according to some estimates, youth who are neither working nor in education or training commit more than 60 percent of all youth crime even though they make up less than 20 percent of the population (Belfield, Levin, and Rosen 2012). Thus, marginalization of large numbers of youth from the working population may sig-nificantly undermine the nation's long-term social well-being, safety, and stability.

What Should Be Done?

As discussed in the previous chapter, the factors producing chronic youth unemployment and disconnection are influ-enced by, but also extend beyond, the performance of the labor market at any given time. Many of the causes are deep-rooted and structural in nature and vary greatly by demographic, edu-cational history, socioeconomic status, and geographic location. While a simple, universal solution to the unique and diverse causes of youth unemployment and disconnection may not exist, a wide range of actors and organizations have sought to better understand the nature of the problem and have worked to address some of the underlying causes of the crisis and to minimize its worst effects.

Expanding Access to and Participation in Higher Education

It is well established that today's youth will have a difficult time achieving gainful employment, economic stability, and upward mobility without some level of postsecondary education or training, whether in the form of a traditional bachelor's degree, an associate's degree, or an occupational certificate. From grade school on, young people are likely to hear repeatedly from teachers, mentors, and guidance counselors that a college education is essential for future employability. Elected leaders across the political spectrum have additionally responded to this reality by offering various proposals to increase access to and enrollment in postsecondary education. In 2016, for example, President Obama announced that his administration would work to make college more accessible, attainable, and affordable in order to advance the goal that, by 2020, America would once again have the highest proportion of college graduates in the world.

Over the past couple of decades, many young people have heeded the advice that they should go to college, and the nation as a whole has made incredible strides toward increasing the number of young people enrolled in various forms of postsecondary education. This progress has been particularly notable when it comes to youth from low-income and disadvantaged backgrounds. For instance, Holzer and Baum (2017) point out that in 1984 only 36 percent of high school graduates from the lowest family income quartile immediately enrolled in a two- or four-year college. By 2014, however, "67 percent of all recent high school graduates—and 52 percent of those from the lowest income group—went straight to college" (3). Although these numbers appear to be a very good sign, researchers are discovering that enrollment alone does not ensure success.

In fact, many of those who set out to pursue a postsecondary degree find themselves in a precarious position. As the costs of attending college have risen more than four times the rate of inflation over the past several decades, students are forced to take on higher levels of debt to finance their education. Securing remunerative employment postgraduation, thus, becomes all the more essential for graduates to maintain a satisfactory standard of living and avoid defaulting on their loans. Yet, data collected in recent years indicates that many college graduates, burdened by debt, have a difficult time finding stable, well-paying employment. As previously observed, nearly half of college graduates in the United States face unemployment, underemployment, or employment in jobs that do not require a college degree (Abel, Deitz, and Su 2014). Graduates who find themselves thousands of dollars in debt without the prospect of remunerative employment risk discovering that they are worse off financially than before they enrolled in school. Such a situation is particularly detrimental for those who are already coming from an economically disadvantaged background.

The most commonly proposed political solution to the growing financial difficulties caused by progressively excessive levels of student debt is to offset such costs by reforming and subsidizing college financing. Over the past several years, representatives at the state and national levels have introduced a variety of legislative proposals to encourage student loan forgiveness, to allow for lower-interest rate refinancing, and to establish repayment plans based on student income following graduation. Senators Elizabeth Warren (D-MA) and Bernie Sanders (I-VT) recently garnered national attention for their joint proposal of the "College for All Act" (Zornick 2017). This plan, based largely on promises that Bernie Sanders and Hillary Clinton made during their 2016 presidential campaigns, aims to make community college free for students of all income levels and to eliminate tuition and fees at four-year colleges and universities for students who come from families that make less than $125,000 a year. The act would authorize the federal government to pay 67 percent of tuition subsidies and requires state and tribal governments to chip in the remaining 33 percent. Supporters laud this and similar legislation as a necessary step toward extending the benefits of higher education to individuals from all backgrounds and income levels. Critics, on the other hand, maintain that such proposals would burden taxpayers and the economy with billions of dollars of debt but would not solve the problem of unemployed graduates and overeducated baristas (Adorney 2017).

Although support for tuition-free public universities has expanded over the past several years, especially at the state level, a growing body of research indicates that increasing students' ability to finance traditional college education through loans and subsidies will not, on its own, improve students' prospects of employability or upward mobility. The reason is that large numbers of students—particularly those who are first-generation college-attenders from disadvantaged backgrounds—do not leave college better prepared for the workforce, either because they fail to enroll in programs or develop the skills that will increase their likelihood of employment success or because they fail to complete their degree at all.

Those who support universal access to college education generally point to data demonstrating significant earning premiums and greater job security associated with the attainment of a college degree. They contend, on these grounds, that the financial gains resulting from the acquisition of a college degree far outweigh the large sums of money used to finance that degree. Such widespread claims, while true in the aggregate, can be extremely misleading. Vedder, Denhar, and Robe (2013) demonstrate, for instance, that the data associating higher levels of income and employment opportunity with a college degree is based on an examination of the average earnings of the entire college graduate population, many of whom graduated 30 or more years ago. Furthermore, such data fails to distinguish between earning potential based on the prestige of the degree program and university and does not account for how individuals' preexisting cognitive skills may contribute to better employment and earning rates. Although many graduates over time have reaped substantial economic benefits from higher education, a large percentage of recent college graduates do not receive a good financial return on their investment. Unfortunately, this is even more the case for many youth born at the bottom of the socioeconomic ladder. Robert Putnam (2016), for example, points out that the class gap in admission to the most selective institutions with the best prospects for employment success has widened in recent years. Summarizing data from several recent studies, Putnam explains, "The fraction of kids from the bottom quartile of the income distribution who ended up at a selective college or university rose from 4 percent in 1972 to 5 percent three decades later, but for kids from the top quartile, the equivalent figures were 26 percent and 36 percent. By 2004, in the nation's 'most competitive' colleges and universities . . . kids from the top quartile of the socioeconomic scale outnumbered kids from the bottom quartile by about 14 to one" (186).

A small fraction of high school graduates from low-income and disadvantaged backgrounds do qualify for and enroll in selective four-year colleges and universities, but most—due to their weak academic backgrounds and other constraints—attend more accessible public colleges and universities, community colleges, or for-profit colleges and institutions. Those who graduate from less selective institutions still, on the whole, have undeniably better prospects than nongraduates. Nevertheless, many of these graduates concentrate in fields with low levels of compensation and are leaving college unprepared for the workforce having few marketable skills. In 2006, the Conference Board, a global, independent business and research association, spearheaded a nationwide study of employers' perception of graduates' readiness for the workforce. More than 90 percent of the hundreds of employers surveyed reported that generic high-order skills—which include those that should be developed in any college degree program—such as written and oral communication, critical thinking, and problem solving were very important for the long-term success of new entrants to the workforce. Yet, a large percentage of employers reported significant deficiencies in these areas among graduates from both two- and four-year institutions. In 2012, *The Chronicle of Higher Education* and America's Public Media *Marketplace* conducted a similar nationwide survey of over 700 employers, asking employers a series of questions pertaining to their perception of how well colleges and universities were preparing their graduates for the workplace (Fischer 2013). Although most of the employers surveyed require applicants to possess a college degree—viewing it as an indicator that an individual can work toward achieving a goal—half of those surveyed reported trouble finding qualified graduates. A third of those surveyed lamented that a large percentage of bachelor's degree holders lack basic workplace proficiencies, such as adaptability; written and oral communication skills; and the ability to problem solve, make decisions, analyze data, and construct cogent arguments. Consequently, most employers surveyed reported that, when given the opportunity, they prefer to hire applicants with a record of workplace competency in addition to possessing a degree. Furthermore, although college major was mentioned as the most important academic credential in evaluating a recent graduate for employment, a large percentage of employers testified that they actually give more weight to the applicant's previous work experience, including internships and employment, than to their academic credentials, including their GPA. Thus, those who graduate from college with a low-demand major and little to no work experience are automatically at a major disadvantage when seeking postgraduate employment.

An additional, and perhaps more serious problem, in terms of viewing college education as a guaranteed pathway to success, is the substantial number of students who enroll in college but don't leave with a degree. In terms of enrollment, the nation has made enormous progress in improving access to two- and four-year institutions for low-income youth from disadvantaged backgrounds. In fact, the number of students from the bottom income quintile who enrolled in college immediately following high school graduation reach a historic high of nearly 70 percent in 2016 (Cooper 2018). Unfortunately, however, the rise in the number of high school graduates attending college has not been accompanied by an increase in the number who graduate from college. Furthermore, while colleges reap financial benefits from admitting large numbers of government-funded students, they are not held liable when a majority of them drop out before receiving a degree. According to the National Center for Education Statistics (2018), only 63 percent of females and 57 percent of males who enrolled at a four-year degree-granting institution in fall 2010 had completed their degree six years later. Only 24 percent of students at public two-year degree-granting institutions and only 60 percent of students at private two-year degree-granting institutions, who enrolled full time in fall of 2013, attained a certificate or associates degree within three years. The completion rates for minority students and those at the bottom of the income scale are even lower than the national averages. Many of these students drop out because of financial constraints associated with limited individual and family resources, but lowering the costs of higher education is not enough to ensure their success. As Holzer and Baum (2017) explain, poor academic preparation in the K-12 years plays a significant role in the completion problem among disadvantaged students, as does a lack of social capital and familiarity with the academic world and what is required for success. Furthermore, many disadvantaged students have significant work and familial responsibilities that make it difficult to maintain their full-time student status.

Improving Higher Education Outcomes

As young people, particularly those from disadvantaged backgrounds, are almost universally encouraged to enroll in college as the most viable path to stable employment and long-term financial security, greater attention should be directed toward ensuring that such enrollment will lead to better, rather than worse, life prospects for those investing their money, time, and other resources. With this goal in mind, many have called for improving the payoff of higher education by arming prospective students with an enhanced awareness of the employment and earning potential of different majors and programs, by expanding efforts to bolster college completion rates for those vulnerable to dropping out, and by developing a stronger link between institutions of higher learning and the labor market.

Increasing Transparency and Accountability

Based on dismal college completion rates and the unreliable employment outcomes, even for those who do manage to graduate from two- and four-year degree-granting institutions, it is clear that major efforts are needed to increase transparency and accountability in higher education. Today, large amounts of public and personal financing are funneled into colleges and degree programs with little consideration of whether that money is being spent on improving higher education quality and overall outcomes. While the movement to provide greater transparency and accountability has gained influence in Washington over the past decade, until recently lawmakers' focus was largely directed toward cracking down on nonaccredited degree programs and for-profit colleges (Van Zandt 2012). In fact, for-profit colleges, designed to provide vocational courses and training to help students move immediately into the job market, are often held to more rigorous standards in terms of completion and labor market outcomes than public and private nonprofit four-year universities. For example, Furchtgott-Roth and Meyer (2015) report that the Department of Education forced Corinthian College to close by withholding Pell Grants and federal loans because it claimed the school fraudulently misrepresented graduates' job prospects; yet, many other institutions that would fail by these same standards continue to operate on the taxpayer dime. Furchtgott-Roth and Meyer, thus, contend that accountability and transparency concerning enrollment and degree outcomes should be extended across the board to public and private not-for-profit institutions as well. This is particularly important considering that, although the federal government distributes financial aid and loans regardless of students' choice of major or program, the ability of students to find gainful employment and to pay back those loans in the future varies greatly based on their choice.

One way to start encouraging greater accountability in higher education is to raise awareness of the costs and benefits of different majors and programs in a way that empowers prospective students to make better decisions regarding their undergraduate education and whether they are investing their time and money wisely. Attempts to measure the value of degrees and programs are undoubtedly subject to immense difficulties and limitations, particularly because individuals pursuing a degree may be seeking different qualities in a college based on personal interest, religion, academic priorities, geography, race and ethnicity, and so on. Popular college-ranking systems tend to reflect the variety of sought-after qualities and outcomes, measuring schools by standards such as faculty research and awards, resources, endowment levels, classroom experience, faculty to student ratio, orientation toward public service, admission of low-incomes students, and level of student body diversity. While rankings have recently begun to focus more narrowly on graduates' labor market returns, opponents of such measures warn against gaging higher education outcomes purely in economic or utilitarian terms. Peter Wood, president of the National Association of Scholars, for example, contends that higher education, rightly understood, aims to prepare graduates for well-rounded citizenship and societal leadership in a free society, qualities that extend beyond a mere concern for material success. He asserts, "Higher education is about entrusting to each new generation the legacy of civilization. We learn—or we should learn—respect for reason, civil dialogue, the great accomplishments of art and science, the enormity of our failures, the profundity of our ideals, and a great deal more that makes us not just capable of carrying forward a society worth living in but an eagerness to do so" (Wood 2015). While there is certainly truth to Wood's concerns, it is nevertheless a modern reality that just as higher education has become progressively more expensive, it has also become more broadly pushed as the primary path for ensuring that members of the general population can obtain upward mobility and economic security. In fact, the choice of college and major may be among the most important lifetime economic investments that many individuals will make. The more widespread college enrollment becomes, the more imperative it becomes for prospective students to understand the economic value of their degree in addition to any intellectual, spiritual, civic, and creative value it might provide.

With this reality in mind, various performance metrics have been proposed and implemented over the past several years. Following the start of the academic year in 2015, for example, President Obama announced the launch of the White House–sponsored College Scorecard with the stated goal of providing federal data to parents and other third parties so they might evaluate institutions of higher learning based on their contributions to student economic success. The College Scorecard, administered by the Department of Education, published information on individual colleges based on a range of variables, including the number of low-income students enrolled, student debt levels, graduation rates, and average graduate earnings. The administration's long-term goal was to make the receipt of federal aid contingent on a high College Scorecard rating. Critics pointed out, however, that the College Scorecard suffered from several major weaknesses. The Scorecard restricted data collection only to institutions that grant more degrees than certificates and to students within those institutions who receive federal aid. It, therefore, excluded analysis of schools with low rates of federal aid, community colleges that offer a large number of certificate programs in addition to associate degrees, and schools where no federal aid recipients are enrolled. An additional shortcoming of the data published in the Scorecard is that it simply listed average alumni employment and salary outcomes without regard to the background and characteristics of enrolled students that might contribute more to such outcomes than the quality of the college. Johnathan Rothwell (2015), a senior economist at Gallup, points out that alumni salary, on its own, is a biased way to measure the quality of a college. Such a measure, he contends, is a weak indicator of a school's economic value "because colleges with high earning alumni also tend to have students who are better prepared academically—as measured by test scores—and come from higher-income families." "These students," Rothwell continues, "would have been well positioned to earn at least moderately high salaries, even if they attended a less prestigious college" (6).

In an effort to solve this latter weakness and more accurately predict which institutions contribute the most to alumni career preparation and economic success, Siddharth Kulkarni and Jonathan Rothwell (2015), conducting research for the Brookings Institution, adopted a more complex measure of investigating the strengths and weaknesses of individual colleges based on what they termed the "value-added" approach. Rather than merely listing data such as graduates' salaries or employment levels, "value-added" measures identify economic outcomes of graduates, such as mid-career earnings, the ability to repay student loans, and level of job skills possessed, and then attempt to determine the effect that colleges themselves had on such outcomes above and beyond what the students' background would predict. In terms of salary, for example, Kulkarni and Rothwell (2015) explain, "a college's 'value-added' is the difference between the actual mid-career salary of alumni and an estimation of what a graduate from a similar school would have earned given his/her characteristics" (2). Drawing on data from a variety of government and private sources, Kulkarni and

Rothwell report that graduates from some two- and four-year colleges enjoy much greater success than their characteristics at the time of initial enrollment would predict, suggesting that students of these schools are receiving a greater value from their education than students similarly situated attending other schools. Kulkarni and Rothwell further conclude that two- and four-year colleges whose alumni receive significant "value" from their education in terms of future economic performance have several key qualities in common. For example, they have high completion rates and tend to focus on training students for careers with higher-than-average earnings, such as those in STEM or technical fields.

In response to a growing emphasis on the importance of accountability and transparency of higher education outcomes, some colleges and universities have voluntarily undertaken their own efforts to provide accessible information on the value of their majors and degree programs to prospective students. In 2018, the University of Texas (UT) System was the first university system to partner with the U.S. Census Bureau to set up a database of its graduates' earnings and student loan averages (Bauer-Wolf 2018). The data site includes information, broken down by majors and programs, identifying the average loans amassed by alumni from each of UT's 14 campuses and their average earnings 5 and 10 years after graduation. The data tool is limited in that it does not include information on loans and earnings for the nearly 30 percent of students who enroll in UT degree programs and acquire student debt but fail to complete their degree within six years. It does, however, offer useful information to prospective students on the variation of average earnings and debt acquired by major and campus for those who complete their degree. Based on an overwhelmingly positive reaction to UT's data tool, the Census Bureau has reported that other institutions are working to set up similarly styled data sites (Bauer-Wolf 2018).

Employers and industry leaders themselves can also serve as a valuable source of institutional accountability and information for prospective students hoping to work in certain fields. In 2008, for example, the Boeing Company—a major employer in the field of aerospace engineering—compiled a ranking of colleges and engineering schools based on how well their graduates performed within the company. In a description of the ranking, Richard D. Stephens, the senior vice president for human resources and management, explained that Boeing's engineers are evaluated based on a combination of technical and nontechnical skills and that the company profits from workers who possess not only strong engineering abilities but also good communication skills, the ability to problem solve, and the ability to work constructively as part of a team (Basken 2008). The rankings were compiled by matching internal data from employees' performance reviews to the colleges they attended with the aim of revealing which colleges were producing the company's most valuable workers. While the results of the rankings were never released to the public, Boeing has used the data to guide its own internal recruitment, hiring, training, and choice of research partners. The company also shared its findings with the colleges ranked in an effort to help them improve the quality of their curriculum and the work record of their graduates. Surprisingly, Boeing's ranking system revealed that several lesser known institutions were producing high-performing engineers and employees. Although similar employer-sponsored ranking systems have yet to catch on nationwide, they provide a potential new paradigm for evaluating college performance and outcomes.

Because labor market outcomes assessments tend to reward institutions and majors that focus primarily in STEM or other technical fields, they are frequently resisted by faculty at non-profit liberal arts and fine arts colleges. It is now well documented that degrees in science, engineering, technology, and health-related fields are on average likely to lead to successful postgraduate careers. That does not mean, however, that students pursuing liberal arts degrees are doomed to a life of unemployment or underemployment. On the contrary, the case can be made that in our rapidly evolving high-tech economy, a liberal arts education is more valuable than ever. Pulitzer Prize–winning reporter George Anders (2017) contends, for instance, that students of the liberal arts have the opportunity to develop much sought-after skills in critical thinking and oral and written communication, in addition to valuable soft skills—including judgment, curiosity, creativity, and empathy—that can open the door to thousands of cutting-edge jobs. Echoing this view, David Van Zandt (2012), president of the New School for Social Research, argues that the fear that accountability measures threaten the core values of liberal arts institutions is based on "an outdated bias." Van Zandt argues that, as the American economy is being driven increasingly by intellectual and creative pursuits, universities that focus on developing students' analytical, critical, and creative thinking through the examination and evaluation of complex texts and project work are helping to shape the country's future economic leaders. According to Van Zandt, assessments demonstrating the significant and measurable contributions of both liberal arts and design degrees should be encouraged by nonprofit institutions. Such assessments could reveal which liberal arts and design degrees at which institutions are producing graduates with the skills and qualities necessary to thrive in the 21st-century marketplace. Indeed, when the UT conducted the assessment of its own majors and programs, its database revealed that "two-thirds of graduates from non-STEM-related programs earned much more than the national median salary for liberal arts graduates, which is roughly $35,400. Music majors from UT campuses earned a median salary of $50,856, and rhetoric and composition graduates' median income was about $46,800" (Bauer-Wolf 2018).

Improving Completion Rates

Increasing institutional accountability and access to information concerning the long-term earning and employment success rates of different programs and majors may help young people make better higher education choices based on their desired labor market outcomes, but it will do little to alleviate low rates of college completion, especially among disadvantaged students. It is, consequently, important to additionally consider practices and strategies for improving degree completion rates among those most at risk of dropping out.

The problem of degree completion over the past two decades has been almost entirely concentrated among students who begin their education at two-year colleges, for-profit schools, or public colleges and universities that are not classified in the nation's top 50 public schools (Bound, Lovenheim, and Turner 2009). Such colleges tend to be more strained for resources and have a harder time hiring quality faculty and offering students the courses or support services they need. Those weaknesses may be further aggravated by the fact that graduation rates are strongly connected to student academic preparation upon entrance and the fact that the concentration of low-performing students in less selective institutions can create a weak peer effect—in which individual outcomes become strongly correlated to the group outcomes—even for those who initially show academic promise. With few exceptions, students from low-income and disadvantaged backgrounds enrolling in postsecondary education are almost certain to attend these nonselective colleges, where their probability of success is reduced in spite of their individual abilities and qualities.

The reason for the concentration of economically disadvantaged students in less selective schools with low graduation rates is primarily academic. As Holzer and Baum (2017) explain, "Many of these students are simply not prepared for the more rigorous classes at more selective institutions and do not qualify for admission" (45). In other words, the problem chiefly lies in the reality that those from well-off families are generally far better prepared for college-level studies during their K-12 education than those from poor families. Holzer and Baum additionally point out, however, that even low-income students with a strong high school academic record, including those in the top achievement quartile, are far more likely than similarly qualified students from higher-income backgrounds to enroll in lower-quality, underperforming postsecondary schools. Based on this fact, many advocates for low-income youth support the implementation of measures to increase the percentage of economically disadvantaged youth in the country's most elite institutions of higher learning.

In their book *Making College Work*, Holzer and Baum (2017) outline three commonly recommended actions for encouraging economically disadvantaged students to enroll in postsecondary programs and institutions that generate stronger outcomes than their less selective counterparts. The first is increasing prospective students' access to information. Many low-income, first-generation college students have little understanding of the educational and financial aid options available to them, and their parents or caretakers may have little knowledge or experience in navigating the higher education system. Furthermore, high school guidance counselors in low-income, low-performing schools often have large caseloads and little training in effective college advising. Additional outreach efforts from the public and private sectors to provide individualized information and assistance filling out applications and forms for prospective students could be extremely valuable in this regard. The second strategy is to improve access by removing financial barriers preventing disadvantaged youth from attending more selective institutions. Although a combination of institutional aid, the federal Pell Grant, and state aid often covers the price of tuition, and sometimes books and fees as well, low-income students are often strained to cover their basic living expenses without further aid. A final commonly recommended strategy is for selective institutions to increase the number of disadvantaged youth through a preferential admissions policy. Opponents argue, however, that this latter attempt to help disadvantaged youth sometimes backfires by diminishing the chance of completion of students who are admitted to institutions that exceed their academic ability.

Although a laudable objective, encouraging exceptional students from disadvantaged backgrounds to enroll in more selective institutions by means of greater informational awareness, financial support, and admission preference will hardly put a dent in the problem of low college completion rates among disadvantaged youth. Even with increased recruitment and assistance efforts, the number of low-income youth who are qualified and equipped for admission and success in the nation's most selective schools is statistically minimal. Until there is a shift in the correlation between socioeconomic background and academic preparation, economically disadvantaged students will inevitably be overrepresented at nonselective institutions with poor completion rates. Moreover, such students frequently face additional personal challenges that make them less likely to complete degrees regardless of where they enroll. As James Piereson (2014) observes, "Even if we do everything in our power to get poor kids into selective colleges, their chances of completion are much lower—not only because they're unprepared academically but also because they lack the support system from families and peers that promote college completion."

Aside from addressing systemic preparation gaps in K-12 education, real change will ultimately require discovering effective practices and strategies to improve student success rates at the vast majority of postsecondary schools attended by high percentages of low-income youth. One proposed strategy for raising degree completion rates involves improving and adapting the process of remediation education for students who enroll in postsecondary education, but who are not prepared for college-level work. Most students upon entering two- and four-year colleges are required to take remedial or developmental education classes that reteach high school and junior high school level content in basic knowledge skills like reading, writing, and math. Although remedial education costs colleges and students billions of dollars annually, there is little evidence that the way these classes are currently structured is improving student success and there is some evidence that they may negatively affect degree attainment (Jaggars and Stacey 2014). One of the leading reasons for this is that many students who are required to take a series of developmental courses before they are permitted to enroll in academic credit courses or courses in their degree program become discouraged and drop out before completing the remediation sequence. Others find that the courses are not well integrated to college-level work. Attempts to reform remedial education at the college level often face resistance from those concerned that such reform will sacrifice academic quality and harm students in the long run. Students with large gaps in preparation may inevitably require intensive instruction in reading, writing, and mathematics in addition to active academic advising and tutoring before they are capable of matriculating into for-credit courses. For those with moderate gaps in preparation, however, evidence increasingly shows that remediation is far more effective at improving student persistence and credit attainment when incorporated directly into for-credit course work or the context of what students intend to study. One successful example of this is the Community College of Baltimore County's Accelerated Learning Program (ALP), which allows developmental-level writing students to enroll in college-level courses but additionally requires them to enroll in a mandatory developmental support course taught by the same instructor (Jaggars, Hodara, and Stacey 2013). Another example is the state of Washington's Integrated Basic Education and Skills Training (I-BEST) model, which provides two teachers for the same course, one to deliver the course content and one to provide needed remediation assistance. Holzer and Baum (2017) explain that rather than relegating remedial education to stand-alone English and math courses, the I-BEST model "embeds remediation into applied job training classes" (142). It thereby provides a context for remedial education, which, consequently, improves student motivation and understanding.

Studies have shown that one of the biggest factors contributing to low rates of college completion among disadvantaged youth is their lack of a social or familial support system and a lack of knowledge of how to manage time, prioritize tasks, effectively complete assignments, and otherwise thrive in an academic setting. Thus, another commonly proposed approach for improving student success rates among those from disadvantaged backgrounds is to provide, and even require, a range of support services such as peer-learning communities, counseling, tutoring, and coaching. While a variety of intervention strategies have been implemented at schools across the country with mixed results, one practice that shows significant promise is the use of coaches to facilitate student persistence and completion. In 2011, Eric Bettinger and Rachel Baker, researchers at Stanford University, evaluated the impact of coaching services provided by InsideTrack, an independent company that works with public and private colleges across the country to improve student success and retention. InsideTrack, in conjunction with each participating college, matches selected students with a trained coach. These coaches then maintain regular contact with assigned students throughout their first year of school. Coaches work with students to develop a clear vision of their goals and to strategize how they might overcome barriers to these goals. Coaches additionally work with students to plan their daily activities in line with their priorities, to manage their finances, and to improve self-advocacy and study skills. In their assessment of the services provided by InsideTrack, Bettinger and Baker found that students who were assigned a coach had significantly higher rates of retention compared to similarly situated students at the same schools who did not participate in the coaching program. Moreover, the retention effects lasted well beyond the coaching period and eventually led to higher rates of college completion. Bettinger and Baker note that the services provided by InsideTrack are more effective in producing desired results than similar services offered internally by individual colleges. This is in part due to the fact that serving multiple institutions enables InsideTrack to invest in personnel, training, processes, and technologies that are typically out of reach for individual schools. Bettinger and Baker ultimately conclude that the coaching provided by InsideTrack was less costly and more effective compared to previously studied interventions, including increased financial aid, and that it provides a highly useful model for improving college completion rates.

Bridging the Gap between Education and Work

According to the Collegiate Employment Research Institute (2018), the job outlook for recent graduates has never been better. The institute projects that "spurred by business growth, employee turnover, and retirements, job opportunities will expand by 19 percent across all degree levels." Nevertheless, many employers report facing extensive hiring challenges, having to compete with other businesses to attract qualified candidates since too many applicants lack the soft and technical skills required for the positions offered. Consequently, as reported in the institute's recent report on recruiting trends, "The available positions will go to those who demonstrate the skills, competencies, work attitudes, and professional behaviors employers want." Whereas, "those who lack experience and are unprepared will likely miss out on this year's opportunities, no matter how many opportunities are available" (1). Thus, while improving degree completion rates among those who enroll in postsecondary education will go a long way to improving youth employment prospects, significantly increasing graduates' potential for labor market success in remunerative skilled careers will require further bridging of the divide between skill supply and demand. Incidentally, institutions of higher learning could drastically improve the prospects of their graduates both by increasing students' opportunities for work-based applied learning experiences and by improving school ties with employers and local industries.

One proposal for improving college affordability and ensuring that students have marketable work experience when they enter the labor market is to expand the number and reach of work colleges (Furchtgott-Roth and Meyer 2015). Work Colleges are accredited institutions of higher education that have a proven record of helping students of limited means—many of whom are first-generation college students—obtain a quality liberal arts college education, while developing transferable real-world professional skills without being burdened by debt. The colleges award bachelor degrees based on a model that incorporates traditional learning with work responsibilities and service. Most students receive full tuition scholarships and are required to work an average of 10 to 15 hours a week and participate in community service in a way that enhances their academic learning. There are currently eight geographically and academically diverse Work Colleges in the United States that run distinctive work programs designed to meet campus need and complement relevant coursework.

Another way postsecondary institutions can encourage hands-on experiential learning and postgraduate employment success is through the support of internships and field projects. Students who participate in internship and classroom-based field projects have the opportunity to acquire real-world experience and develop valuable professional connections for future employment. An online survey of major employers who hire more than 25 percent of their employees from two- and four-year colleges conducted for the American Association of Colleges and Universities found that 78 percent of the hundreds of respondents mentioned that completing an internship or a community field-based project plays a major role in enabling students to successfully transition to work following graduation (Hart Research Associates 2013). Internships, in particular, provide a means for students not only to gain valuable experience but also to demonstrate their capacity to work in a professional environment to potential employers. In fact, more and more companies, reluctant to hire college graduates with little to no work experience, are increasingly hiring from their intern pools. Recent estimates predict employers hire around 50 percent of their interns and in some industries, such as construction, accounting, and scientific services, employers offer full-time employment to more than 75 percent of their interns (Selingo 2016). The benefits of internship experiences additionally appear to extend beyond the increase in immediate employability. In 2016, a Gallup survey demonstrated that applied internship experiences "are strongly linked to increased employee engagement, higher well-being later in life, and graduates' feeling that their degree was worth the cost" (12). Although abundant evidence demonstrates that internships play a critical role in helping graduates secure gainful employment, not all internships offer the same career payoff. In comparison to paid internships, which have a fairly strong record of leading to postgraduation job offers, unpaid internships are more of a mixed bag in terms of whether or not they give participants a boost in the job market. Higher education expert Jeffrey Selingo (2016), thus, encourages students to consider two factors when determining whether the time they invest in an unpaid internship will pay off—first, whether the internship allows participants to gain experience in more than just menial work; and second, whether those who have secured the same internship in the past were hired into paid positions.

Educators and business leaders are increasingly working together to adopt additional strategies for students to apply what they are learning in the classroom to the actual world of work. One such strategy is cooperative education programs that provide students with the opportunity to alternate between semesters of academic study and semesters of full-time off-campus employment that is integrated with their educational and career goals. Participating students are able to earn money while they apply the principles and techniques they are learning in the classroom to a practical real-world environment. Participants also acquire the type of work experience and professional connections that greatly increase their opportunity for full-time employment after college. Cooperative education programs are most common in engineering and technology-related fields but are also expanding into other fields, including business and liberal arts. Hundreds of companies and several government entities such as the National Aeronautics and Space Administration (NASA) and the Defense Intelligence Agency (DIA) are now working with universities to offer students a range of cooperative education opportunities.

Partnerships between employers and institutions of higher learning can be especially valuable at the community college level. Although most guidance counselors advise young people to go directly into four-year degree programs, community colleges provide the most promising path to high-quality education and careers for millions of America's youth, particularly those whose circumstances, resources, and high school achievement level would make it difficult for them to thrive in a traditional four-year setting. Community colleges not only serve a valuable role in helping prepare students to transfer to four-year institutions, but they also contribute to social mobility by providing students—many of whom are low-income and low-achieving youth—the opportunity to earn an occupational certificate or associates degree in a range of high-paying, high-demand professions, such as the building trades, health care, and computer programing. In fact, students who earn credentials or associates degrees in high-income fields experience significant lifetime-earning gains and mobility outcomes (Belfield and Bailey 2011). Moreover, because community colleges serve students who live within a defined geographic area, they are well suited to partner with local industries to develop flexible, affordable, and relevant training programs that meet business and regional economic needs. Jeffrey Selingo (2017) notes, "Faced with a skills gap, employers are increasingly working with community colleges to provide students with both the academic education needed to succeed in today's work force and the specific hands-on skills to get a job in their company." Selingo cites the example of the collaboration between John

Deere dealerships and several community colleges to illustrate this point. John Deere donates its equipment and provides curriculum to participating colleges to train technicians for its dealer network. In addition to taking courses on topics ranging from customer service to hydraulics, participants in the John Deere Tech Program are paid to work part time and participate in hands-on training with seasoned technicians at a sponsoring dealership. Students who complete the seven quarter program earn an associate degree in applied arts and sciences and most receive a full-time, salaried position with John Deere upon graduation.

Expanding Access to Nontraditional Education and Career Pathways

Postsecondary education has undeniably become the most effective, and often only, means to gainful employment and upward mobility for many of America's youth. Nevertheless, some argue that the widely accepted "college-for-all" mantra prevents the growth of promising educational and career pathway alternatives by stigmatizing anything other than a four-year college degree as second best. Yet, there are several other reliable and effective alternative paths to learning—outside of enrollment in traditional postsecondary programs—that can help youth obtain the skills, capacities, and experiences to thrive in the labor market and improve their postsecondary education outcomes should they eventually choose that route. Among these promising routes to occupational success are apprenticeships, career and technical education beginning as early as high school, and national service or job training programs.

Apprenticeships

One proven method of helping young people gain work experience while they acquire the knowledge and skills they will need for career success are apprenticeships. Apprenticeships refer to programs, lasting anywhere from one to six years, in which participants are paid by a sponsoring employer to engage in hands-on training under the direct supervision of a skilled expert in a specific occupation or industry. In addition to supervised work-based learning, apprentices are generally required to take academic courses on related technical and professional skills in order to complete the program. Apprenticeship programs are sponsored by a range of employers, including private businesses and nonprofits, labor groups, industry associations, government agencies, and the military.

Although apprenticeships have long been prevalent in Europe, particularly Germany and the Scandinavian countries, as a highly respected means of preparing a majority of youth for professions in a variety of fields from manufacturing to hospitality and banking, they have had trouble catching on in the United States where they are often discounted as second-choice options for underachievers or those who are not college material. Furthermore, until recently, apprenticeship opportunities in the United States were largely available only to those going into manual labor occupations and the construction trades. Nevertheless, over the past decade, in response to ever-growing levels of college debt and mounting evidence of a skills gap between graduates seeking work and available job opportunities, the country has shown rising interest in and openness to expanding the number of apprenticeship opportunities in a wider variety of fields. Consequently, policy makers at the national and state levels from all sides of the political spectrum have begun to give apprenticeships a closer look.

The benefits that young people receive from participating in apprenticeships are hard to ignore. Because apprentices receive wages for the time they spend in on-the-job training, they accumulate little to no student debt and are able to pay for their living expenses while they learn. This makes apprenticeships a more viable educational path for many youth from economically disadvantaged backgrounds. Robert I. Lerman (2010), a research fellow at the Urban Institute, contends that the combination of earning and learning makes apprenticeships a particularly effective way to successfully integrate minorities, particularly minority young men, into the labor market. Lerman explains, "Having learning take place mostly on the job, making the tasks and classroom work highly relevant to their careers, and providing participants wages while they learn can give minorities increased confidence that their personal efforts and investment in skill development will pay off. In addition, mastering a skill by completing an apprenticeship gives graduates a genuine sense of occupational identity and occupational pride" (2). Moreover, some industries are beginning to augment the educational benefit of apprenticeships by partnering with postsecondary institutions, so that participants in paid apprenticeships can simultaneously pursue a degree in a related field. Thus, in the words of former U.S. Secretary of Labor Thomas Perez, "Apprenticeship is the other college, except without the debt" (Selingo 2017).

Apprenticeships additionally provide participants with a huge competitive advantage in the job market compared to those who graduate from college with minimal on-the-job experience. A major reason for this is that because apprenticeships are driven by employer demand, they are less likely to create the kind of mismatch between skills taught and those desired in the workplace compared to education and training that are provided solely in academic, school-based courses. Consequently, after completing their program, apprentices generally transition seamlessly into full-time positions with middle-class starting salaries. Apprentices also have an easier time advancing throughout their career due to their level of experience and the social and professional networks they are able to form early on through their one-on-one interaction with direct supervisors and their contact with fellow industry professionals.

In light of these clear and substantial benefits, the number and variety of businesses and industries offering apprenticeships have grown over the past several years. Nevertheless, apprenticeships remain an underutilized worker training strategy in the United States. Less than 1 percent of American workers have enrolled in an apprenticeship program, and the supply of available apprenticeships falls far short of the demand. Part of this shortage results from the federal government's meager support for apprenticeships in comparison to billions of dollars allocated to support traditional postsecondary education and other alternative training methods. In fact, even with modest federal subsidies, the costs of apprenticeships are financed almost entirely by employer or industry sponsors who pay for apprentices' on-the-job training costs and wages and often a portion of the tuition and fees for classroom instruction. The minimal amount of federal funding that is allocated to support apprenticeships is funneled through the Department of Labor's Office of Apprentice (OA) that administers the country's "Registered Apprenticeship" program. As part of its oversight responsibilities, the OA oversees approval and registration of apprenticeships sets standards for training duration, quality, and competency; regulates worker health and safety; ensures equality of access; and issues nationally recognized certificates of completion. Toward the end of his second term, President Obama significantly increased the amount of grant funding allocated to the OA to study the potential for improving public–private partnerships and to expand Registered Apprenticeships into new industries. Yet, at the end of 2016, the Department of Labor reported only a half million active Registered Apprenticeships, over 80 percent of which were in construction and manufacturing (Department of Labor 2017). In his first year in office, President Donald Trump renewed efforts to expand available apprenticeships under the Department of Labor's Registered Apprenticeship Program by issuing an executive order to increase the level of funding allocated to subsidize apprenticeships and to give private entities—such as companies, labor unions, and industry groups—more flexibility to design their own apprenticeships standards outside of the OA's specific guidelines.

Over the past few years, the states themselves have played a significant role in expanding apprenticeship opportunities to youth. Whereas federally governed Registered Apprenticeships typically have age limits and require participants to possess a high school diploma or GED, a growing number of states are working to prepare high school students and low-achieving young adults for a career pathway or entry into Registered Apprenticeships through the launch of pre-apprenticeship programs. The programs that generally involve partnerships between high schools, businesses, and community colleges are geared toward providing work-based learning opportunities for those who are still enrolled in high school that create a pipeline to postsecondary education opportunities and careers. Robert Lerman (2010) suggests that states additionally expand the reach of apprenticeships by using discretionary funding allocated for job training under the federal Workforce Innovation and Opportunity Act (WIOA) to promote apprenticeship opportunities for youth most vulnerable to unemployment and disconnection, such as those with a history of involvement in the criminal justice system. Some states have started encouraging businesses to participate in apprenticeship opportunities by offering tax credits or other subsidies to help offset the costs. In 2007, in response to the state's shortage of skilled workers, South Carolina adopted a $1,000 business tax credit per apprentice for up to four years to help offset the costs of maintaining apprenticeship opportunities. The state simultaneously sponsored the creation of Apprenticeship Carolina, one of the largest and fastest-growing apprenticeship programs in the country. The program is based on a partnership between private and public employers in the state and the 16 technical colleges in the South Carolina Technical College System. In addition to job-related training with a partner company, participants in the apprenticeship program must complete over 100 hours of job-related education in one of the technical colleges.

Career and Technical Education

Programs that link classroom education with employer partnerships and work-based learning as early as high school
have additionally demonstrated potential to improve the
labor market outcomes of young people—particularly those
whose family background, neighborhood characteristics, and
economic situation put them at high risk for dropping out of
school. Lamentably, however, the way vocational education
was applied in the past has created significant cultural barriers to the expansion of what is now referred to as career and
technical education (CTE). Dating back to the first half of
the 20th century, vocational education in the United States,
or "voc ed" as it was commonly referred to, was consistently
low in quality. As Holzer and Baum (2017) report, "The academic content was weak, the skills imparted were limited,
and the jobs for which students were prepared were often
low-wage and low-skill. Voc ed was where students went
if they were not 'college prep,' and it was clearly seen as a
last-resort option. Indeed, many of the skills taught were for
declining occupations and industries, taught by instructors,
far from the frontier of knowledge and the contemporary
labor market." "Even worse," Holzer and Baum continue,
"there was a long tradition of tracking those with lower perceived achievement into voc ed, [and] in many cases, race
and class, as opposed to measured achievement through
test scores, determined the tracks into which students were
sorted" (194). Due to this historically checkered past, career
and technical education became widely stigmatized as a form
of lower quality education for those who are less capable or
have few ambitions and was frequently criticized as a dis-
criminatory means of relegating lower-income and minority
students to a second-class education regardless of their abilities or aspirations. Consequently, many of the opportunities
for career preparation in high school were eliminated rather
than improved.

Nonetheless, the past couple decades have witnessed a resurging experimentation with CTE for some students that is relevant to the jobs and careers of the 21st century, and growing evidence shows that students involved in modern career and technical education outperform students in more traditional academic settings. While such evidence has begun to change attitudes toward CTE, outdated stereotypes against vocational education still persist. On the whole, most educators steer students away from high school vocational education entirely, instead viewing high school through the narrow lens of prepping students for immediate enrollment in college. Standard courses and measures of achievement for high school students are almost entirely driven by college entry requirements. In the face of evidence that the sophistication and quality of such preparation varies substantially from school to school and that many students leave high school academically ill-equipped in math and literacy, the general thrust of K-12 reform is to raise the academic standards across the board. Rarely do national educational outcome goals focus on improving occupational and career prospects or bolstering school-employer partnerships to allow for hands-on learning. Ironically, many of the states that have sought to raise requirements and standards for all students in academically rigorous subjects like math and science have suffered a decrease in high school completion rates (Symonds, Schwartz, and Ferguson 2011).

A number of prominent experts in education policy now contend that the current system places far too much weight on a single pathway to success—that is, graduating from a four-year bachelor's degree program after completing an academically oriented course of study in high school—especially considering that only 30 percent of young people successfully achieve this goal in spite of decades-long concerted efforts to raise that number (Symonds, Schwartz, and Ferguson 2011). Furthermore, among those who do graduate with a bachelor's degree, many still lack a clear understanding of what career they want to pursue or the steps necessary to achieve their professional goals. According to Nicholas Wyman (2015), in spite of the low levels of completion and postgraduate success rates, popular misconceptions that "the lack of a bachelor's degree is akin to a life sentence of low-wage, low-skill service jobs with limited advancement opportunity" continue to fuel the restricted view of the purpose of high school education (72). Yet, as Wyman points out, "The reality is that vocational high school graduates with certifications and some work experience are not only highly employable, they often earn *higher* salaries than their counterparts who graduate from traditional high schools and complete a few years of college—often even higher than college graduates without any skills training" (72–73). Thus, Wyman and others suggest that it is high time to broaden the range of quality career pathways offered to high school students by incorporating elements of CTE and workplace-training into the more traditional elements of the school curriculum and to allow students seeking to pursue occupations that require fewer academic requirements the ability to start taking steps toward a viable career. In fact, students who participate in many of today's work-based learning programs in high school are often better prepared for a variety of postsecondary options, whether they choose to pursue a traditional academic four-year degree or to continue their learning in the workplace or in another educational setting suitable for their chosen career path, such as an apprenticeship or occupational certificate program.

According to researchers at Harvard's Graduate School of Education, work-based learning and CTE are beneficial not only for helping high school students develop 21st-century skills and a clearer sense of direction in the marketplace, but they are also a powerful way to engage students who are bored or turned off by conventional classroom instruction (Symonds, Schwartz, and Ferguson 2011). In fact, considering that a majority of high school dropouts report that lack of interest is one of their primary reasons for leaving school, work-based learning—which engages students in a range of school-related activities and provides a clear and immediate payoff—has enormous benefits for economically disadvantaged students and those at greatest risk of dropping out. According to Robert Lerman (1999), schools provide a great service to students at risk of disconnection when they help them develop good work habits and allow them to earn money and pursue personal interests in jobs and careers as a way of motivating them to learn effectively. Lerman explains, "The use of learning in context not only helps students see the relevance of what they are studying, but also helps them gain the self-confidence many of these students lack through their capability to accomplish tasks" (205). In this way, work-based learning can ultimately encourage young people to remain engaged in school and to achieve their academic goals as well.

Not all CTE or workplace learning programs are equal in quality or outcomes, but over the past two decades several high-quality national models have emerged. One proven model of success is the Career Academy Movement, which began in Philadelphia in 1969 and now operates in thousands of schools across the nation. The program sets-up mini-academies within already-established high schools that allow students to interweave career-themed courses into their college-prep curriculum and to participate in hands-on, work-based learning in their chosen field. One well-known evaluation of the program found that it had strong and lasting effects on the future earnings of participants, especially young men, and improved the high school performance of at-risk students (Kemple and Willmer 2008).

The state of Massachusetts has additionally developed a successful statewide network of over two dozen regional vocational technical high schools. During their freshman year, students attending these schools are able to spend time sampling and learning about a wide range of occupationally oriented disciplines. Once they reach their sophomore year, students select a focus area. From then on, they spend half of their time in hands-on career education and the other half in traditional academic and technical education. Students are also given the opportunity to take a course in small business entrepreneurship. The schools have a lower dropout rate than the state average and have a much higher graduation test pass rate than students at the state's more conventional high schools. Nicholas Wyman (2015) reports that at one of these schools, Minuteman Regional High School, more than 48 percent of students are classified as having physical or other learning disabilities, and yet one year after graduation, 95 percent of the school's graduates are either working, in college, or in the armed forces.

Other successful CTE programs are based on a more narrow approach to career education. Project Lead the Way, for example, was launched in several New York high schools in 1997 as an effort to introduce high school students to engineering. It has since expanded to several thousand high schools in all 50 states. Student participants enroll in a four-year sequence of rigorous course work that introduces them to the foundations and principles of engineering as well as its more specific components. The program concludes with a team-based project, in which participants work to solve an open-ended engineering problem. Approximately, 80 percent of graduates go on to study engineering, technology, or computer science, and their college retention rate in these courses is higher than those who did not participate in the program (Symonds, Schwartz, and Ferguson 2011).

National Job Training and Service Programs

Most employment-related youth training programs target those who are enrolled in high school or some form of post-secondary education, yet over 5 million American youth have become completely disengaged from both school and work. Many of these youth face life circumstances that impose multiple barriers to reconnection. Over the years, a variety of "second chance" initiatives have been proposed to meet the unique needs of high school dropouts and youth who are out of school and out of work. From World War II through the Vietnam

War, military service provided an opportunity for youth who had dropped out of school and lacked vocational direction to re-engage, develop a sense of purpose, and eventually transition into the civilian labor market. Eventually, however, the military stopped accepting high school dropouts and became less inclined to offer remedial training to those with educational deficits. Beginning with Lyndon B. Johnson's declaration of a "War on Poverty" in his 1964 State of the Union Address, Congress began to authorize funding for job training and educational programs for low-income youth and those at high risk of disconnection. Job Corps, the central program of the Johnson administration's War on Poverty, was first established under the Economic Opportunity Act of 1964 to provide educational and job-training opportunities to youth in both residential and nonresidential settings. A year later, Congress authorized the enactment of Volunteers in Service to America (VISTA) as the domestic version of the Peace Corps. The program, which funds and deploys volunteers to assist nonprofits focused on addressing the economic challenges of the long-term poor living in low-income communities, was intended to give young people the opportunity to learn valuable skills, while aiding communities in need. Over the years, the number of federal job-training grants and national services programs has expanded to include such well-known entities as AmeriCorps, YouthCorps, Youth-Build, and the National Guard ChalleNGe Corps. While each program has a distinct approach, they all typically provide some combination of education, training, community service, leadership development, subsidized temporary jobs, and support services—including housing, child care, and health care. Many of the programs additionally offer financial awards to participants who complete at term of service that can be used to finance higher education, career training, or student loans.

Members of Congress, and most recently President Trump, have at times questioned the effectiveness of such programs and threatened them with discontinuation or defunding based on their high costs and on indications that training and education services provided to youth participants have few long-term effects and often do not effectively develop the particular skills demanded by local labor markets (Hossain and Bloom 2015). Nevertheless, recent studies sponsored by the Corporation for National and Community Service Programs have found that youth who participate in volunteer and job-training service programs experience increased likelihood of finding employment and receive higher incomes following their service—this is especially true for participants who lack a high school diploma (Price et al. 2011; Spera et al. 2013). In a report compiled for the Center for American Progress, Ross, Sagawa, and Boteach (2016) suggest that national service as a workforce development strategy can be strengthened in several ways, including incorporating employment models for in-demand fields and ensuring that workers who experience barriers to securing and sustaining employment are supported through enhanced mentor services.

Although they have not been studied or covered as extensively as federally sponsored and publically funded service and job-training programs, a wide array of private community-based organizations and employers are engaged in substantial job-related intervention efforts and are working in diverse ways to help disconnected youth overcome significant barriers to employment. Many of these organizations and their endeavors are highlighted in Chapter 4, "Profiles."

Reforming Policies That Discourage Youth from Pursuing Jobs and Employers from Creating Them

As explained in the previous chapter, over time, federal, state, and local policy makers from both major parties have proposed and adopted well-intentioned labor policies that have actually thwarted young people's entry into the job market. Efforts to prepare youth to succeed in the marketplace will have minimal impact, as long as policies are in place that inhibit the aspirations of young people and discourage employers from expanding opportunities. Although a variety of labor market regulations and policies may be impeding the creation of entry-level jobs, entrepreneurship, and youth employment prospects, two of the most prominent policies that have captured the attention of youth employment advocates in recent years are occupational licensing restrictions and minimum-wage mandates.

Calls to reform occupational licensing—the process by which governments establish qualifications to practice a trade or profession—have become more and more prevalent in recent years in response to concerns that they are no longer narrowly adopted to protect the public from serious harm. In a review of the literature on occupational licensing, Morris Kleiner (2015) observes that "the current proliferation of occupational regulations does not appear closely related to health and safety considerations" (3). In fact, over the past several decades, professional associations rather than consumer advocacy and public interests groups have been behind the rapid growth of state occupational licensing requirements, which impose significant restrictions on market entry and now extend to seemingly innocuous fields as cosmetology, interior design, computer repair, and tourism. Furthermore, these regulations often include "grandparent provisions" exempting current practitioners from new requirements. As occupational licensing mandates are more frequently imposed to protect established businesses and professionals from competition, they serve as a substantial barrier to new market entrants and contribute to a decline in entrepreneurship. They, consequently, restrict young people's ability to start their own businesses or pursue employment in certain industries, making it harder for them to put their skills to work and launch a career.

In the 2014 documentary, *Locked Out: A Mississippi Success Story*, director Sean Malone chronicles the struggles of Melony Armstrong, who fought to become the first professional African hair braider in Mississippi and to remove arbitrary regulations that stood in the way of other aspiring entrepreneurs seeking to enter the profession. After learning how to braid hair, Armstrong sought to use her skills to earn a living. When she tried to open the first professional hair-braiding salon in Mississippi, however, she was blocked by the Mississippi State Board of Cosmetology (MSBC). The MSBC demanded that Armstrong first obtain a cosmetology license costing nearly $10,000 and attend over a year of board-approved training, none of which had anything to do with hair braiding. Although Armstrong did not have the means to meet these onerous requirements, she did not give up. Instead, she engaged in a legal battle against the state restrictions, which eventually sparked statewide reform and set a precedent for several other states to remove their own hair-braiding licensing requirements. Armstrong not only established her own successful business where she employed several individuals, but she also opened the door to hundreds of other aspiring entrepreneurs seeking to enter the hair-braiding business. Armstrong's victory revealed how reforming occupational licensing can encourage entrepreneurship and drastically improve employment opportunities for young people. As filmmaker Sean Malone explains, "For a lot of people, entrepreneurship—and even simply access to a variety of employment options—is the way to wealth and empowerment. Yet restrictions like the ones Melony faced push people into poverty, trap them in cycles of dependency, and prevent people from earning a good living doing something they actually want to do."

In a Brookings Institution report on reforming occupational licensing policies, Morris Kleiner (2015) offers a series of four actionable recommendations for how states might improve and streamline occupational licensing practices to make them more consistent with ensuring quality, health, and safety, while still allowing for the expansion of employment opportunity, such as that sought by individuals like Melony Armstrong. First, Kleiner suggests that state officials should be required to conduct a cost-benefit analysis based on research by outside experts or academic researchers to determine whether regulations are warranted and absolutely necessary before they decide to license an occupation or impose new requirements. If regulations are deemed necessary, states should pursue the least restrictive means of meeting desired goals. Kleiner, secondly, advocates for the implementation of a competitive federal grant program to encourage states to establish best practices with regard to occupational regulation. Third, Kleiner contends that states ought to recognize occupational licenses granted in other states so that licensed workers can move across state lines without having to undertake burdensome and expensive retraining and residency requirements. Finally, Kleiner argues that, when politically feasible, licensed occupations that do not pose a significant risk to health or safety should either be reclassified to a system of lesser regulation, such as certification, or deregulated altogether. Unlike licensing, a system of certification allows anyone to perform a service for pay, but only those who earned certification can claim the certified title. Kleiner concludes by asserting that "if governments were to undertake these proposals, available evidence suggests that employment in these regulated occupations would grow, consumer access to goods and services would expand, and prices would fall" (3).

In addition to advocating change in occupational licensing requirements, those seeking to improve labor market outcomes for youth have called for policy reform in response to the problem of young, unskilled workers who have been priced out of valuable job training experiences because of increased wage mandates. Although a small number of youth advocates endorse higher minimum-wage mandates believing they will spur wage growth, higher wages for some minimum-wage workers generally come at the expense of young, inexperienced workers. As explained in the previous chapter, the bulk of economic research now confirms that mandated wage increases negatively affect the employment opportunities of teenagers and young adults, who make up more than half of all minimum-wage workers. Employers faced with additional labor costs imposed by mandated wage increases generally react by hiring fewer low-skilled workers and relying more on labor-saving technology. By removing the incentive for companies to hire workers with few skills and little experience who are expensive to train, minimum-wage increases have the unintended effect of pushing the least-skilled employees, usually teenagers, out of the labor market altogether. One proposal to combat the negative effect that mandated wage hikes have on the employment prospects of youth is to allow young people to work for a lower wage than older Americans. While some business owners are reluctant to hire young, inexperienced, and untested job applicants with few professional skills at higher wages, they might reconsider employing and training them if they are able to offer a lower wage for a short period. One frequently proposed policy solution based on this logic is for states and localities to legalize a "youth minimum-wage" or YMW. The federal government has already adopted a YMW under which workers up to the age of 20 may earn a wage of $4.25 an hour for their first 90 days on the job on the grounds that a YMW will incentivize employers to hire young people who lack experience and relevant skill. The federal YMW has had a minimal effect, however, both because it only applies to a teen's first 90 days on the job and because many states have failed to adopt a YMW in their state labor code, which means that the adult minimum-wage imposed by the states applies across the board. Preston Cooper (2016), a policy analyst at the Manhattan Institute, contends that if all 50 states and the federal government adopted a YMW with no 90-day limit for individuals aged 16 to 19, the teen employment rate would improve by nearly 9 percent and employers would generate almost half a million jobs in the first year following enactment. Those who advocate for a YMW rationalize that it will eventually lead to higher wages, since working in an entry-level position will provide teenagers with the experience and professional references they need to obtain higher-paying jobs in the future.

Conclusion

As the chapter makes clear, in spite of improved economic growth, the United States faces a crisis of chronic and widespread youth unemployment, underemployment, and disconnection that present significant immediate and long-term challenges. High levels of youth unemployment, underemployment, and disengagement are damaging to the economic, psychological, physical, social, and civic well-being of individuals and of the nation as a whole. They lead to lost earnings, slower economic growth, and greater reliance on the social welfare system. They are additionally correlated with the deterioration of physical and mental well-being and an increase in personally and socially harmful and delinquent behavior. Finally, they inhibit the successful transition to adulthood for many youth and threaten the social fabric of society by restricting social mobility and undermining civic engagement and social cohesion.

Because the factors producing youth unemployment and disconnection vary in nature and scope, addressing its underlying causes and minimizing its worse effects require action on many different fronts. Over the past several decades the crisis has received special attention from policy makers and private individuals alike. One of the most central areas of focus has been on improving outcomes in postsecondary education. As it has become well established that today's youth will have a difficult time achieving gainful employment, economic stability, and upward mobility without some level of postsecondary education, a great deal of attention has been directed toward making traditional four-year bachelor's degrees more accessible, attainable, and affordable. Yet, as enrollment levels have increased across all demographics, they have not led to equivalent increases in college completion. As a consequence, many young people, especially those from economically disadvantaged backgrounds, enroll in college and acquire student loan debt, but do not meaningfully enhance their employment prospects through achieving a degree. Furthermore, even among those who do graduate, many fail to participate in programs, develop skills, or obtain the work experience and professional connections necessary for employment success. Consequently, strengthening youth employment prospects through traditional avenues of postsecondary education will require concerted efforts to bolster accountability and transparency in terms of degree outcomes, to improve students' success in the programs in which they enroll, and to create more effective partnerships between employers and institutions of higher learning.

Given the reality that a large percentage of American youth do not have the means, desire, or inclination to thrive in traditional forms of higher education, any comprehensive approach to improving youth employment outcomes will also require destigmatizing additional routes to occupational success and working to strengthen and expand access to high-quality alternatives, such as apprenticeships and career and technical education, beginning in high school. Special attention must also be given to reaching out to those unlikely to engage in the workplace due to life challenges or a history of involvement with the criminal justice system, as well as to reforming policies that inhibit young people's opportunity to gain experience, develop skills, and pursue gainful employment. Such efforts to improve and increase quality education options and outcomes and to alleviate economic, social, and political barriers to employment success will help ensure that America's youth are better suited to effectively transition into adulthood, contribute to their communities as productive citizens, and thrive in the 21st-century marketplace.

References

Abel, Jaison R., Richard Dietz, and Yaqin Su. 2014. "Are Recent College Graduates Finding Good Jobs?" *Current Issues in Economics and Finance*, 20(1): 1–8. Federal Reserve Bank of New York. Accessed March 10, 2018. https://www.newyorkfed.org/medialibrary/media/research/current_issues/ci20-1.pdf

Adorney, Julian. 2017. "How Tuition-Free College Education Hurts Young People." *National Review*. April 21. Accessed

June 10, 2018. https://www.nationalreview.com/2017/04/
bernie-sanders-elizabeth-warren-tuition-free-college-
proposal-hurts-students/

Aguiar, Mark, Mark Bils, Kerwin Kofi Charles, and Erik
Hurst. 2017. *Leisure Luxuries and the Labor Supply of Young
Men.* Cambridge, MA: National Bureau of Economic
Research. Accessed February 26, 2018. http://www.nber
.org/papers/w23552

Anders, George. 2017. *You Can Do Anything: The Surprising
Power of a "Useless" Liberal Arts Education.* New York: Little,
Brown and Company.

Arum, Richard, and Joseph Roksa. 2014. *Aspiring Adults
Adrift: Tentative Transitions of College Graduates.* Chicago:
University of Chicago Press.

Ayres, Sarah. 2013. "The High Cost of Youth Unemployment."
Center for American Progress. April 5. Accessed March 28,
2018. https://cdn.americanprogress.org/wp-content/
uploads/2013/04/AyresYouthUnemployment1.pdf

Basken, Paul. 2008. "Boeing to Rank Colleges by Measuring
Graduates' Job Success." *Chronicle of Higher Education,*
55(4): A1–A16.

Bauer-Wolf, Jeremy. 2018. "A 'Workaround' to US Ban on
Student-Level Data: The University of Texas Releases a
New Breakdown of Student Earnings." *Inside Higher Ed.*
March 27. Accessed June 20, 2018. https://www
.insidehighered.com/news/2018/03/27/university-
texas-system-releases-new-student-outcome-database

Belfield, Clive R., and Thomas Bailey. 2011. "The Benefits
of Attending a Community College: A Review of the
Evidence." *Community College Review,* 39(1): 46–68.

Belfield, Clive R., Henry M. Levin, and Rachel Rosen.
2012. *The Economic Value of Opportunity Youth.* Civic
Enterprises. January. Accessed March 12, 2018. http://

www.civicenterprises.net/MediaLibrary/Docs/econ_value_
opportunity_youth.pdf

Bettinger, Eric, and Rachel Baker. 2011. *The Effects of
Student Coaching in College: An Evaluation of Randomized
Experiment in Student Mentoring.* Working Paper 16881.
Cambridge, MA: National Bureau of Economic Research.
March. Accessed June 22, 2018. http://www.nber.org/
papers/w16881.pdf

Bound, John, Michael Lovenheim, and Sarah Turner. 2009.
*Why Have College Completion Rates Declined? An Analysis
of Changing Student Preparation and Collegiate Resources?*
Working Paper 15566. Cambridge, MA: National Bureau
of Economic Research. December. Accessed June 15, 2018.
http://www.nber.org/papers/w15566.pdf

Busteed, Brandon, and Mona Mourshed. 2016. "The Health
Effects of Youth Unemployment." *Harvard Business
Review.* October 3. Accessed June 10, 2018. https://hbr
.org/2016/10/the-health-effects-of-youth-unemployment

Casner-Lotto, Jill, Linda Barrington, and Mary Wright.
2006. *Are They Really Ready for Work? Employers'
Perspectives on the Basic Knowledge and Applied Skills of
New Entrants to the 21st Century U.S. Workplace.* Report
of the Conference Board. Washington, DC: Conference
Board. Accessed June 1, 2018. https://files.eric.ed.gov/
fulltext/ED519465.pdf

Collegiate Employment Research Institute. 2018. "Recruiting
Trends 2017–18." 47th edition. Executive Summary.
Accessed June 21, 2018. http://www.ceri.msu.edu/
wp-content/uploads/2018/03/Recruiting-Trends-2017-
Executive-Summary.pdf

Cooper, Preston. 2016. *Reforming the U.S. Minimum Wage.*
New York: Manhattan Institute. August 9, Accessed
March 13, 2018. https://www.manhattan-institute.org/
html/reforming-us-youth-minimum-wage-9134.html

Cooper, Preston. 2018. "College Enrollment Surges among Low Income Students." *Forbes*. February 26. Accessed June 15, 2018. https://www.forbes.com/sites/prestoncooper2/2018/02/26/college-enrollment-surges-among-low-income-students/#4ea5091d293b

Eberstadt, Nicholas. 2016. *America's Invisible Crisis: Men without Work*. West Conshohocken, PA: Templeton Press.

Fischer, Karin. 2013. "The Employment Mismatch." *The Chronicle of Higher Education*. March 4. Accessed June 15, 2018. https://www.chronicle.com/article/The-Employment-Mismatch/137625

Fry, Richard. 2016. "For First Time in Modern Era, Living with Parents Edges Out Other Living Arrangements for 18- to 34-Year-Olds." *Pew Research Center*. May 24. Accessed June 1, 2018. http://www.pewsocialtrends.org/2016/05/24/for-first-time-in-modern-era-living-with-parents-edges-out-other-living-arrangements-for-18-to-34-year-olds/

Fry, Richard. 2017. "5 Facts about Millennial Households." *PEW Research Center*. September 6. Accessed June 1, 2018. http://www.pewresearch.org/fact-tank/2017/09/06/5-facts-about-millennial-households/

Furchtgott-Roth, Diana, and Jared Meyer. 2015. *Disinherited: How Washington Is Betraying America's Youth*. New York: Encounter Books.

Gallup. 2016. *Great Jobs. Great Lives. The Value of Career Services, Inclusive Experiences and Mentorship for College Graduates*. The Gallup-Purdue 2016 Index Report. Accessed June 21, 2018. https://www.luminafoundation.org/files/resources/great-jobs-great-livees-3-2016.pdf

Golub, Harvey. 2013. "The Tragedy of Teen Unemployment." *Real Clear Markets*. December 5. Accessed March 12, 2018. https://www.realclearmarkets.com/articles/2013/12/05/the_tragedy_of_teenage_unemployment_100777.html

Hart Research Associates. 2013. *It Takes More Than a Major Employer Priorities for College Learning and Student*

Success. An Online Survey among Employers Conducted on Behalf of the American Association of Colleges and Universities. April 10. Accessed June 17, 2018. https://www.aacu.org/sites/default/files/files/LEAP/2013_EmployerSurvey.pdf

Holzer, Harry J., and Sandy Baum. 2017. *Making College Work: Pathways to Success for Disadvantaged Students.* Washington, DC: Brookings Institution Press.

Hossain, Farhana, and Dan Bloom. 2015. *Toward a Better Future: Evidence on Improving Employment Outcomes for Disadvantaged Youth in the United States*. MDRC. February. Accessed June 17, 2018. https://www.mdrc.org/sites/default/files/Toward_Better_Future.pdf

Houle, Jason N., and Cody Warner. 2017. "Into the Red and Back to the Nest? Student Debt, College Completion and Returning to the Parental Home among Young Adults." *Sociology of Education*, 90(1): 89–108.

Jaggars, Shanna S., Michelle Hodara, and Georgia W. Stacey. 2013. *Designing Meaningful Developmental Reform.* Community College Research Center. Teachers College, Columbia University. February. Accessed June 20, 2018. https://files.eric.ed.gov/fulltext/ED539912.pdf

Jaggars, Shanna S., and Georgia W. Stacey. 2014. *What We Know about Developmental Education Outcomes.* Community College Research Center. Teachers College, Columbia University. January. Accessed June 20, 2018. https://files.eric.ed.gov/fulltext/ED565668.pdf

Kemple, James, and Cynthia Willmer. 2008. *Career Academies: Long-Term Impacts on Labor Market Outcomes, Educational Attainment and Transitions to Adulthood.* MDRC. June. Accessed June 15, 2018. https://www.mdrc.org/sites/default/files/full_50.pdf

Kleiner, Morris M. 2015. *Reforming Occupational Licensing Policies.* Discussion Paper. The Hamilton Project. Brookings Institution. March. Accessed May 14, 2018.

https://www.brookings.edu/wp-content/uploads/2016/06/ THP_KleinerDiscPaper_final.pdf

Kroger, Teresa, and Elise Gould. 2017. *The Class of 2017.* Washington, DC: Economic Policy Institute. Accessed March 15, 2018. http://www.epi.org/publication/ the-class-of-2017/

Kulkarni, Siddharth, and Jonathan Rothwell. 2015. *Beyond College Rankings: A Value-Added Approach to Assessing Two- and Four-Year Schools.* Brookings Institution. April 29. Accessed June 15, 2018. https://www.brookings.edu/wp-content/uploads/2015/04/BMPP_CollegeValueAdded.pdf

Lerman, Robert I. 1999. "Improving Links between High Schools and Careers." In Douglass J. Basharov, ed. *America's Disconnected Youth: Toward a Preventive Strategy*, 185–212. Washington, DC: Child Welfare League of America, Inc. and American Enterprise Institute for Public Policy Research.

Lerman, Robert I. 2010. *Expanding Apprenticeship: A Way to Enhance Skills and Careers.* The Urban Institute. October. Accessed June 23, 2018. https://www.urban.org/sites/ default/files/publication/29691/901384-Expanding-Apprenticeship-A-Way-to-Enhance-Skills-and-Careers.PDF

Locked Out: A Mississippi Success Story. 2014. Directed by Sean W. Malone. Honest Enterprise.

Mitnik, Pablo A., and David B. Grusky. 2015. *Economic Mobility in the United States.* PEW Charitable Trusts. July. Accessed June 1, 2018. https://web.stanford.edu/~pmitnik/ EconomicMobilityintheUnitedStates.pdf

Morsy, Hanan. 2012. "Scarred Generation." *Finance and Development*, 49(1): 15–17. Accessed June 1, 2018. http:// www.imf.org/external/pubs/ft/fandd/2012/03/pdf/ morsy.pdf

Mossakowski, Krysia. 2009. "The Influence of Past Unemployment Duration on Symptoms of Depression among Young Women and Men in the United States." *American Journal of Public Health*, 99: 1826–1832. Accessed June 1, 2018. https://www.ncbi.nlm.nih.gov/pmc/articles/PMC2741513/pdf/1826.pdf

Mroz, Thomas, and Timothy Savage. 2006. "The Long-Term Effects of Youth Unemployment." *The Journal of Human Resources*, 41(2): 259–293.

National Center for Education Statistics. 2018. "Undergraduate Retention and Graduation Rates." May. Accessed June 20, 2018. https://nces.ed.gov/programs/coe/indicator_ctr.asp

Obama, Barack. 2016. "President Obama Delivers Remarks on Higher Education." *The White House*. October 17. Accessed June 10, 2018. https://obamawhitehouse .archives.gov/photos-and-video/video/2016/10/17/president-obama-delivers-remarks-education

Peck, Don. 2011. *Pinched: How the Great Recession Has Narrowed Our Futures and What We Can Do about It*. New York: Crown Publishers.

Piereson, James. 2014. "The *Times* Tries a New College Ranking." *Minding the Campus*. September 10. Accessed June 15, 2018. https://www.mindingthecampus.org/2014/09/10/the-times-tries-a-new-college-ranking/

Price, Christofer et al. 2011. *National Evaluation of Youth Corps: Findings and Follow-Up*. Washington, DC: Prepared for the Corporation for National and Community Service. Cambridge, MA: Abt Associates Inc. Accessed June 10, 2018. https://www.nationalservice.gov/pdf/nat_eval_youthcorps_impactreport.pdf

Putnam, Robert D. 2016. *Our Kids: The American Dream in Crisis*. New York: Simon and Schuster.

Ross, Tracey, Shirley Sagawa, and Melissa Boteach. 2016. *Utilizing National Service as a 21st Century Workforce Strategy for Opportunity Youth*. Center for American Progress. March. Accessed June 10, 2018. https://cdn.americanprogress.org/wp-content/uploads/2016/02/29105313/NatlServiceReport.pdf

Rothwell, Jonathan. 2015. *Using Earnings Data to Rank Colleges: A Value-Added Approach Updated with College Scorecard Data*. Brookings Institution. October 29. Accessed June 15, 2015. https://www.brookings.edu/research/using-earnings-data-to-rank-colleges-a-value-added-approach-updated-with-college-scorecard-data/

Sawhill, Isabel, and Quentin Karpilow. 2014. "Youth Unemployment Is a Problem for Social Mobility." Brookings Institution Social Mobility Memo. March 5. Accessed April 30, 2018. https://www.brookings.edu/blog/social-mobility-memos/2014/03/05/youth-unemployment-is-a-problem-for-social-mobility/

Selingo, Jeffrey J. 2016. *There Is Life after College: What Parents and Students Should Know about Navigating School to Prepare for the Jobs of Tomorrow*. New York: Harper Collins.

Selingo, Jeffrey J. 2017. "Wanted: Factory Workers, Degree Required." *The New York Times*. January 30. Accessed April 7, 2018. https://www.nytimes.com/2017/01/30/education/edlife/factory-workers-college-degree-apprenticeships.html

Spera, Christopher et al. 2013. *Volunteering as a Pathway to Employment: Does Volunteering Increase Odds of Finding a Job for the Out of Work?* Washington, DC: Corporation for National and Community Service. Accessed June 10, 2018. https://www.nationalservice.gov/sites/default/files/upload/employment_research_report.pdf

Symonds, William C., Robert B. Schwartz, and Ronald Ferguson. 2011. *Pathways to Prosperity: Meeting the Challenge of Preparing Young Americans for the 21st Century*. Pathways to Prosperity Project, Harvard Graduate School

of Education. February. Accessed May 15, 2018. https://
www.gse.harvard.edu/sites/default/files/documents/
Pathways_to_Prosperity_Feb2011-1.pdf

U.S. Department of Labor. 2017. Registered Apprenticeship
National Results. Accessed June 23, 2018. https://www
.doleta.gov/OA/data_statistics.cfm

Van Zandt, David. 2012. "Holding All Universities
Accountable for Student Outcomes." *Huffington Post.*
October 22. Accessed June 10, 2018. https://www
.huffingtonpost.com/david-van-zandt/holding-all-
universities-_b_2001008.html

Vedder, Richard, Christopher Denhart, and Jonathan Robe.
*Why Are Recent College Graduates Underemployed? University
Enrollments and Labor-Market Realities.* Washington, DC:
Center for College Affordability and Productivity. Accessed
February 25, 2018. https://files.eric.ed.gov/fulltext/
ED539373.pdf

Vogel, Peter. 2015. *Generation Jobless? Turning the Youth
Unemployment Crisis into Opportunity.* New York: Palgrave
Macmillan.

Wood, Peter. 2015. "College Scorecard: How Much Will
you Earn?" *National Association of Scholars.* October 2.
Accessed June 10, 2018. https://www.nas.org/articles/
college_scorecard_how_much_will_you_earn

Wyman, Nicholas. 2015. *Job U: How to Find Wealth and
Success by Developing the Skills Companies Actually Need.*
New York: Crown Business.

Zornick, George. 2017. "Bernie Sanders Just Introduced His
Free College Tuition Plan." *The Nation.* April 3. Accessed
June 10, 2018. https://www.thenation.com/article/
bernie-sanders-just-introduced-his-free-college-tuition-plan/

3   Perspectives

Introduction

The chapter includes nine essays written by authors from a variety of perspectives and professional backgrounds on a range of topics related to the issue of youth employment. The chapter opens with essays by authors Matthew Marko and Siobhan Gallagher Kent, who recount how their experiences in a NASA apprenticeship program and in AmeriCorps contributed to their long-term success. The next essay, written by Rebecca Burgess, an advisory board member of iCivics, explores how a lack of civic education is both caused by and contributes to the problem of youth unemployment and disconnectedness. The fourth and fifth essays explore examples of regulatory and nonregulatory barriers to employment. Hadley Heath Manning examines how the Affordable Care Act, although well-intentioned, has negatively affected youth employment, and Riane Castro recounts the barriers young people face in seeking employment as convicted felons with a record of incarceration. Essays six and seven offer advice for young people seeking employment and a career. Cynthia Sakamoto, a human

A graduate receiving a Master's degree from the University of New Orleans. Although education and training are essential for stable employment, wage growth, and social mobility, a disconnection commonly exists between institutions of higher learning and the labor market. Evidence suggests that today's higher education system is preparing large numbers of students for jobs that no longer exist or are in short supply. (Aviahuismanphotography/Dreamstime.com)

resources professional, discusses the mistakes young people make when going through the recruiting process, and educator Melanie Warren emphasizes the importance of finding the correct motivation for study. The chapter concludes with two essays advocating various ways to combat the problems of youth disconnectedness and unemployment. Vicki Alger makes the case for Educational Savings Accounts and Stephen Monteros discusses the importance of bridging the skills gap and Linked Learning programs.

My First Step into a Successful Career
Matthew Marko

Whenever someone asks me about my first job, I briefly gloss over the summer when, at 16 years old, I ripped tickets and stamped hands for Six Flags. I made very little money, I worked only part-time on the weekends, and overwhelming everything I used and enjoyed was thanks to Mom and Dad, including the ride to the park on the days that I worked. Although I was costing my parents a lot more in food, gas, and electricity than the minimal amount I earned working, I did gain valuable experience interacting with people and learning how to be a dependable employee. I was also able to enjoy the spending money I earned.

A year later, fortunately, I got a big promotion, when I was selected for the NASA Summer High School Apprenticeship Research Program (SHARP) Plus program. The program provided participants with ten weeks of food and housing and the opportunity to work on a research project at Hampton University, just outside of Norfolk, Virginia. The opportunity to have my expenses paid while I worked on a university research project full time was a big deal for me as a 17-year-old about to start my senior year of high school! While the pay was less than minimum-wage once the room and board allowance was deducted, this experience was my first time away from my home in New Jersey, and the first time I wasn't dependent on my parents for anything I did. In a way, it was my first taste of adulthood.

The NASA SHARP Plus program consisted of 7 guys and 7 girls, from all over the country and Puerto Rico—all of us just 16 and 17. A 40-year-old teacher named Cornelius was our counselor and helped us get settled. Living away from home for the first time was a bit of a shock, as the dorm building we were staying in was old and far from luxurious—especially compared to my parents' house. For an entire week a water main was broken outside, and we only had scalding hot water in the shower. Outside there were rats as large as cats, and inside there were cockroaches. One of which managed not only to survive being smashed with a phone book but also to carry the phone book on its back afterward! The food was greasy cafeteria style; I gained nearly ten pounds over those few months!

Despite the modest living conditions, the campus itself, which was situated on the edge of the Hampton River as it spilled out into the much larger James River, had a pretty, collegiate vibe that I greatly enjoyed. It was common for all of us program participants to hang out at the peaceful riverbank park on campus, overlooking a quiet recreation boat dock on the other side; this peaceful scenery was a stark contrast to the large and imposing naval base visible in the distance. While on campus, I enjoyed a certain freedom I had never before experienced. Other than the time spent working and our 10 P.M. curfew, I was free to go wherever and whenever I wanted. If I wanted to eat, if I wanted to go to the gym, if I wanted to go to the Chinese takeout place, it was up to me and nobody else. Previously, I had only gone where adults took me; I had never owned a car at this point, and there were no stores or restaurants in my parents' town that I could walk or ride my bike to. For the first time in my 17 years, I was free to move around on my own to different places and new experiences.

The work I was assigned to do was quite interesting for a 17-year-old high school student. At the time, the European Organization for Nuclear Research (CERN) was constructing its Large Hadron Collider particle accelerator, and I worked for a lab run by the late professor Ken McFarlane, built to assemble components for the ATLAS detector. It was tedious work, requiring great attention to detail. An overly simplified description of my job was that I had to assemble large straws into white foam cotton sheets. It wasn't simple construction, as everything had to be precisely aligned, and these properly spaced straws would eventually contain ionizing gas and electrical wires designed to detect the faintest of signals from split atoms in that particle accelerator for decades. All of the foam needed to be completely cleaned of any dirt and impurities and had to be just the right density and weight. As a 17-year-old high school student, this was my first real foray into the world of fundamental science. The experience helped me to understand and see firsthand a purpose for all of the fundamentals I was learning in high school.

Another meaningful aspect of my experience in the NASA SHARP Plus program was that everything I did and enjoyed during that trip was paid for by what I had earned. While my salary was a part of a grant from NASA for high school students, there was the expectation I EARNED my pay and board working in the lab. The work was hard, but also invaluable, as it helped to shape my work ethic and appreciation for what is involved in advance research. Even though my pay was less than minimum-wage (after room and board), it was the first money I had fully earned with no assistance from my parents. Whenever we were done with work, Cornelius made sure we all had a lot of fun and opportunity to spend our earned money during our time down; we went to the movies every Friday night, we went to DC and Virginia Beach, and all sorts of different attractions in the city of Norfolk. As I participated in these activities, I enjoyed the satisfaction of being able to pay for them myself.

My summer experience in the NASA SHARP Plus program was 17 years ago, and I am now twice as old. In the years following my completion of the program, I managed to graduate from college and complete my PhD in engineering from Columbia. I have since been working as a physicist and engineer with the Navy for 12 years. I did not get where I am today overnight, but by consistently applying myself through college and graduate school and my first jobs as a new employee with the Navy. At more times than I can count, I considered quitting the difficult study of science and engineering, but the memories of the fun times and satisfaction I had while working with the NASA SHARP Plus program inspired me to keep going. There is a very good chance that had it not been for that opportunity 17 years ago, I would not be where I am today, and for that I am forever grateful.

Matthew Marko holds a PhD in mechanical engineering and works as a physicist and engineer for the U.S. Navy.

Skipping Grad School to Find My Career: An AmeriCorps Story
Siobhan Gallagher Kent

When I was a senior in college, I wanted to save the world. I didn't have grand aspirations of becoming a superhero or a world leader. I was *realistic* about my goal: I was going to help people improve their lives by becoming a social worker. I knew that a big step toward my goal was getting a master's degree in social work. My life, however, took an unexpected turn. The year I graduated from college as a double-major, I suffered a stress-induced nervous breakdown that left me mostly confined to a small bedroom at my parents' house, barely eating, sleeping, or bathing for several months.

I couldn't go straight to grad school. I could *not* do it. I wasn't ready to jump back into the stress, deadlines, and competitive atmosphere that had contributed to my breakdown. I needed time to rebuild and work with a therapist. But I still wanted to save the world! So I started looking into community service programs and discovered the AmeriCorps

Community Health Corps, an arm of the Corporation for National Community Service that has since been absorbed into other program areas.

Around the same time that I decided to apply for Ameri-Corps, one of my best friends graduated from college in Albany, New York, and was looking for a roommate. I didn't really care where I was stationed, so I applied for and was hired for a ten-month placement at Albany's community health center.

I was originally assigned to serve in the health center's social work unit, assisting the staff social workers and their student interns with case management. It seemed perfect! Not only would I get to spend ten months trying out my chosen field, I would also be able to learn from the health center's social work director, Jeannie (name has been changed), who was also a professor in the local university's social work master's program.

On my first day, Jeannie explained that she taught her students that they must be able to detach from their clients at the end of the day.

"You can't take their problems home with you," she said. "You'll drive yourself crazy if you do."

Jeannie was right. Unfortunately, I have *never* been able to compartmentalize my thoughts and experiences, and I learned the hard way that such compartmentalization is a critical skill for social work.

Having grown up in a small but diverse city with friends from various races and economic backgrounds, I thought I understood the challenges of poverty and was well prepared to work with the health center's target population—a community plagued by widespread poverty, addiction, chronic health issues (including one of the highest childhood asthma rates in the state), underfunded schools and youth programs, and a city government unable to do much about it.

After a few weeks, however, it became obvious that the social work program wasn't a good fit for me. I wasn't able to stop thinking about our clients' problems once I left the office and I did not receive the mentorship and guidance I needed as an inexperienced AmeriCorps worker to thrive in the position. I went home every night feeling defeated—I spent every day just making sure our clients had heat, food, and power at home, but was completely useless in helping them overcome their massive social and economic obstacles. In hindsight, I had wildly unrealistic expectations of what one person could do in a social worker role.

It's hard to admit you aren't the right person for a job. It's even harder when it's your first real job and your intended profession. I finally realized I just wasn't mentally strong enough to be a social worker. I had to make a change.

I talked with Jeannie, and she helped me develop a new schedule. I started spending half my time at the health center's methadone clinic, where I helped people recovering from opiate addiction get into schools and job-training programs and the other half with the center's community outreach program, where I worked with people with chronic health conditions, such as diabetes and HIV, and helped them stay on-track with their treatment plans.

I thrived in my new positions. I enjoyed helping people get into GED programs and develop resumes and working with my chronic condition clients. I wasn't solving major life issues for people, but I was able to help them take small steps toward better health and stable employment.

I was a few months away from finishing my AmeriCorps term when I met Lynn (name has been changed), the owner of the company that handled marketing and public relations for the health center. Lynn had built her own communications firm over 20 years that worked almost exclusively with non-profit organizations.

I'd written up some information for Lynn on an upcoming community health fair. It was going to be a big event, and we needed lots of publicity to get people in the door for free screenings and open consultations with the center's staff. Lynn liked my writing and kept me involved with the press outreach and advertising work for the event.

The health fair was a big success, and I learned the ins and outs of promotions and communications from Lynn. I hadn't taken a single college class on public relations and always thought it was soulless and corporate, but now I saw that PR could be used to make a positive difference.

And best of all, Lynn thought I was good at it! She offered me a job after I completed my AmeriCorps term. She took me under her wing and taught me everything there was to learn about marketing, PR, graphic design, and advertising for non-profits. I worked with her for four years and have worked in nonprofit communications ever since.

I now spend my days spreading the word about my organization and our services, supporting our work in regional economic development, and connecting with the media and other partners. I also serve in leadership roles with several professional societies and mentor younger communicators at local nonprofits. I even work with local AmeriCorps members from time to time, and I always tell them I'm an AmeriCorps alumna!

I ended up in a niche field that I didn't even know existed when I was an unbalanced college senior. If I'd gone straight to grad school, I would have spent tens of thousands of dollars on a degree for work that I was fundamentally unfit to do. AmeriCorps was the right solution: my program and the people in it provided me with the flexibility to try out different professional roles. AmeriCorps gave me the time and experience I needed to figure out the best way for me to accomplish what I really wanted to do—help people.

My experience with AmeriCorps taught me that the path toward accomplishing your goals rarely looks the way you expect, and that you need to be flexible and honest with yourself in order to keep moving forward. It's one of the most important lessons I've ever learned, and I didn't need to spend a single penny to learn it.

Siobhan Gallagher Kent, APR, is communications director for a large nonprofit funding organization in Albany, New York. She also chairs the Northeastern U.S. District of the Public Relations Society of America and does volunteer communications and marketing for local nonprofit organizations.

Youth Civic Engagement and Unemployment: What Cause and What Effect?
Rebecca Burgess

Several years after the "Great Recession" of 2008, it was obvious that communities across the geographic and demographic board were not feeling the effects of the economic downturn similarly. Curious, the National Conference on Citizenship (NCoC) and the Center for Information and Research on Civic Learning & Engagement (CIRCLE) decided to examine whether the "economic resilience" of particular communities (those with low levels of unemployment) was significantly related to "civic health" (the level of civic engagement within a community). In two successive reports, NCoC and CIRCLE argue that they found evidence of a correlation between the two: Communities with higher levels of civic engagement in 2006 suffered less from unemployment in the wake of the 2008 recession.

There is a qualifier to that statement, however; researchers found that it is "stronger social cohesion within a community" that "strongly predict[s] a smaller increase in the unemployment rate" (CIRCLE 2012). Social cohesion is a broad concept, but it is generally defined as the "degree to which residents socialize, communicate, and collaborate with one another" (CIRCLE 2012). Civic engagement, on the other hand, usually refers to a variety of disaggregated behaviors, ranging from voting in local and national elections to protesting, to joining a community group, or volunteering with a church or other association (Flanagan and Levine 2010). Civic engagement can refer to both nonpolitical and political participation—but some political participation can actively undermine social cohesion. Civic engagement is thus not simply identical with social cohesion; civic engagement arguably can be understood as the result or expression of a prior social cohesion even as it can also be understood as a measurement of the same.

The correlation between social cohesion, civic engagement, and unemployment is complex not only because cohesion and engagement are broad and generalized concepts but also because employment and unemployment appear to have a separate bearing on an individual's civic presence and behavior. Employment has been shown to positively affect an individual's civic behavior and engagement, while civic engagement has been shown to positively affect an individual's employment status. While this seems to amount to a classic chicken-and-egg situation in determining which causes which, examining the various components in more depth yields important insights into how educators, policy makers, and communities should understand the components as both a sequence and a cycle, each part of which is especially relevant to youth.

If we begin from the standpoint of unemployment, we find that those not in the workforce are typically not devoting their time to volunteering or to other civic activities. In *Men without Work*, political economist Nicholas Eberstadt focuses on un-working, prime-age men (unemployed males who normally ought to be in the labor force), and then examines what activities they pursue in place of a job. Using the General Social Survey and the American Time Use Survey, Eberstadt uncovers that un-working males typically don't devote their extra time to helping others in their family or community; don't engage more in religious activities; and don't have purposeful movement outside of the house.

This has further ramifications: un-working men are less likely to volunteer, read daily newspapers, or vote in presidential election years than their working peers. Simultaneously, un-working men have much higher rates of tobacco and drug use, illegal drug use, and gambling than working men, and spend considerably more hours than the latter on sleeping and self-grooming (Eberstadt 2016). Furthermore, the more time those not in the workforce in general spend not being employed, the likelier they are to develop antisocial and anti-civic behaviors and to never return to the workforce.

When we introduce the youth component to unemployment and civic engagement, we see the more nuanced interconnectedness of both, denoting a cycle that may begin in youth and continue throughout the life course. In part, the civic skills, habits, and motivations of young adults result from opportunities for engagement during childhood and adolescence. "Children and teens who have opportunities for involvement in extracurricular activities and community institutions are more likely to vote and participate in other forms of civic engagement as young adults" (Center for the Study of Social Policy 2011).

Crucially, building effective ties through participation in community organizations where members hold each other accountable for group goals shapes a young person's civic disposition through producing trust among peers (Flanagan 2003). Building and maintaining trust with one's peers is as key to civil and democratic societies as it is to the workplace, as it both nourishes and produces the sense of being equal stakeholders within and throughout a community. In fact, a high level of social trust is often taken for a sign of social solidarity and cohesion—and has been linked to strong economic performance (Rahn and Transue 1998). Where there is strong social trust, individuals typically embark on their social interactions assuming that those around them are of good will and benign intentions, and so give even those they do not know the benefit of the doubt. Without that social trust, individuals are unlikely to take risks in their personal or professional life, stymieing their entrepreneurial, social, and civic potential.

It's unsurprising then, that research has shown that taking part in community service "strengthens intrinsic work values, [and] leads youth to rethink their vocational priorities, and encourages a less individualistic approach" (Flanagan and Levine 2010, 168). Civic engagement prepares young men and women for later success in the workforce because it gives the youth practical experience in accomplishing group tasks, while also familiarizing them with political institutions and social issues, and the need to consume news about and discuss with others the issues of the day. In turn, holding down a job has been linked to the "success sequence" of adulthood, in which a steady job, marriage, and parenting lead to personal success and stable patterns of continued civic engagement, which includes political participation (voting).

Civic engagement is a key part of the transition between adolescence and mature adulthood, precisely because it is through participating in community-based organizations and institutions that young people learn what it means to belong to a community—to develop shared goals, to exercise rights and fulfill obligations toward the execution of those goals, to connect personal goals to the group's goals and thus learn to see themselves as members of the public with a shared interest in the common good (Flanagan 2003).

Typically, political engagement increases as one's life, roles, and institutional connections in the community become more stable. But today's youth experience a lengthening or delayed transition to adulthood, meaning that contemporary youth are taking longer to establish stable patterns of civic engagement just as they are taking longer to finish their education and to get married (Flanagan and Levine 2010). This raises the question of whether youth today have permanently weaker connections to civic life than their predecessors. There is evidence to support this, tied to the prolonged absence of meaningful civic education within public education over the past few decades. Students today spend only 7.6 percent of their school time in social studies, only one part of which is civic education—the most crucial vehicle of transmitting an appreciation of the value of the democratic political order, and inspiring the individual to invest in the practice of democracy through civic engagement broadly understood (Burgess 2017 and 2016).

For the overall social and democratic health of local communities and the nation at large, it's vital for educators, employers, and policy makers to understand how civic education helps establish the foundation for social trust and cohesion, which in turn influences especially youth to engage civically in their larger communities and gives them the tools to transition to adulthood via steady employment. Employment and civic engagement is both a sequence and a cycle, with the most crucial intersection of both happening in the moment of youth.

References

Burgess, Rebecca. 2016. "Disgusted with Trump vs. Clinton? Blame America's Civic Education." *The Hill.* October 4. Accessed April 30, 2017. http://thehill.com/blogs/punditsblog/education/299261-disgusted-with-trump-v-clinton-blame-americas-civic-education

Burgess, Rebecca. 2017. "Our Veterans Deserve Better." *InsideSources.* November 10. Accessed April 30, 2017. http://www.insidesources.com/veterans-deserve-better/

Center for the Study of Social Policy. 2011. "Promoting Youth Civic Engagement." November 15. Accessed April 30, 2018. https://www.cssp.org/policy/papers/Promoting-Youth-Civic-Engagement.pdf

CIRCLE. 2012. "Civic Health and Unemployment II: The Case Builds." The Center for Information and Research on Civic Engagement. September 12. Accessed April 30, 2018. https://civicyouth.org/civic-health-and-unemployment-ii-the-case-builds/

Eberstadt, Nicholas. 2016. *Men without Work: America's Invisible Crisis* (New Threats to Freedom Series). West Conshohocken, PA: Templeton Press.

Flanagan, Constance. 2003. "Developmental Roots of Political Engagement." *PS: Political Science and Politics*, 36(2): 257–261.

Flanagan, Constance, and Peter Levine. 2010. "Civic Engagement and the Transition to Adulthood." *Future Child*, 20(1): 159–179.

Rahn, Wendy M., and John E. Transue. 1998. "Social Trust and Value Change: The Decline of Social Capital in American Youth, 1976–1995." *Political Psychology*. Special Issue: Psychological Approaches to Social Capital, 19(3): 545–565.

Rebecca Burgess is the program manager for the American Enterprise Institute's Program on American Citizenship, which produces original research on civic education, the health of America's public institutions, and the principles of American democracy. Rebecca is also an advisory board member of iCivics, an educational nonprofit developed in response to the declining quality of civics education in U.S. schools.

The Impact of the ACA on Youth Unemployment
Hadley Heath Manning

In March 2010, Congress passed and then-president Obama signed the Patient Protection and Affordable Care Act, a significant overhaul of U.S. health policy. The law was intended to expand health insurance coverage via a system of taxes, subsidies, regulations, and mandates. Several of the law's provisions had a direct impact on employment and a disproportionate impact on youth employment.

The Affordable Care Act (ACA) did not create the link between health insurance and employment in the United States. During World War II, price controls on labor fostered the market for new compensation benefits (including employer-based health coverage), and shortly after the war (1953), Congress granted a tax exemption for health insurance benefits offered through work.

As a result, most privately insured Americans (both before and after the passage of the ACA) obtain health insurance via an employer plan.

This means that as the cost of health insurance increases, employers must pass along more costs in various forms: increases in cost sharing for employees, reductions to hours or wages, reductions to other benefits, or increases in price for consumers. Employers might also simply stop providing health insurance, although this might put them at a disadvantage in attracting and retaining their workforce.

The ACA worsened this problem in several ways, contributing to higher levels of unemployment, especially among certain demographics, including youth.

First, the ACA mandated that employers of 50 or more workers provide insurance. This mandate was accompanied by myriad regulations on what plans must include, what employees were eligible, and what portion of costs employers must cover. Employers in violation of the mandate would pay penalties of $2,000 or $3,000 per worker.

Importantly, the employer mandate only applies to workers above a 30-hour threshold. This means that one way employers could circumvent the mandate is to cut hours. Younger workers (and female workers) are more likely to hold jobs just above the 30-hour-per-week threshold, making them prime targets of this practice.

Various economic studies have examined this effect. A Vanderbilt University study estimated that "the ACA resulted in an increase in low-hours, involuntary part-time employment of a half-million to a million workers in retail, accommodations, and food services, the sectors in which employers are most likely to reduce hours if they choose to circumvent the mandate, and also the sectors in which low-wage workers are most likely to be affected" (Dillender et al. 2016)

A study from the National Bureau of Economic Research similarly concluded that "between 28,000 and 50,000 businesses nationwide appear to be reducing their number of full-time-equivalent employees to below 50 because of that mandate. This translates to roughly 250,000 positions eliminated from those businesses" (Mulligan 2017).

Second, the ACA not only decreased labor *demand* through a mandate that punished employers for creating and maintaining a full-time workforce, but it also created a system of subsidies for non-employer coverage that ultimately served to reduce labor *supply* and discourage work.

As economist Casey Mulligan (2014) explains in "The Affordable Care Act and the New Economics of Part-Time Work," the employer mandate acts as an explicit tax on full-time work. But the law's tax credits and subsidies, made available on the law's health insurance exchanges to those who earn between 100 and 400 percent of the federal poverty level, act as an implicit tax on full-time work and higher incomes.

Mulligan estimates that 20 percent of the U.S. workforce would be better off working part-time and using the law's subsidies for ACA-exchange plans than working full time. The ACA subsidies do not extend to full-time workers unless their employer fails to offer "affordable" coverage as defined by the law.

While some might rightly celebrate a strong market for individual (non-employer) insurance plans as an antidote to "job lock"—the condition of being stuck in a job only for the sake of using the employer-sponsored health plan—the ACA approached this problem in a convoluted way. Rather than income-based subsidies (that phase out as workers earn more), a better policy would be to equalize the tax treatment of all insurance plans, both those offered by employers and those purchased individually, regardless of income level or employment status.

Third and finally, the ACA failed to contain health insurance costs. In fact, all of the evidence suggests that the ACA (contrary to its title) spurred increases in health insurance premiums in both employer-sponsored plans and non-employer plans. The law also significantly increased regulatory compliance costs for employers, compounding its anti-growth, anti-employment effect.

How did the ACA affect employer-sponsored coverage costs? The law imposed new requirements on employer plans, including a rule that dependent coverage would extend to age 26 and a provision requiring all preventive services to be covered from the first dollar (meaning, with no co-pays or cost-sharing).

These requirements are not as extensive as those that the law applied to non-employer plans (available in the state-based "exchanges"), and therefore the impact on premiums was not as great (non-employer plans saw premium increases of 105 percent on average between 2013 and 2017).

But new requirements on employer plans were not without cost. A 2016 survey of employers from the International Foundation of Employee Benefit Plans found the ACA increased employer health care costs by 5.8 percent (Mrkvicka et al. 2016).

Direct health insurance costs aren't the only burden that the ACA put on employers: The state and private-sector regulatory compliance cost of the law has reached $53 billion (and approximately 177 million paperwork hours), according to a tracker from the American Action Forum (2018). These increased costs depress wage growth and job creation as well.

Taken together, the impact of the law's employer mandate, subsidy system, and regulations contributed to higher levels of unemployment. In any labor market, the easiest jobs to change or eliminate are those held by low-wage, low-skill workers. Naturally, younger workers congregate in these jobs due to a lack of experience and skill. Therefore, youth bear the worst of the ACA's burdens on employment.

The intentions of the ACA were noble, but its impact on youth employment has clearly been negative. A better policy would aim to eliminate the link between health insurance and employment and control costs in both insurance and health care through stronger market competition and greater choice in plans. This would allow businesses of all types to focus on maximizing profit and offering competitive wages so that workers could make individual decisions about what coverage suits them best. And, they would face better employment opportunities.

References

American Action Forum. 2018. Regulation Rodeo. Analysis of Affordable Care Act Regulations 2010–2018. http://regrodeo.com

Department of Health and Human Services. 2017. "Average Health Insurance Premiums Doubled since 2013." https://www.hhs.gov/about/news/2017/05/23/hhs-report-average-health-insurance-premiums-doubled-2013.html

Dillender, Marcus, Carolyn Heinrich, and Susan Houseman. 2016. *Effects of the Affordable Care Act on Part-Time Employment: Early Evidence*. Nashville, TN: Vanderbilt University. https://my.vanderbilt.edu/carolynheinrich/files/2016/06/DHH_Effects-ACA-on-Part-time-employment-6-9-16.pdf

Mrkvicka, Neil, Justin Held, and Julie Stich. 2016. "Employer-Sponsored Health Care: ACA's Impact." International Foundation of Employee Benefit Plans. http://www.ifebp.org/pdf/aca-impact-survey-2016.pdf

Mulligan, Casey. 2014. "The Affordable Care Act and the New Economics of Part-Time Work." Mercatus Center. https://www.mercatus.org/publication/affordable-care-act-and-new-economics-part-time-work

Mulligan, Casey. 2017. "The Employer Penalty, Voluntary Compliance, and the Size Distribution of Firms: Evidence from a Survey of Small Businesses." National Bureau of Economic Research. http://www.nber.org/papers/w24037

Hadley Heath Manning is director of policy at the Independent Women's Forum (www.iwf.org).

Addressing the Setbacks Incarcerated Youth Encounter in the Job Hunt
Riane Castro

Whether one has recently graduated college, is switching careers, or has been laid off, finding employment can be difficult. Often overlooked is the even greater challenge formerly incarcerated individuals face in the job hunt. For incarcerated youth—many of whom have experienced trauma, have developed little social capital, and have acquired few professional mentors—finding employment opportunities can seem impossible. Policy makers and nonprofits seeking to reduce the effects of youth unemployment should therefore strive to assist this vulnerable group.

Ninety percent of youth, aged 16 to 24, who are involved in the juvenile justice system or criminal justice system have admitted to experiencing some trauma in their lifetime (Olafson et al. 2016). Trauma includes anything from neglect of basic needs, such as food or water; all forms of assault, such as physical, sexual, or verbal; or the witnessing of traumatic scenarios (Kerig 2016). The average adult brain is not fully developed with a frontal lobe until about 25 years old, and trauma prior to this point can hinder further brain development (Adams 2010). The critical brain structures developed early on regulate emotion, memory, and behavior. The impression trauma makes on a child's brain, therefore, can be tremendous—if development in the emotional and aggression centers of the brain is disrupted, youth may fail to develop empathy and are more prone toward aggressive, violent, and sociopathic behavior (Adams 2010). In fact, young adults who experience trauma are more likely to develop lifelong psychiatric conditions including personality disorders, ADHD, depression, anxiety, substance abuse disorders, and posttraumatic stress disorder as well as developmental delays, decreased cognitive abilities, learning disabilities, and even lower IQ levels (Adams 2010). Therefore, a large population of youth who are incarcerated have major brain development issues, and many receive limited to no developmental assistance while behind bars. Moreover, further trauma can occur during incarceration, minimizing any chance of changed behavior and growth for the individuals. Nevertheless, once these young people are released they are often expected to secure employment to meet parole standards.

The job hunt can cause any individual to feel unqualified and unsure of himself or herself, as it is usually filled with a vast amount of rejection. The job hunt for those who have stunted maturation and a criminal record can be even worse. Many employers are reluctant to hire formerly incarcerated youth because they are fearful of the negative effect that those who have been involved in the system may have on their business. In a study of formerly incarcerated individuals, 70 percent of a sampled group noted that their record was a major barrier to employment in their job search post-incarceration (Ray et al. 2016). This difficulty is further aggravated by the fact that many incarcerated youth are often removed from school in the prime of high school. Involvement in school allows youths to begin establishing their network. It further allows them to work on their writing and verbal communication skills and to develop the mannerisms required in different social settings. Furthermore, many schools offer youth assistance in creating a resume and applying for higher education and financial aid. When young people are removed from these resources and are placed in correctional facilities, they lack the chance to develop the social capital obtained by many of their peers. Thus, although some former inmates find jobs eventually, they traditionally do so at much lower rates than the general population.

Over the past several years, a number of federal and state level actions have been taken to improve the employment finding capabilities of formerly incarcerated youth. In 2016, the

Department of Education partnered with the Department of Justice to secure $5.7 million in grants for youth who have been involved in the criminal justice system. These grants specifically focused on funding career and technical education programs, reentry services, and employment training opportunities for students (Department of Education 2016). As of January 1, 2018, California attempted to improve the employment opportunities of the formerly incarcerated by restricting employers from requiring job applicants to disclose their conviction history. Only once a conditional offer has been made are employers able to conduct a criminal history background check, and such checks are only permitted if a criminal history would have a direct and adverse relationship on specific duties of the job. In addition to California, ten other states—Connecticut, Hawaii, Illinois, Massachusetts, Minnesota, New Jersey, Oregon, Rhode Island, Vermont, and Washington—have followed suit by passing "ban the box" legislation prohibiting employers from inquiring about criminal history (Ray et al. 2016). Evidence demonstrates that individuals who are not required to reveal their record have a higher rate of employment and are offered better salaries (Selbin et al. 2018).

In addition to federal and state policy makers, private individuals, organizations, and businesses have also attempted to increase opportunities for employment and rehabilitation to formerly incarcerated youth. This past October, the nonprofit organization Campaign for Youth Justice sponsored an "Action Month" to promote employment opportunities to formerly incarcerated youth. A few of their partners included Drive Change, Pop! Gourmet Popcorn, and Flikshop (Kenderdine 2017). Drive Change was founded in 2013 by a former prison teacher. She started the company to hire individuals, aged 17 to 25, who have recently been released from correctional facilities. These individuals then participate in a yearlong program designed to help them develop professional skills and work experience. Pop! Gourmet Popcorn was founded in Seattle, Washington, in 2011 by a formerly incarcerated individual. Today, formerly incarcerated individuals make up over 20 percent of the company's staff. Flikshop was also created by a formerly incarcerated individual who established a school of business to help his colleagues create coding and technological skills.

While such programs and policies exist to increase opportunity, access is limited and is available only to individuals who live in proximity. Former inmates who live in states without employment protections or assistance programs are unlikely to find work and are more than likely to return to criminal activity. Thus, greater public and private efforts are necessary to help formerly incarcerated youth overcome the barriers to employment and successfully reintegrate into society.

References

Adams, Erica J. 2010. *Healing Invisible Wounds: Why Investing in Trauma—Informed Care for Children Makes Sense.* Justice Policy Institute. July. Accessed January 1, 2018. http://www.justicepolicy.org/images/upload/10–07_REP_HealingInvisibleWounds_JJ—PS.pdf

Department of Education. 2016. *Education Department Announces New Tools to Support Successful Reentry for Formerly Incarcerated Youth and Adults.* Accessed April 18, 2018. https://www.ed.gov/news/press-releases/education-department-announces-new-tools-support-successful-reentry-formerly-incarcerated-youth-and-adults

Kenderdine, Rachel. 2017. *Businesses Building a Better Way for Formerly Incarcerated Youth.* Center for Youth Justice. October. Accessed April 28, 2018. http://cfyj.org/yjam/blog/item/businesses-building-a-better-way-for-formerly-incarcerated-youth

Kerig, Patricia. 2016. *Psychosocial Interventions for Traumatized Youth in the Juvenile Justice System: Research, Evidence Base, and Clinical/Legal.* Accessed January 11, 2018. https://www.researchgate.net/profile/Patricia_Kerig/

publication/298969956_Psychosocial_Interventions_for_Traumatized_Youth_in_the_Juvenile_Justice_System_Research_Evidence_Base_and_ClinicalLegal_Challenges/links/56eda17208ae4b8b5e7436fa/Psychosocial-Interventions-for-Traumatized-Youth-in-the-Juvenile-Justice-System-Research-Evidence-Base-and-Clinical-Legal-Challenges.pdf

Olafson, Erna, et al. 2016. "Implementing Trauma and Grief Component Therapy for Adolescents and Think Trauma for Traumatized Youth in Secure Juvenile Justice Settings." *Journal of Interpersonal Violence*. February. Accessed January 11, 2018. https://www.ncbi.nlm.nih.gov/pubmed/26872505

Ray, Bradley, Eric Grommon, and Jason Rydberg. 2016. "Anticipated Stigma and Defensive Individualism during Post-Incarceration Job Searching." *Sociological Inquiry*, 86(3): 348–371. Accessed January 11, 2018. https://doi.org/10.1111/soin.12124

Selbin, Jeffrey, Justin McCray, and Joshua Epstein. 2018. "Unmarked? Criminal Record Clearing and Employment Outcomes." *Journal of Criminal Law and Criminology* 108(1). Accessed April 28, 2018. https://scholarlycommons.law.northwestern.edu/cgi/viewcontent.cgi?article=7617&context=jclc

Riane Castro recently graduated with a BA in political science from California State University, San Bernardino. She plans to pursue a career as an advocate for incarcerated and formerly incarcerated individuals.

Arrogance or Ignorance, but Not Confidence
Cynthia Sakamoto

Young job seekers tend to make common mistakes during recruitment and employment that leave employers skeptical about their abilities in the workplace. Specifically, Millennials and Generation Zers frequently exhibit certain behaviors from the recruiting phase to the exit interview that leave employers with the view that young candidates or employees are at best arrogant, at worst ignorant, but definitely not confident. Ultimately, this contributes to youth unemployment.

One common mistake that young professionals make during the recruiting process is to exhibit a demanding tone as early as the initial phone screen interview. Recruiters are frequently taken aback when a recent college graduate, with little to no experience, immediately asks about his or her ability to promote within the organization in the next year. Other presumptuous topics young, inexperienced professionals commonly bring up during their initial interviews include: salary negotiations, vacation accrual compromises, casual dress preferences, dual career ladder possibilities, and accommodating or flexible work schedules. Candidates may sincerely want answers to these questions, but it is better that they first prove themselves desirable to an employer before making such inquiries. Young candidates should realize that they will be more successful in the interview stage if they highlight their potential for growth. When candidates show maturity throughout recruitment, organizations may be open to hiring them, even if they have little experience. The experience they gain from initial employment will then make them better suited to promote and negotiate for better salary and benefits. For example, a vice president (VP) of manufacturing for a start-up car company recently explained to me that when he applied for his current position he let his recruiter know that he required relocation to California, a minimum salary, a company car, a full-time assistant, and a specific amount of money if he was terminated from his position before three years. The VP was only able to make these demands because he is a seasoned professional with over 35 years of experience. Working in similar positions for companies like General Motors, both in America and abroad, the VP earned the ability to lay out his conditions for a job out-front. In contrast, young, inexperienced job seekers should not take an arrogant position when considering where to work. Instead, they should be open to any opportunity that might give them valuable experience and enable them to be more selective and demanding in the future. Negotiation works only when both parties have something valuable to offer. In the case of employment, that translates to compensation and benefits from the employer and experience and accomplishments from the candidate.

Additionally, many young people in the workforce are making it difficult for their generational equals to obtain work because of the negative impression their behaviors leave on their employers. For example, young people increasingly relying on their parents as they transition from school to work and are frequently unable to accept the consequences for breaking the rules. It is common for concerned parents to call HR professionals on behalf of their children because they were disciplined at work. Other behaviors widely observed in young professionals include: a lack of sense of urgency, hasty use of sick time, repetitive pay increase requests, disregard for start times, and quitting without notice. Unfortunately, impressions conveyed by professional networks and bloggers, who target recent college graduates and young professionals, may contribute to these youthful behaviors. Student-oriented websites like Vault serve as a perfect example with headlines such as, "You Should Be Interviewing Even If You're Not Looking for a Job." Another site, The Ladders, recently sent out a newsletter titled, "How Swearing at Work Can Help You Succeed." At the risk of sounding old fashioned, new professionals should focus on learning a trade and doing their jobs correctly—not on how interviewing can make them better negotiators or how saying swear words can make them more approachable.

The Society for Human Resource Management (SHRM) recently gave rise to the concept of the Employee Value Proposition (EVP). According to the SHRM, an organization's EVP answers two questions: "Why would a talented person want to work for an organization?" and "What is going to keep them there?" (Hasan, Loftus, Malhotra, and Walters 2017). Although these are valid questions for employers to ask themselves, SHRM does not specify which audience ought to be concerned with this concept. They speak in general and this may confuse those with little experience about how the real-world workforce operates. There is a short window of time to gain work experience as a young professional. It behooves young people to learn humility in the process of building a career, which will ultimately lead to the experience and confidence they need for success.

References

Capitol Standard. 2016. "You Should Be Interviewing Even If You're Not Looking for a Job." *Vault*. http://www.vault .com/blog/interviewing/interview-when-youve-got-a-job-to-help-your-career/

Hasan, E., C. J. Loftus, R. P. Malhotra, and V. C. Walters. 2017. *SHRM Learning System for SHRM-CP/SHRM-SCP People*. Alexandria, VA: Society for Human Resource Management.

Salyer, K. 2017. "How Swearing at Work Can Help You Succeed." *The Ladders*. https://www.theladders.com/ career-advice/swearing-work-can-help-succeed

Cynthia Sakamoto was born in 1983 and is technically a millennial. She has worked in human resources for eight years. She has a master's degree in human resources and employee relations from the Graduate School at Pennsylvania State University and is a SHRM-CP.

Institutional Motivation versus Personal Motivation
Melanie Warren

Walking into Texas State Technical College at 17, I was awe-struck by the glaring signs promising that I would be making at least 100k in computer networking in less than two years. Having dropped out of high school at 15, I didn't think I would ever get a chance to go to college and be anything besides a minimum-wage worker. I was sold.

The year I spent at Texas State Technical College was a learning experience but not the typical one you would think. The teachers were some of the "best in the field," as they proclaimed, and I passed most of my classes and learned a lot about computers. Yet, I never completed the program. Why didn't I finish? After deeply pondering this question, I realized that it is because I was sold an education, and I did not follow what I was passionate about or good at. I wasn't ready to be in the field nor did I have the passion and motivation to be an actual computer networker. The motivation needed to excel in that field cannot be taught even by "the best in the field."

After a few semesters, I quickly figured that I had no real interest in computers and that my main reason for attending Texas State Technical College was that I had been sold a dream. As soon as prospective students walk in, they are greeted with enthusiasm and handed a list of possible associate degrees and certifications. "Just pick one!" "From commercial art to computer programming we have many options." I did what I thought I was supposed to do and picked one. At this point in my life, I didn't know much about computers, but I did know that people working in the field make a lot of money! I wanted to make money, who doesn't? While financial security motivates most people, the institution itself is also motivated by the goal of making money from students' education. Thus, they feed off of students' motivation for financial success to sell them an idea.

Does this mean alternative forms of higher education are all useless? Should we give up on the idea of promoting alternative forms of education? No. Like traditional forms of higher education, however, they are not for everyone. The important thing is that students know what they hope to obtain from such institutions. This requires research and following what really motivates you as opposed to the motives of the institution you are considering attending. Education is a big business and alternative forms are popping up everywhere for pretty much every field. Some are predatory and will leave students in debt with a possibly worthless certification or worse, they will be students like myself, who never complete the program, with nothing other than debt.

After my failed attempt at a technical college, I tried various jobs that only required a GED. I tried one more time to attend an alternative college, this time a cosmetology school. I did not finish. I was a beauty school dropout. This was because I was not great at it—and, although I could get a job at a mediocre salon, I wouldn't make any more money than I currently did as a bartender. I cut my losses after acquiring another $20,000 in debt.

At this point, I was tired of trying to find the answer in education and resigned myself to a life of customer service. I was great at bartending and made excellent money. The only drawbacks were the fact that I lacked health care benefits and the idea of being 60 still tending bar with no real retirement plan was hard to fathom. I was lost. One day while riding the bus to work in Austin, Texas, I noticed Austin Community College. I saw smiling faces and college students with their backpacks ready for class. I wanted that. But, my experience with alternative higher education had not been good. Why would community college be any different? The next day I went online to research Austin Community College and made an appointment with an advisor. At my first appointment, the advisor asked me what I WANTED to do. She didn't try to sell me a career but told me I had time to explore and to create my own education. She did rattle off some of the certification programs the college offered, but she didn't try to make me choose one at that moment. There I was, at 25, about to start at a traditional community college. Every undergrad class I took excited me! At one point I wanted nothing more than to be an art historian and then I took a geography class! Maybe I will pursue that!?

These classes were all required no matter what major I chose and they exposed me to a wide range of fields. It was through this more traditional route to a college degree that I found my calling as an educator. I ended up graduating from Austin Community College and transferring to Texas State University where I finished my bachelor's degree in elementary education, and where I am now pursuing my master's degree. I went from a high school dropout at 15 to a college grad at 34. Everyone's path is different. Finding what motivates you and being aware of what motivates others is key to your success at any school, whether alternative or traditional. Just because you are pushed in one direction does not mean you have to go down that path. Not everyone is suited for or motivated to be the top computer programmer or hair designer and those dream institutions often try to sell can be misleading. So why not pursue something that truly excites and motivates you?

Melanie Warren is an educator currently pursuing an MA in Education at Texas State University in San Marcos, Texas. She is a nontraditional student and mother of two. She has a passion for the education of those who are less advantaged.

Transforming Disconnected Youth through Educational Opportunity
Vicki Alger

Many young people today may doubt whether the American Dream will ever become a reality for them.

Some experts even predict that the current generation may be the first since the Great Depression to earn less than their parents. Yet, today's youth have more educational options than their predecessors, and those options are helping a growing number of young people beat the odds—which are daunting, to be sure.

Today, there are 4.9 million American teenagers and young adults aged 16 to 24 who are not employed or in school, commonly referred to as disconnected youth. That's roughly one in eight teenagers and young adults (Ross and Svajlenka 2016, ii).

Access to high-quality K-12 education is one of the best ways to be prepared for college and beyond. Yet, only one-third of people in fragile communities, which are characterized by high rates of residents who struggle to meet daily necessities and have limited social mobility, report that children in their communities have access to high-quality public schools (Gallup, Inc. 2018, 8, 21, and 23). What's more, many experts agree that at-risk youth often need options beyond the traditional public school system (Dobbs et al. 2016, 75; NYEC 2008, 11).

Thankfully, K-12 education options are growing and are already helping transform disconnected youth into opportunity youth. Phoenix, Arizona, is a case in point.

In 2012, Phoenix ranked the worst of the country's 25 largest metropolitan areas for its youth disconnection rate of almost one in five (Burd-Sharps and Lewis 2012, 5). Within five years, however, Phoenix reduced its youth disconnection rate from nearly 100,000 people to less than 74,000 people (Burd-Sharps and Lewis 2017, 5).

The Maricopa County Education Service Agency (MCESA) spearheaded efforts by government, community, nonprofit, and philanthropic leaders to reduce youth disconnection. These efforts focused on high school completion, preventing youth from entering or returning to prison, job creation and training, and internship programs (Burd-Sharps and Lewis 2017, 5). Expanding K-12 education options also helps improve opportunities for disconnected youth, and Arizona is considered a national leader in this regard.

Arizona students can enroll in virtually any district public school regardless of where they live. Such freedom puts powerful pressure on all public schools to be responsive and increases the likelihood that students can attend the schools that work best for them without having to move. Research also shows that open enrollment helps increase high school graduation rates, as well as college attendance and completion rates (Miku-lecky 2013, 4).

Public charter schools, which follow the same admissions and accountability requirements as district public schools, have the flexibility to offer innovative programs. Arizona charter schools are so popular, 17 percent of all public school students statewide attend them (Gilbertson 2017). A growing number of charter schools throughout the state also specializes in serving disconnected youth.

Aseelah, for example, loved high school. Then a series of family health issues arose, and she left school to help out by working two part-time jobs. Aseelah enrolled in online classes, but they didn't offer her the support she needed. She found the right fit at Ombudsman Arizona Charter Metro School, where a flexible schedule and shorter school day meant Aseelah could balance her family and academic responsibilities. Not only has Aseelah caught up, she says that "the scholarship and career resources we receive are all preparation for my next goal—college." She plans to attend the University of Arizona as a pre-med student so she can help others who struggle with health issues (Muhammad 2016).

Things were much different for Lilly, who attended a traditional high school for three months before being "kicked out." Her negative views about school changed after she gave birth to her daughter. "I don't want her to [make] the mistakes I did." Lilly, now 17, is on track to graduate soon from Hope College and Career Readiness Academy in Phoenix, and she's sad to leave. Yet, she feels prepared for the next chapter in her life thanks to the parenting, life-skills, and job training she received (HCCRA n.d.).

Arizona also offers extensive K-12 private school options. It has five scholarship programs, and it's the first state to offer education savings accounts (ESAs). Parents and guardians of students who are not thriving at their current public schools sign a contract promising not to re-enroll their children as long as they are using an ESA. The state then deposits at least 90 percent of the formula funding it would have sent to students' public schools into students' ESAs instead. Parents receive a type of dedicated-use debit card to pay for approved education expenses, including private school tuition, tutoring, special education therapies, online courses, and testing fees. Leftover funds roll over from one year to the next for future education expenses, including college.

Students eligible for these programs include those who are or are at risk of becoming disconnected youth, including students who are from low-income families, would otherwise be assigned to failing public schools, have special needs, are from the foster-care system, reside on Indian reservations, are military dependents, or students whose parents were killed in the line of duty. These programs put the specialized schools students' need within reach and encourage partnerships with foundations such as the Pappas Kids Schoolhouse Foundation, which focuses helping disadvantaged and homeless students, like Briana.

Thanks to her scholarship, Briana is now finishing college and plans to become a nurse. "I am actually the first to graduate high school in my family from the last four generations," says Briana, who received financial assistance as well as ongoing support from the foundation. "I received calls and emails asking how I am, how is school, and if I needed anything . . . all the emails and checking up on me made me work harder to make everyone proud" (Pappas Kids 2017).

Seventeen-year-old Antonio Gibson also comes from a low-income family and has Asperger's syndrome, a condition on the higher functioning autism spectrum. He "felt like I was teaching myself at my public school," where he was not receiving the services he needed and was failing most of his classes. With an ESA, he was able to attend Gateway Academy in Phoenix, which focuses on special needs and gifted education. Now, says Antonio, "I'm actually learning from my teachers," and he did so well he earned a college scholarship (AFC 2017).

Arizona's educational options are already changing students' lives for the better, and similar programs are proliferating nationwide.

All students deserve the chance to become a success story instead of a statistic. Educational options give them that chance and help transform disconnected youth into opportunity youth prepared to achieve their hopes and dreams.

References

Arizona Federation for Children (AFC). 2017. "Autistic Kids Tell Their Stories to Help All Other Arizona Children Have School Choice." May 1. Accessed March 3, 2017. https://az4children.org/2017/05/autistic-kids-tell-their-stories-to-help-all-other-arizona-children-have-school-choice

Ayres, Sarah. 2013a. "The High Cost of Youth Unemployment." Washington, DC: Center for American Progress. April 5. Accessed November 23, 2017. http://www.americanprogress.org/wp-content/uploads/2013/04/AyresYouthUnemployment1.pdf

Ayres, Sarah. 2013b. "America's 10 Million Unemployed Youth Spell Danger for Future Economic Growth." Washington, DC: Center for American Progress. June 5. Accessed November 23, 2017. https://cdn.americanprogress.org/wp-content/uploads/2013/06/YouthUnemployment.pdf

Burd-Sharps, Sarah, and Kristen Lewis. 2012. *One in Seven: Ranking Youth Disconnection in the 25 Largest Metro Areas.* Brooklyn, NY: Measure of America, of the Social Science Research Council. Accessed November 23, 2017. http://ssrc-static.s3.amazonaws.com/moa/MOA-One_in_Seven09-14.pdf

Burd-Sharps, Sarah, and Kristen Lewis. 2017. *Promising Gains, Persistent Gaps: Youth Disconnection in America.* Brooklyn, NY: Measure of America, of the Social Science

Research Council. Accessed November 23, 2016. https://ssrc-static.s3.amazonaws.com/moa/Promising%20Gains%20Final.pdf

Dobbs, Richard, et al. 2016. *Poorer Than Their Parents? A New Perspective on Income Inequality*. London, England: McKinsey & Company, McKinsey Global Institute. Accessed November 23, 2016. https://www.mckinsey.com/~/media/McKinsey/Global%20Themes/Employment%20and%20Growth/Poorer%20than%20their%20parents%20A%20new%20perspective%20on%20income%20inequality/MGI-Poorer-than-their-parents-Flat-or-falling-incomes-in-advanced-economies-Full-report.ashx

EdChoice. 2018. "School Choice in America." Indianapolis, IN: EdChoice. Last modified March 16, 2018. Accessed March 20, 2018. http://www.edchoice.org/school-choice/school-choice-in-america

Education Commission of the States. 2016. "Open Enrollment 50-State Report—All Data Points." Denver, CO: Education Commission of the States. Accessed November 26, 2017. http://ecs.force.com/mbdata/mbquest4e?rep=OE1605

Faller, Mary Beth. 2013. "Alternative Education Scores High in Arizona: Schools for Struggling Students Continue to Show Improvement; 9 Given Top Marks (Phoenix)." ChanceLight. August 23. Accessed November 26, 2017. http://chancelight.com/news/alternative-education-scores-high-phoenix-az/

Friedman Foundation for Educational Choice. 2016. "How Does School Choice Affect Public Schools?" Indianapolis, IN: Friedman Foundation for Educational Choice. Last modified February 26, 2016. Accessed November 26, 2017. http://www.edchoice.org/school_choice_faqs/how-does-school-choice-affect-public-schools

Gallup, Inc. 2018. "The State of Opportunity in America."
Washington, DC: Center for Advancing Opportunity.
Accessed March 3, 2018. http://www.advancingop
portunity.org/wp-content/uploads/2018/01/The-State-of-
Opportunity-in-America-Report-Center-for-Advancing-
Opportunity.pdf

Gilbertson, Megan. 2017. "More Families Choosing
Arizona Public Charter Schools." Phoenix, AZ:
Arizona Charter Schools Association. Accessed
November 23, 2017. https://azcharters.org/
more-families-choosing-arizona-public-charter-schools/

Henderson, J. Maureen. 2013. "Millennials Earn Less Than
Their Parents and the Recession Isn't to Blame." Forbes.
com. November 30. Accessed November 23, 2016. https://
www.forbes.com/sites/jmaureenhenderson/2013/11/30/
millennials-earn-less-than-their-parents-and-the-recession-
isnt-to-blame/#375971c95946

Hope College and Career Readiness Academy (HCCRA).
n.d. "Student Spotlight Story." https://www.mcrsd.org/
hopeacademy

Kellogg, Bob. 2017. "'School Choice' Leader AZ Jumps Ahead."
One News Now. April 17. Accessed November 26, 2017.
https://www.onenewsnow.com/education/2017/04/17/
school-choice-leader-az-jumps-ahead

Mikulecky, Marga Torrence. 2013. "Open Enrollment
Is on the Menu—But Can You Order It?" Denver,
CO: Education Commission of the States.
Accessed November 26, 2017. https://ecs.org/
clearinghouse/01/07/96/10796.pdf

Muhammad, Aseelah. 2016. "Education Is Helping Me
Overcome Obstacles to Pursue My Dreams." Ombudsman
Charter Metro Blog. March 9. Accessed March 3, 2018.
http://www.ombudsman.com/alt-ed/education-is-helping-
me-overcome-obstacles-to-pursue-my-dreams-phoenix/

National Youth Employment Coalition (NYEC). 2008. Expanding Options: State Financing of Education Pathways for Struggling Students and Out of School Youth. Washington, DC: NYES. Accessed November 26, 2017. http://nyec.org/wp-content/uploads/2016/12/ NYECexpandopt_w_cvr-FULLDOC.pdf

Pappas Kids. 2017. "Letter from Brianna." June. Pappas Kids Schoolhouse Foundation Testimonials. Accessed March 3, 2018. https://pappaskidssf.org/testimonials/

Ratcliffe, Caroline, and Signe-Mary McKernan. 2013. "Lost Generations? Wealth Building among Young Americans." Washington, DC: Urban Institute, Urban Wire. March 19. Accessed November 23, 2016. https://www.urban.org/ urban-wire/lost-generations-wealth-building-among-young

Ross, Martha, and Nicole Prchal Svajlenka. 2016. "Employment and Disconnection among Teens and Young Adults: The Role of Place, Race, and Education." Washington, DC: Brookings Institution. Accessed November 26, 2016. https://www.brookings.edu/research/ employment-and-disconnection-among-teens-and-young- adults-the-role-of-place-race-and-education/

Steuerle, Eugene, et al. 2013. "Lost Generations? Wealth Building among Young Americans." Washington, DC: Urban Institute. Accessed November 23, 2016. https://www.urban.org/sites/default/files/ publication/23401/412766-lost-generations-wealth- building-among-young-americans.pdf

Viteritti, Joseph P. 1999. "A Way Out: School Choice and Opportunity." *Brookings Review*. Fall. Accessed November 26, 2017. https://www.brookings.edu/wp- content/uploads/2016/06/viteritti.pdf

Wall Street Journal. 2017. "Arizona's Grand School Choice." *Wall Street Journal*, Review and Outlook Editorial. April 11. Accessed November 26, 2017. https://www.wsj

.com/articles/arizonas-grand-school-choice-1491865839

West, Martin R. 2016. "Schools of Choice: Expanding Opportunity for Urban Minority Students." *Education Next*. 16: 2. Accessed November 26, 2017. http://educationnext.org/schools-of-choice-expanding-opportunity-urban-minority-students/

Vicki Alger, PhD, is a research fellow at the Independent Institute in Oakland, California, and author of Failure: The Federal Misedukation of America's Children.

Just a Little More
Stephen Monteros

I recently attended a workforce board meeting that opened with a very interesting fact. Ten years ago, employers were asked whether they would rather hire a young, educated person with no experience or a person with more experience, who would require tenure and a higher salary, for an entry to mid-level professional position. The overwhelming response was the young person. The comments in response were based on the rationale that young workers would be less expensive, easier to manage, and more enthusiastic. The same survey was recently reconducted and, surprisingly, the employers' preference had now shifted to the more experienced person.

One would expect that the problem of youth unemployment would solve itself over the long term based on the retirements of more experienced workers. Companies, however, are paying more and more to attract experienced employees rather than bringing in new talent with longer work horizons. Having personally witnessed the recent shift in preference toward older, more experienced workers in my own business caused me to consider what has led to the shift in employer preference over the past ten years.

My business employs a mix of both experienced and non-experienced workers, so I asked my staff what they thought had caused the change in hiring preferences. My staffers explained the need to exercise caution when hiring non-experienced workers. Employees are often required to work on-site with customers based on very tight deadlines. If customer engagement goes poorly, we can lose customers that negatively impact the business and could possibly cost someone a job. The stakes are very high. As I mentioned, my company employs a mix of both experienced and newer, less-experienced employees. The newer employees are performing well and are generally well received. So I interviewed these newer employees to determine what had contributed to their hiring. It was immediately apparent that the newer, less-experienced employees possess and exercise something we refer to as, "just a little more."

Research shows that the most common complaints against younger workers are their lack of professionalism, appropriate dress, and knowledge of the company and their inability to identify and articulate their talents (Workopolis 2014). According to an article in *US News and World Report*, companies should prefer to hire older workers because they have more experience, confidence, reliability, and loyalty and are better suited to help a company save money (LaPonsie 2015).

My best advice to younger employees—in light of these stereotypes in favor of older, more experienced workers—is that they need to show, *just a little more*. Younger workers entering the workforce face negative stereotypes, competition from older more experienced workers, and resumes that look very similar to those of all the other inexperienced young people vying for the same job. They need some way to stand out. The process of standing out can be implemented as late as graduation but is best started early.

Starting early requires a young person to have some knowledge or idea of what career they might wish to pursue. These ideas can be general or based on a personal interest and talent, such as an interest in computers and technology. Once an interest is identified, young people can start preparing themselves for a future career as early as middle and high school using a program and concept called Linked Learning, which is now supported by many school districts, especially in California.

Linked Learning is an approach to academic learning that promotes the core principles of rigorous academics, career technical education, work-based learning experiences, and comprehensive support services to ensure that students who graduate from high school are college and career ready. According to the 2015 SRI International Report, "Taking Stock of the California Linked Learning District Initiative," students in a Linked Learning program are more likely to earn a diploma and are better prepared for college and careers.

The Linked Learning model is geared to begin a student's exploration of career possibilities as early as elementary school. The model takes students through a process of a work-based learning continuum, which encompasses career exploration, and then moves into an integrated application of skills. For example, at Bing Wong Elementary in San Bernardino School District, students learning about communications not only apply the fundamentals of writing, but they are also required to work on projects in teams and apply specific skills such as public speaking—in this case, by producing a news show to broadcast on a school network to their peers (Linked Learning 2012). Within any given chosen career track, students learn to overcome the "soft skills" obstacles many employers see as an impediment to employing young adults.

Students who have participated in Linked Learning and similar programs present themselves with more confidence, improved written and verbal communication skills, and a better understanding of what will be expected of them in a real-world job. Students who choose a particular career pathway are not necessarily confined to that course of study. The most important aspect of the program is that it provides a rich experience of rigorous classroom work tied with application, which better prepares students for college courses or to take on a position when they graduate from high school.

There are many things in life that are out of our control. The best advice I can give young people is to control what they can. This requires that they start practicing a craft as early as possible and work a little harder. In giving a little more, they will be able to distinguish themselves as they search for employment. Linked Learning and programs like it help students gain that competitive edge that will aid them on the path to career success.

References

Guha, Raneeta, et al. 2014. *Taking Stalk of the California Linked Learning District Initiative: Fifth Year Evaluation Report Executive Summary*. Menlo Park, CA: SRI International. https://www.sri.com/sites/default/files/publications/ year5linkedlearningevaluationexecsummmdec2014.pdf

LaPonsie, Maryalene. 2015. "5 Reasons Employers Should Hire More Workers Over Age 50." *US News and World Report*. https://money.usnews.com/money/retirement/ articles/2015/09/18/5-reasons-employers-should-hire-more-workers-over-age-50

Linked Learning. 2012. "Work Based Learning in Linked Learning: Definitions, Outcomes, and Quality Criteria." http://www.connectedcalifornia.org/direct/ files/resources/WBL%20Definitions%20Outcomes%20 Criteria_pg_120512_v2.pdf

Linked Learning. n.d. "About Linked Learning." http://www .linkedlearning.org/en/about/

Workopolis. 2014. "Employers Say There Are Three Reasons Why They Don't Like to Hire Younger Workers." https:// careers.workopolis.com/advice/three-reasons-young-people-arent-getting-hired-and-how-to-fix-them/

Stephen Monteros is a member of the California Workforce Development Board, an adjunct instructor at the University of LaVerne, and the vice president of operations and strategic initiatives at ConvergeOne. Maral Hernandez, a government and legislative affairs analyst for San Bernardino County, assisted Stephen Monteros in writing this essay.

4 Profiles

Introduction

Over the past several decades, hundreds of organizations and individuals have been and continue to be involved in attempts to alleviate the crisis of youth unemployment in the United States and to respond to its most pernicious effects. This chapter highlights some of the key public and private organizations through which individuals and groups have drawn attention to or have worked to resolve the crisis. The chapter begins with a description of some of the most well-known government organizations and programs designed to alleviate youth unemployment and then overviews important businesses and non-profit organizations that have responded to the crisis in various and unique ways. Among these organizations are policy and research institutions that work to uncover the nature of the problem and shape the debate over policy reform. The chapter additionally highlights the efforts of organizations involved in providing direct services to youth who are at risk of or affected by unemployment and disconnection.

A young job seeker fills out a name tag during a Shades of Commerce Career Fair in the Brooklyn borough of New York on February 17, 2018. The factors producing chronic youth unemployment are often deep-rooted and structural, extending beyond the performance of the labor market at any given time. (Gabby Jones/Bloomberg via Getty Images)

Government-Sponsored Organizations and Programs

Career Academies

Developed more than 40 years ago, Career Academies are one of the oldest and widely used high school reforms in the United States. Today, they operate in thousands of schools across the country. Career Academies generally have three distinguishing features. First, they are designed to create a supportive and personalized learning environment by operating as a school-within-a-school. Second, their curriculum combines academic and theme-based occupational-related course work to promote applied learning and satisfy college entrance requirements. Third, the academies form partnerships with local employers who provide workplace learning opportunities for participating students. Although Career Academies were originally established to provide increased workplace preparation for high-risk youth, with the goal of preventing them from dropping out of high school, they are now designed to prepare students for both work and college. As a result, enrollment in Career Academies includes both students at risk of dropping out as well as those who are highly engaged in school.

After studying more than 1,400 students who were randomly assigned to Career Academies and their non-academy peers over the course of 15 years, the Manpower Demonstration Research Corporation (MDRC), a nonpartisan education and social policy think tank, found that "investments in career-related experiences during high school can produce substantial and sustained improvements in labor market prospects and transitions to adulthood of youth" (Kemple 2008). Specifically, the research showed that Career Academy participants produced sustained earning gains and employment stability in the eight years following graduation and were more likely to live independently with children and a spouse or partner. Participation in a Career Academy had a particularly beneficial impact on the labor market prospects of young men.

Federal Work Study

Originally established under the Economic Opportunity Act of 1964, the Federal Work Study program was modeled after the Depression-era National Youth Administration program that provided federally funded work opportunities to low-income high school and college students who needed earnings to remain in school. Today, the program continues to fund part-time employment for college students with financial need by subsidizing the wages of eligible students. Student participants may be employed by educational institutions, government agencies, or private nonprofit and for-profit organizations as long as they meet the legal requirements established by law. According to Department of Education regulations, participating institutions and employers must also use at least 7 percent of their Work Study allocation to fund students engaged in community service jobs such as tutoring or emergency preparedness and response.

The program maintains the three-pronged goal of helping students earn money to subsidize their education costs, providing students with work experience relevant to their chosen major or career field, and improving relations between institutions of higher education and the surrounding community.

Job Corps

First enacted under the Economic Opportunity Act of 1964, the Job Corps program aims to provide disadvantaged youth with intensive social, academic, career, and technical education and service learning opportunities through contractor organizations, including nonprofit and for-profit entities as well as the U.S. Department of Agriculture's Forest Service. To qualify for Job Corps, participants must be low-income and face specific barriers to employment, such as basic skill deficiency, pregnancy or teen parenthood, homelessness, or involvement in the foster care system. Job Corps is one of the only employment programs geared toward youth that provides residential centers, where participants are able to live, receive health care, child care, and other services.

National Guard Youth ChalleNGe Corps

Founded in 1993, the National Guard Youth ChalleNGe Corps is a residential, quasi-military program that aims to intervene in the lives of at-risk youth in order to help them develop the values, life skills, education, and self-discipline that will enable them to live rewarding and successful lives as productive citizens. The program, which is operated by participating states through their state National Guard organizations with support from federal funds, accepts 16- to 18-year-olds who have dropped out of high school or are not progressing in a traditional high school setting and are either unemployed or underemployed.

Participants spend a regimented five and a half months on a military base, where they participate in a curriculum structured around eight core components: leadership/followership skills, responsible citizenship, community service, life-coping skills, physical fitness, health and hygiene, job skills, and academic excellence. The largest portion of each day is spent in intensive academic instruction with the goal of helping participants earn their high school diploma or pass the GED exam. This Residential Phase is followed by a 12-month Post-Residential Phase, in which participants are paired with National Guard mentors who support and advise participants as they pursue further education, employment, or military service.

Today, the program serves thousands of youth annually at 40 sites in 29 states, the District of Columbia, and Puerto Rico. The program has been recognized as one of the country's most effective and cost efficient programs for targeting youth who are at the greatest risk for substance abuse, teen pregnancy, delinquency, and criminal activity. One evaluation of the program found that participants were more likely to obtain a high school diploma or GED certificate, to enroll in continuing education, and to be employed with higher earnings than members of a control group (Millenky et al. 2011).

National Service Programs

Dating back to the Depression era's Civilian Conservation Corps, national service programs are federally established institutions that serve the community, while providing experience and training to youth participants. These programs generally create full-time, year-long public service positions—financed by public and private resources—that provide participants a minimal stipend and health care and child care benefits. National service programs additionally offer financial awards to participants who complete a term of service that can be used to finance higher education, career training, or student loans. National service programs are not designed to replace long-term careers, but they can help prepare difficult-to-employ young adults and recent college graduates for future employment in the private or public sector. Although Congress has at times questioned the effectiveness of such programs, studies sponsored by the Corporation for National and Community Service Programs have found that youth who participate in volunteer service programs experience an increased likelihood of future gainful employment following their service—this is especially true for participants who lack a high school diploma (Price et al. 2011; Spera et al. 2013).

The federal government currently funds national service opportunities for youth through a variety of programs and focus areas.

AmeriCorps

AmeriCorps is the largest national service program in the country. Created by federal law in 1993, AmeriCorps provides grants to state and national organizations, including nonprofits, colleges, government agencies, and faith-based groups to provide recent college graduates, veterans, and at-risk youth with direct service opportunities. Most service opportunities are designed to respond to critical community needs in the areas of education, public health and safety, and environmental protection. One major aim of AmeriCorps' programs is to create a pathway for young adults to enter into public service careers that might otherwise experience substantial workforce shortages.

In July 2013, the Corporation for National and Community Service, which oversees AmeriCorps, announced the launch of the president's Task Force on Expanding National Service. This Task Force led to the creation of several collaborative programs between federal agencies and the private sector designed to provide service opportunities for vulnerable youth. One of these programs, Youth Opportunity AmeriCorps, established in 2014 under the Justice Department's Office of Juvenile Justice and Delinquency Prevention, creates opportunities for formerly incarcerated youth to reconnect to society by enrolling in direct service activities throughout the nation. Also founded in 2014, ServiceWorks is a collaborative program sponsored by AmeriCorps, the Citi Foundation, and the international non-profit Points of Light, which aims to help low-income youth in ten major cities across the United States develop the skills they need to prepare for college and careers while engaging in service. Participants first receive training courses taught by field professionals in 21st-century leadership and workplace skills. Then, under the guidance of a mentor, they participate in and lead volunteer service projects. Additional partnerships have been established with the U.S. Forest Service and U.S. Department of Transportation to provide opportunities for youth and veterans to work to protect and restore the nation's forest and grasslands or to improve state and regional transportation.

National Association of Service and Conservation Corps

The National Association of Service and Conservation Corps (NASCC), also known as the Corps Network, directs and supports a network of nearly 150 locally based organizations that engage youth, aged 16 to 25, and veterans up to the age of 35, in various service and conservation projects involving infrastructure, public lands, and disaster response. The Corps Network is supported in part by AmeriCorps funding and in part by private donations—including sizeable contributions from the Ford, Hewlett, and Mott Foundations. Participants or "Corps members" are compensated with a stipend, while participating in work activities designed to preserve and improve the nation's public lands, such as building and enhancing rails, increasing access to public lands and waters, creating and maintaining urban parks, removing invasive species, and restoring communities and resources following disasters. Corps members also receive education, training, and certification in skills such as wildland firefighting, carpentry, HAZMAT remediation, and heavy equipment operation. Many also work simultaneously on completing their GED or high school diploma.

Volunteers in Service to America

Volunteers in Service to America (VISTA), originally founded in 1965 as the domestic version of the Peace Corps, was incorporated into AmeriCorps in 1993 and renamed AmeriCorps VISTA. The program funds and deploys volunteers to assist nonprofits focused on addressing the economic challenges of the long-term poor living in low-income communities. Volunteers are tasked with recruiting additional volunteers, raising funds, developing new programs, and building community partnerships.

Youth Conservation Corps

Youth Conservation Corps is an eight- to ten-week summer employment program for youth, aged 15 through 18. Participants are paid minimum-wage to work alongside federal employees in national parks, forests, wildlife refuges, and fish hatcheries. Assignments may include projects such as building and maintaining trails and fences, cleaning campgrounds, improving wildlife habitat, environmental education planning, and historical building preservation.

YouthCorps

YouthCorps is a network of services programs focused on recruiting youth, aged 16 to 24, who are not in the labor force and not in school and are economically, physically, or educationally disadvantaged. YouthCorps programs encourage participants to earn a General Educational Development high school equivalency, while they acquire job-related skills through service projects in energy conservation, human services, and urban construction.

Office of Apprenticeship

Operating under the Department of Labor, the federal Office of Apprenticeship (OA) administers the National Apprenticeship Act, which authorizes the federal government in cooperation with independent State Apprenticeship Agencies (SAAs) to manage the nation's apprenticeship system. The primary function of OA is to oversee and set guidelines for the federal Registered Apprenticeship programs. Registered Apprenticeships are programs that have been certified by the Department of Labor's Office of Apprenticeship or by a State Apprenticeship Agency because they meet specified standards. As part of its oversight responsibilities, the OA oversees program approval and registration, sets standards for training quality and worker health and safety, ensures equality of access, and issues nationally recognized certificates of completion. The OA directly administers the Registered Apprenticeship program in 25 states and delegates operational authority to independent State Apprenticeship Agencies (SAAs) in 25 states and in Washington, D.C.

In order to qualify to participate in the OA Registered Apprenticeship program, an occupation must involve skills that are customarily learned in a practical way through supervised on-the-job training. Registered Apprenticeships generally last between one and six years and require the completion of at least 2,000 hours of on-the-job learning in addition to 144 annual hours of supplemental classroom instruction in technical subjects related to the occupation. Today, thousands of employers and companies in a variety of industries—including construction, manufacturing, information technology, health care, the military, and others—offer Registered Apprenticeship training opportunities to nearly half a million apprentices.

In June 2017, President Donald Trump signed an Executive Order calling for the expansion of available apprenticeships under the Department of Labor's Registered Apprenticeship Program. The order also shifted the role of developing and issuing guidelines for government-funded apprenticeship programs from the OA to private entities—such as companies, labor unions, and industry groups—pending Department of Labor approval.

Reentry Employment Opportunities Program

The Reentry Employment Opportunities Program is designed to provide job training and other services for individuals with a criminal record. While Congress never explicitly authorized this program, the Department of Labor has appropriated funding for its operation under the Workforce Innovation and Opportunity Act and the Second Chances Act. Through the allocation of grants to community-based organizations, school districts, and state departments of correction, the youth component of the program aims to increase employment opportunities and educational services for youth who have been involved with the juvenile justice or criminal justice system or who are at risk of dropping out of school and becoming involved with the justice system. Services provided under the program include pre-release mentoring, housing, and employment services.

State and Local Youth Apprenticeship Programs

A growing number of states have worked with businesses, labor market professionals, and educators to establish youth apprenticeship and pre-apprenticeship programs geared toward providing skills training and work-based learning opportunities for those who are still enrolled in high school. Several of the most prominent state youth apprenticeship programs are listed here.

Apprenticeship Carolina

Apprenticeship Carolina in South Carolina is one of the fastest-growing and largest apprenticeship programs in the country. It was launched in 2007, in response to the state's shortage of skilled workers, as a partnership between several of the state's private and public employers and the 16 technical colleges in the South Carolina Technical College System. In addition to job-related training with a partner company, participants in the apprenticeship program must complete over 100 hours of job-related education in one of the technical colleges. The program additionally sponsors a youth component that offers pre-apprenticeships for 16- to 17-year-olds who are still in high school but are on a career trajectory. The state offers participating companies a $1,000 tax credit per apprentice for up to four years to help offset the costs of maintaining apprenticeship opportunities.

CareerWise Colorado

CareerWise Colorado is a public-private collaboration funded in part by a $9.5 million donation from Bloomberg Philanthropies and JPMorgan Chase. The program is inspired by the Swiss model, in which 70 percent of high school students participate in apprenticeships in over 200 different occupations. Launched in fall of 2017 with 250 apprenticeships, CareerWise Colorado aims to serve approximately 10 percent of the state's eligible high school students by 2027. Since the program's inception, 51 school districts have signed on, and a wide range of employers have committed to working with CareerWise apprentices, including JPMorgan Chase, Intertech Plastics, Mountain Medical, Pilatus Business Aircraft, Research Electro-optics, TeleTech, and many others.

Participants, all juniors or seniors in high school, spend up to half of their day working on-site with employers, while earning a training wage, and the other half in the classroom working to complete their high school diploma. After graduation, participants spend another year of apprenticeship preparing either to directly enter the workforce or to continue their education at a community or four-year college. During this time, they have the opportunity to earn up to a year's worth of college credit debt free, and upon completion of the program, they receive a nationally recognized industry certification.

Tech Ready Apprentices for Careers in Kentucky Program

The Tech Ready Apprentices for Careers in Kentucky Program (also known as the TRACK program) is a youth preapprenticeship program cosponsored by the Kentucky Labor Department and the Kentucky Department of Education's Office of Career and Technical Education, which provides high school students with an early pipeline for entering into a postsecondary Registered Apprenticeship. The program initially began in the 2013–2014 academic year in 13 high schools with a focus on manufacturing. It has since expanded to high schools throughout the state and has added programs in construction, electrical technology, welding, and health science.

Wisconsin Youth Apprenticeship Program

The Wisconsin Youth Apprenticeship Program, established in 1991 as part of a state-led school-to-work initiative, is one of the oldest and largest youth apprenticeship programs in the country. The one- to two-year elective program offers apprenticeships to several thousand high school juniors and seniors based on partnerships between the state school districts and participating employers. During this time, students complete between 450 to 900 hours of paid work-based learning with a sponsoring employer and several semester-long technical courses, while simultaneously working to complete the academic requirements for their high school degree. With the help of a counselor, students choose an apprenticeship career option that best meets their needs or goals. Apprenticeships are offered in a wide range of fields including manufacturing, agriculture, hospitality, and information technology. Each student participant is additionally assigned a work-site mentor who provides individualized evaluation and instruction, creates a training schedule, and encourages progress. Upon completion of the program, student participants receive a Wisconsin Department of Workforce Development Certificate of Occupational Proficiency, and many receive college credit as well. According to a study by Harvard Graduate School of Education, over 85 percent of participants are employed after graduating high school and 60 percent go on to complete degrees in a technical college or university, a percentage much higher than the national average (Symonds, Schwartz, and Ferguson 2011).

YouthBuild

First established under the Cranston-Gonzalez National Affordable Housing Act of 1992, YouthBuild was administered by the Department of Housing and Urban Development until it was transferred to the Department of Labor in 2007. YouthBuild is a competitive grant program intended to engage disadvantaged, low-income youth in employment and other activities related to housing and construction. YouthBuild participants are generally taught construction skills while working on community service projects, such as building parks and community centers and improving low-income housing and schools. Participants are required to spend at least 40 percent of their time in work and skill development activities and at least

50 percent of their time in education or activities designed to meet their educational needs, including training in industry rules and requirements.

Youth Workforce Investment Activities Program

The Youth Workforce Investment Activities Program, also referred to as the Youth Activities Program, is a formula grant program that allocates funding to state and local workforce development boards to provide year-round employment opportunities and other services to youth. Although most federally funded youth employment and training programs accept participants only from low-income backgrounds, the Youth Activities Program accepts those who are not low income if they have dropped out of high school. Workforce development boards are required to provide a variety of different services to participants, including mentoring services, tutoring, study skills training, alternative secondary school services or dropout recovery services, and paid and unpaid work experiences—which could include summer employment, preapprenticeships, or internships.

Nongovernmental Organizations and Programs

After School Matters

After School Matters (ASM) was founded in 1991 by former Chicago mayor Richard M. Daley's wife Maggie Daley and Chicago Department of Cultural Affairs Commissioner Louis Weisberg, to offer after school and summer project-based programs in the arts, communications and leadership, sports, and STEM (Science, Technology, Engineering, and Math) to Chicago teens. Thanks to partnerships with over 200 organizations and corporate entities and over 1,000 workplace professionals throughout the city, After School Matters is annually able to provide more than 15,000 teens with the opportunity to explore future career possibilities and develop critical skills for college and employment. Student participants have access to professional development courses taught by volunteer instructors and receive a small stipend to participate in pre-apprenticeships, apprenticeships, and internships in local industries.

Every year, After School Matters hosts an annual fundraising gala that allows participants to showcase their work.

American Enterprise Institute

The American Enterprise Institute (AEI) is a public policy think tank dedicated to making the intellectual, moral, and practical case for expanding freedom, increasing individual opportunity, and strengthening the free enterprise system in America and around the world. The work of Institute scholars explores ideas that further these goals and is based on data-driven research and broad-ranging evidence. Research fellows conduct analysis and make policy recommendations on a range of issues related to youth unemployment, including minimum-wage mandates, workplace regulation, job training, and secondary and postsecondary education reform.

Two of the institute's research fellows, Andy Smarick and John P. Bailey, host a weekly podcast titled "The New Skills Marketplace," on which they interview some of the most innovative thinkers and practitioners across the landscape of education and workforce development and explore new and innovated approaches to education, human capital development, and preparation for the workforce. Together with their guests, Smarick and Bailey attempt to answer the question: "How can today's and tomorrow's social entrepreneurs, employers, schools, and others better serve all of our citizens, young and old, so they possess the information, skills, habits, and beliefs needed to succeed in the world of work?"

AT&T Aspire

AT&T Aspire is a $100 million initiative to address high school success and workforce readiness by connecting students to the world of work, providing one-on-one mentoring, and leveraging technology to enable personalized and mobilized learning. Starting in 2008, the initiative began matching AT&T employee volunteers with high school students and funding various other job-shadowing programs so that students could learn firsthand about different careers and gain a better understanding of the educational background and skills they will need to succeed on the job.

Based on the belief that technology is fundamentally altering education by removing the barriers so that everyone regardless of their age or background has the opportunity to make their dreams a reality, AT&T Aspire works with different institutes and academies to develop tools for anytime and anywhere learning. Recently, AT&T Aspire teamed up with Udacity to expand online educational pathways to industry-relevant skills through the Nanodegree program. Nanodegree courses are online, project-based courses taught by leaders in tech, with the support of coaches. Today, thousands of learners are enrolled in various Nanodegree credential programs, and hundreds of AT&T employees have earned a credential.

Black Male Initiative

In 2004, the City University of New York (CUNY) launched the Black Male Initiative to increase the educational and employment attainment of young black males. The initiative initially provided funding to the campuses in the CUNY system to establish demonstration projects. These projects include mentorship opportunities, academic support, and career counseling to black males and other disadvantaged youth, as well as support geared specifically to formerly incarcerated individuals. The program was designed to provide a model for other universities and colleges around the country, and similarly styled initiatives have since been adopted by several additional schools.

Brookings Institution

The Brookings Institution, one of the oldest and most influential think tanks in the United States, is a nonprofit public policy organization based in Washington, D.C., that seeks to conduct quality, in-depth research and analysis and to influence policy debates with proposals firmly rooted in observed facts, empirical evidence, and experience rather than political ideology. Its scholars conduct research on a variety of issues related to domestic and foreign policy, many of which are related to the crisis in youth unemployment and disconnection. Two institute fellows, Martha Ross and Isabel V. Sawhill, have produced substantial research and analysis on the topic. Martha Ross has authored and coauthored reports on employment trends among young adults, improving educational options and career pathways for low-income or low-skilled workers, and increasing access to youth summer jobs programs. Isabel V. Sawhill is a senior fellow and economist, who served as the vice president and director of the institute's Economic Studies Program from 2003 to 2006. Her research covers an array of economic and social issues, but over the past decade she has largely focused on how to improve opportunities for the country's disadvantaged youth.

In 2006, the Brookings Institution launched an economic policy initiative titled "The Hamilton Project," which is administered by an advisory council of academics, business leaders, and former public policy makers. The project provides a platform for economic thinkers to develop innovative and pragmatic policy options. The project is named after Alexander Hamilton, the nation's first treasury secretary, who, as an immigrant born into poverty, symbolizes the American values of opportunity and mobility that motivated the project's work. Over the past decade, the Hamilton Project has produced thoughtful analysis of the long-term effects of the Great Recession on America's Youth and improving economic opportunity for low-income youth.

Center for Advancing Opportunity

The Center for Advancing Opportunity (CAO), a research and education initiative headquartered in Washington, D.C., was founded after Johnny C. Taylor, the former president and CEO of the Thurgood Marshall College Fund (TMCF), heard Charles Koch, the CEO of Koch Industries and cofounder of the Koch Foundation, give a television interview about removing barriers to opportunity. Taylor sent Koch a letter proposing a partnership between Koch Industries and TMCF, which led to the establishment of CAO shortly thereafter. Thanks to a more than $25 million grant from the Koch Foundation, CAO now financially supports faculty and students at Historically Black Colleges and Universities (HBCUs) and other postsecondary institutions to research barriers to opportunity for those living in fragile urban, rural, and suburban communities and to develop research-based solutions to challenging issues in education, criminal justice, and entrepreneurship. The center defines fragile communities as areas in the United States characterized by high proportions of residents struggling in their daily lives and possessing limited opportunities for social mobility. In addition to faculty and student research, CAO additionally sponsors an annual State of Opportunity in America Summit to examine and discuss the latest findings and best practices regarding the problems in fragile communities.

CAO-sponsored research adopts a different approach than much of the previous research conducted on poverty-stricken urban and rural communities. Whereas most research is conducted by academics who view themselves as responsible for solving the problems of those they study, CAO seeks to include those living in impacted communities as active participants in the problem-solving. In an effort to gain insight into the lives and experiences of individuals living in fragile communities nationwide, CAO partnered with Gallup to conduct a comprehensive six-month qualitative and quantitative survey of thousands of residents from low-income areas in Birmingham, Alabama; Cleveland, Ohio; Fresno, California; and Chicago, Illinois. The survey sought to reveal residents' feelings, opinions, and perceptions on education, criminal justice, entrepreneurship, optimism, and self-efficacy.

The CAO recently established three research hubs at HBCU's: the Center for the Study of Economic Mobility at Winston-Salem State University in North Carolina, the Center for Criminal Justice Research at Texas Southern University, and the Center for Educational Opportunity at Albany State University in Georgia.

Conrad N. Hilton Foundation

The Conrad N. Hilton Foundation is a nonprofit charitable foundation established and funded by the late hotel entrepreneur Conrad N. Hilton with the mission to "relieve the suffering, the distressed, and the destitute." In March 2012, the Foundation Board approved the launch of the first phase of the organization's Foster Youth Strategic Initiative Strategy. The goal of the initiative is to support one of the nation's most challenged populations, foster youth between the ages of 16 and 24, and to work with partners to ensure that as these youth age out of the foster system they are able to become self-sufficient and thriving adults. The Strategic Initiative aims to achieve its vision in variety of ways, but the core focus is to bring about systemic policy change by developing and advocating a new framework for addressing the unique needs of "transition age youth" (TAY) and by creating new education and career pathways to ensure their success. According to the initiative report, research and frontline experience have demonstrated that expanding knowledge, skills, and opportunities in career pathways have the most significant impact on a young person's ability to become self-sufficient. Between 2012 and 2017, the foundation invested $53.5 million and joined with community partners and others investors in New York and Los Angeles to move public child welfare systems and policies away from a one-size-fits-all approach that narrowly focuses on foster TAY's safety and basic needs toward an approach that emphasizes TAY's potential to succeed in education, careers, and life. The partnerships have spurred policy reform and the successful passage of more than 120 new state and local legislative proposals in Los Angeles County and New York City that expand educational and career services for older youth in foster care.

Cristo Rey Network

The Cristo Rey Network is a network of 35 Catholic work-preparatory high schools that exclusively serve underprivileged students. The network was established in 2000 to increase the number of schools modeled after Cristo Rey Jesuit School, which was founded in 1996 in Chicago. Network schools adopt an effective and innovative approach to inner-city education designed to equip students from underserved, economically disadvantaged communities to develop their minds and become lifelong contributors to society. It is the only network of high schools in the country that integrates four years of rigorous college preparatory academics with four years of professional work experience through its Corporate Work Study Program. This program operates as a temporary employment agency within the schools. Throughout the academic year, each student is employed in an entry-level, professional job five days a month. Work experiences are offered in a variety of fields including law, finance, health care, and technology. Students typically earn $18 an hour in education support and are able to use their earnings to defer most of their education expense.

In 2009, the network established a University Partners program to forge collaborative relationships between select colleges and Cristo Rey schools and students. University partners commit to supporting, mentoring, and recruiting Cristo Rey students, many of whom are first-generation college students. This partnership not only benefits students, it also benefits university partners by providing them with access to a national pipeline of diverse, motivated, and well-prepared students. Although the average Cristo Rey student begins about two grade levels behind their peers, the school has been successful at catching students up academically and 90 percent of graduates enroll in college.

Economic Policy Institute

The Economic Policy Institute is a liberal leaning think tank funded in part by labor unions. The institute was founded in 1986 by several economists to assesses current economic policies and propose new policies aiming to address economic inequalities and to protect and improve the living standards of low- and middle-income workers. Areas of research and analysis include education, immigration, public investment, raising wages, trade and globalization, and unions and labor standards. Every year the institute publishes a flagship manual, *The State of Working America*, which examines the U.S. economy's impact on wages, employment, wealth, and poverty.

Employment Policies Institute

The Employment Policies Institute is a conservative leaning think tank that publishes research conducted by independent economists on employment-related issues. Of central concern to the institute is the impact particular policies have on employment growth and entry-level employment. Institute-sponsored research largely aims to quantify the effects of minimum-wage mandates, health care mandates, and employment taxes credits on low-wage labor markets and the degree to which higher labor costs inhibit job creation.

Homeboy Industries

Homeboy Industries is a nonprofit community organization based in Los Angeles, California, that provides support and employment training to formerly gang-involved and previously incarcerated men and women. It was originally started in 1988 as a small jobs program in one of the most gang-ridden parishes in Los Angeles by a Jesuit priest, Father Greg Boyle, who recognized the need to provide community support, jobs, and education as an alternative to gangs. It has since grown to become one of the largest, most comprehensive, and most successful gang intervention, rehabilitation, and reentry programs in the country.

The organization offers services including educational courses, tattoo removal, substance abuse treatment, legal assistance,
and job placement services to more than 1,000 members of
the community each month. It also provides full-time employment to more than 200 men and women at a time through
an 18-month program designed to help participants reidentify
who they are in the world and develop workplace skills that
enable them to redirect their lives and become contributing
members of the community. Since its inception, the organization has inspired the establishment of more than 40 other
organizations across the country based on similar models.

Jim Casey Youth Opportunity Initiative

A branch of the Annie E. Casey Foundation, the Jim Casey
Youth Opportunity Initiative works to promote practices and
policies that help foster youth (aged 14 to 26) successfully transition to adulthood. The initiative sponsors the Opportunity
Passport, a program designed to build the financial capability of foster youth by providing financial literacy training, a
bank account, and matched-savings program to help them pay
for assets such as a car, books for school, and initial housing-
related costs. Foster youth who purchase these assets through
the matched-savings programs more than double their chances
of having a full-time job.

Jobs for America's Graduates

Jobs for America's Graduates (JAG) is a national nonprofit network dedicated to helping at-risk youth graduate from high
school and either enroll in postsecondary education or secure
a quality entry-level job with career advancement potential.
Originally founded in Delaware in 1980 by former state gov-
ernor Pete du Pont, the network now includes 34 state organizations and over a thousand program affiliates, including
middle schools, high schools, community colleges, and government agencies. The state-based organizations and affiliates
work together to provide youth who face serious barriers to

graduation and employment with mentoring, dropout recovery services, employability skills development, and career and academic counseling—including one-on-one assistance with finding and keeping a job after graduation.

Jobs for the Future

Based in Boston, Washington, D.C., and Oakland, California, Jobs for the Future (JFF) is a leading national workforce and education nonprofit that provides expert consulting and analysis to transform workforce and education systems to create economic advancement opportunities for low-income young adults who face significant barriers in the labor market, especially as automation and technology reshape the economy. JFF works with key stakeholders in a community—including employers, system leaders, youth leaders, community-based organizations, schools, and postsecondary institutions—to help them develop collaborative career pathways that will enable young adults to prepare effectively to transition into occupational training programs that lead to skilled jobs with advancement potential or into degree-granting postsecondary programs of study. For the past 15 years, JFF has additionally convened the Postsecondary State Network to advance policies and practices that hasten community college completion rates and career advancement through guided career pathways.

Junior Achievement USA

Junior Achievement (JA) is the nation's largest organization dedicated to helping young people understand the opportunities and realities of work in the 21st century, plan for their futures by making smart academic and economic choices, and obtain the skills they need for economic success. JA programs that are taught and administered by corporate and community volunteers provide relevant, hands-on experiences designed to give students from kindergarten through high school knowledge and skills in financial literacy, work readiness, and entrepreneurship. JA helps students realize the various paths and possibilities for success, whether through pursuing college or a trade or in starting their own business.

JA programs, which are taught by volunteers in inner cities, suburbs, and rural areas, now reach nearly 5 million students in classrooms and afterschool locations throughout the country. The organization also sponsors a National Student Leadership Summit contest in business skills, ingenuity, and innovation. Student participants devise a product that fills an unmet consumer need, recruit investors, and market and run their enterprise under the guidance of a volunteer from the local business community.

InsideTrack

InsideTrack is an independent company that provides professional coaching services to students in four-year nonprofit institutions, for-profit institutions, and community colleges to improve student success, retention, and degree completion. The company was founded in 2001 in response to studies showing that, in addition to purely academic reasons, one of the biggest factors contributing to low rates of college completion, especially among disadvantaged youth, is students' lack of a social or familial support system and inadequate knowledge of how to manage time, prioritize tasks, effectively complete assignments, and otherwise thrive in an academic setting.

InsideTrack, in conjunction with each participating college, matches selected students with trained coaches who work out of call centers in San Francisco, California; Nashville, Tennessee; and Portland, Oregon. These coaches then maintain regular contact via phone with assigned students usually during their first year of school—although the company has begun to offer pre-enrollment advising services as well. Coaches work with students to develop a clear vision of their goals and to strategize how they might overcome barriers to these goals. Coaches additionally help students plan their daily activities in line with their priorities, manage their finances, and improve self-advocacy and study skills.

In 2011, two researchers at Stanford University conducted an analysis of the coaching services provided by InsideTrack and found that students who were assigned a coach had significantly higher rates of retention compared to similarly situated students at the same schools who did not participate in the coaching program. Moreover, the retention effects lasted well beyond the coaching period and eventually led to higher rates of college completion (Bettinger and Baker 2011). The same study found that the services provided by InsideTrack are more effective in producing desired results than similar services offered internally by individual colleges. This is in part due to the fact that serving multiple institutions enables InsideTrack to invest in personnel, training, processes, and technologies that are typically out of reach for individual schools. In fact, some colleges have now begun to send their own in-house advisors to train with InsideTrack.

Manhattan Institute

The Manhattan Institute (MI) is a leading free-market policy think tank that aims to develop and disseminated new ideas that foster economic choice and individual responsibility. MI recruits experts that work to shape public discourse and influence policy in a variety of areas—including economic growth, education, energy and the environment, health care, race, and urban policy—by authorizing reports, essays, and books; testifying at government hearings; and communicating directly with citizens through op-eds, podcasts, and television interviews. MI often collaborates directly with cities and public officials to put policy prescriptions into practice. For example, in 2007, the institute partnered with Newark, New Jersey's mayor Cory Booker to implement a new approach to prisoner reentry based on the "work-first" strategy of connecting ex-offenders with paid work immediately upon release (a long-standing research area of the institute). In 2017, the institute launched a project to identify ways to expand funding to New York charter schools and enable them to educate more students.

MENTOR: The National Mentoring Partnership

MENTOR: The National Mentoring Partnership is a national network committed to increasing the quantity and quality of mentoring relationships for disconnected youth and those who are risk of disconnection. The organization dates back to 1990 when Wall Street financiers Geoffrey Boisi and Raymond Chambers cofounded One-to-One partnership to serve as a resource for mentors and mentoring networks nationwide and to advocate for the expansion of mentoring. In 1991, they produced the first edition of the manual *The Elements of Effective Practice for Mentoring*. Now in its fourth edition, the manual outlines national-adopted standards that serve as guide to assist organizations in starting and operating quality mentor programs.

One-to-One partnership was officially rebranded MENTOR in 1997, after the organization received a $4 million grant from the federal Office of Juvenile Justice and Delinquency Prevention for a juvenile mentoring program. Today, MENTOR oversees, advises, and provides infrastructure for more than 2,000 mentoring program partners across the country and continues its commitment to ensuring that at-risk youth have access to caring adults who will help them overcome personal and institutional obstacles as they pursue their interests and work to develop their skills. MENTOR additionally supports mentor recruitment and connects volunteers to these local programs by operating the Mentor Connector, the only national database of quality mentoring programs across the country that allows volunteers to search for a local program that meets their criteria. Every year, MENTOR convenes the National Mentoring Summit in Washington, D.C., which brings together more than 1,000 practitioners, researchers, philanthropists, government and civic leaders, and youth serving organizations from across the country to discuss and share emerging research, program models, and innovative practices. MENTOR additionally engages with elected and public officials to advocate for policy that supports positive youth development and mentoring relationships as a solution to community challenges.

National Academy Foundation

The National Academy Foundation (NAF) is an educational nonprofit that facilitates bringing businesses, educators, and community leaders together to expose high school students to career options and workplace experience through a national network of over 500 career academies. NAF was originally started by banker, financier, and philanthropist Simon I. Weill in 1982 who, in conjunction with the New York City Board of Education, opened the first Academy of Finance in a Brooklyn public high school. NAF, which has grown to hundreds of academies serving thousands of students in high-need communities throughout the country, now focuses on five career themes finance, engineering, hospitality and tourism, information technology, and health sciences. The academies operate as small, focused learning communities within existing high schools and encourage both preparation for college and technical training in a career path. Following the high school work-based learning portion, the NAF program culminates with the opportunity for each student to participate in six- to ten-week summer internships sponsored by more than 2,500 corporate partners. NAF provides each academy with rigorous, industry-validated, career-themed curriculum that incorporates current industry standards and practices, literacy strategies, and STEM integration. NAF also supports educational quality by hosting a professional development program for teachers who want to develop their skills and strengthen their academies through effective practice and leadership. In addition, NAF sponsors and maintains myNAFTrack, an online professional network connecting NAF students, alumni, and NAFTrack Certified Hiring employees. MyNAFTrack allows students to build a professional profile and portfolio and to access a wide range of potential internship and job opportunities. It additionally benefits employers by enabling them to easily search for talented students who have been certified through a rigorous and industry-developed assessment system.

The foundation has an extremely impressive record of success. Over 90 percent of participants graduate from high school. More than 80 percent of participants go on to college, and 52 percent complete their degree within four years. Participants additionally earn 11 percent more on average than those who do not attend (Symonds, Schwartz, and Ferguson 2011).

National Youth Employment Network

The National Youth Employment Coalition (NYEC) is a national membership network of organizations—including nonprofit service providers, city agencies, local workforce development boards, and research entities—that work with, study, and advocate for disconnected youth. NYEC's primary mission is to improve the effectiveness of organizations and systems that seek to help disconnected youth become productive citizens. To advance this mission, NYEC engages in four kinds of activities. First, NYEC keeps the field up to date on recent innovations in practice and the latest research on best practices and service models. Second, NYEC builds its members' capacities to effectively serve opportunity youth by providing professional development services and working to help organizations implement best practices, expand their reach, and adapt to changing policy contexts. Third, NYEC serves as a unique line of communication between practitioners and policy makers and regularly solicits of the views of members on how policy affects their service to youth. Based on this information, NYEC analyzes policy developments that affect disconnected youth, such as workforce development and K-12 and higher education reform. NYEC then uses these analyses to inform policy recommendations at the federal, state, and local levels. Finally, NYEC promotes the establishment and expansion of models based on research findings.

Network for Teaching Entrepreneurship

The Network for Teaching Entrepreneurship (NFTE) is an international nonprofit that seeks to activate an entrepreneurial mind-set and build entrepreneurial skills in low-income urban youth. Founded by business executive and entrepreneur Steve Mariotti, a former public high school teacher in New York City's South Bronx neighborhood, NFTE provides schools and partners with high-impact, award-winning entrepreneurship curriculum and teacher training and support. NFTE materials—which include versions for middle school, high school, and young adult students—can be implemented in semester or year-long courses in schools, in after school programs, and in summer business camps. Over a thousand schools and organizations across the country currently use NFTE's program, and more than 400 educators have joined NFTE's Teacher Corps, which provides training on how to effectively deliver project-based learning and the NFTE curriculum.

Besides providing schools and nonprofit organizations with high-quality curriculum that helps students work through the process of creating, refining, and implementing an original business concept, NFTE hosts two-week, intensive summer BizCamps for at-risk students between the ages of 13 and 18, which include daily course work, guest speakers, and field trips. At the end of the camp, students present their business plan in competitions for cash awards. NFTE also sponsors regional business competitions that lead up to a yearly national competition. Winning students receive an all-expense paid trip to the annual awards dinner in New York City and a grant that can be applied toward establishing a business or college tuition.

100,000 Opportunities Initiative

Launched in 2015 by Starbucks CEO Howard Schultz and his wife Sheri, the 100,000 Opportunities Initiative began as a partnership between several local governments; the MacArthur, Rockefeller, Walmart, JPMorgan Chase, and W.K. Kellogg Foundations; and leading companies—including Alaska Airlines, Cintas, CVS Health, Hilton Worldwide, J.C. Penney, Lyft, JPMorgan Chase, Macy's, Microsoft, Taco Bell, Walgreens, and Walmart. The initial goal was to establish the nation's largest employer-led coalition and, within three years, to provide internships, apprenticeships, and jobs to at least 100,000 16- to 24-year-old Opportunity Youth—those who face systemic barriers to jobs and education and who are neither currently employed nor in school. The initiative began on August 13, 2015, with an Opportunity Fair & Forum for Opportunity Youth in Chicago and has since sponsored similarly styled events around the country. The coalition continues to grow and has already surpassed its initial hiring and training goals.

Opportunity America

Opportunity America is a Washington-based think tank that aims to restore and advance economic mobility for poor and working Americans through the promotion of work, careers, ownership, and entrepreneurship. The organization works to advance equal opportunity and economic mobility by influencing state and federal policy makers and encouraging civic engagement by workers and employers alike. Primary activities include research, policy development, dissemination of policy ideas, and working to build consensus around policy proposals. In recent years, Opportunity America has published a volume on new ways of thinking about poverty and economic mobility, and several reports on improving community colleges, workforce education, and high school career and technical education.

Opportunity America additionally sponsors the Opportunity America Jobs and Careers Coalition, a Washington-based business coalition focused on drawing attention to the need for workforce training, changing national perceptions of technical careers and career training, and highlighting successful state initiatives. Members include employers and employer associations from a broad range of industries—such as IT, manufacturing, construction, and hospitality—that are currently experiencing skills mismatches and worker shortages.

Opportunity Nation

Opportunity Nation is a bipartisan coalition of more than 350 organizations and individuals—including employers, educational institutions, nonprofits, philanthropies, policy makers, and young Americans—seeking to reduce the opportunity gap by expanding economic mobility. Opportunity Nation maintains an opportunity index to measure factors that contribute to upward mobility and opportunity at both the state and county level and seeks to promote bipartisan policy approaches to increase access to education, tackle the skills gap, and expand opportunity for young adults. Opportunity Nation recently published the pamphlet, *We Got This: A Call to Action for Youth Unemployment*, outlining how private and public groups and individuals can collaborate and form cross-sector partnerships to connect young people to meaningful, seamless education and career pathways.

Prison Entrepreneurship Program

The Prison Entrepreneurship Program (PEP) was established in Texas in 2014 in response to the state's vast prison population and the reduced prospects that individuals with a previous record of incarceration have for securing legitimate work that pays livable wages. Based on the goal of preparing inmates with the tools, skills, and support structure they need to successfully reintegrate into society and pursue healthy, fulfilling, and productive lives, PEP has developed a series of rehabilitative programs focused on character and career development, including entrepreneurship training and mentorship, that begin in the prison system prior to release and continue after release.

PEP's program starts with a rigorous selection process that begins when the Texas Department of Criminal Justice provides PEP with a list of approximately 10,000 eligible inmates. PEP then sends information to these inmates inviting them to apply. On average, 2000 candidates return the nearly 20-page application. PEP staff selects the top 1,500 candidates, whom they send a study packet, including the AP Writing Style Guide, a list of PEP's Ten Driving Values, and a Basic Business Vocabulary reference. Two weeks after sending the study packets, PEP recruiters visit prisons to interview candidates. Each candidate who scores higher than 70 percent on the test moves on to a personal interview, in which PEP staff determine whether the candidate has the work ethic and commitment to succeed in the program. At this stage, the top 450 to 500 candidates are selected for a final round of interviews with the program manager and several recently released graduates.

Once inmates are accepted into the program, they are transferred to one of two prison facilities where PEP operates, either the Estes Unit south of Dallas or the Cleveland Correctional Facility outside of Houston. The program begins with a three-month character development and leadership program called the Leadership Academy where participants work through curriculum in *The Quest for Authentic Manhood* series. Mentors work with participants to help them live out PEP's Ten Driving Values: Integrity, Accountability, Wise Stewardship, Love, Fun, Fresh Start Outlook, Servant-Leader Mentality, Innovation, Execution, and Excellence.

Following the Leadership Academy is a six-month in-prison "mini-MBA" boot camp, in which PEP staff and business executives teach businesses courses on topics related to their areas of expertise. Participants additionally work through a college textbook titled, *Entrepreneurship: A Small Business Approach*, and several Harvard and Stanford Business School case studies. During this time, each student is required to research and develop a business plan for the Business Plan Competition. Participants additionally complete a financial literacy course, an employment workshop, a business etiquette course, and a Toastmasters class. Finally, after completing the in-prison program, participants graduate in a cap-and-gown ceremony attended by family and friends. PEP often financially subsidizes the travel costs of family members who wish to attend the graduation. In recognition of the intensity of the program, the Baylor University Hankamer School of Business provides each graduate with a Certificate of Entrepreneurship.

In addition to coordinating the in-prison program, PEP provides extensive post-release support to its participants. Upon release, PEP alumni are supported with a variety of reentry services including case management, transition housing, and assistance in finding employment and connecting to social services.

The PEP model has proven remarkably successful at preventing recidivism and maximizing self-sufficiency. To date, the program has helped over 1,300 prisoners reintegrate into society with a less than 7 percent three-year recidivism rate, compared to an average recidivism rate of 50 to 70 percent in Texas. A study conducted by researchers at Baylor University found that PEP outperformed all nine other rehabilitation programs in Texas in reducing recidivism rates (Johnson, Wubbenhorst, and Schroeder 2013). Moreover, PEP graduates have launched over 200 businesses, and almost 100 percent are employed within 90 days of their release and continue to be employed after 12 months. The Baylor study concluded that every dollar donated to PEP produces a 340 percent return on investment due to avoided incarceration, increased child support payments, and reduced reliance on government assistance.

Project CRAFT

Project CRAFT (Community, Restitution, and Apprenticeship-Focused Training) was established in 1994 after the Home Builders Institute (HBI), the workforce development and educational arm of the National Association of Home Builders, received a Youth Offender demonstration grant from the U.S. Department of Labor's Employment and Training Administration. Project CRAFT aims to improve educational levels, teach vocational skills, and reduce recidivism among court adjudicated youth, while simultaneously addressing the home-building industry's ongoing shortage of entry-level workers.

The Project CRAFT model includes ten main components: outreach and recruitment, assessment and screening; individualized development plans; case management services; industry-validated, trades-related training; building industry-related academics; community service; academic preparation and substance abuse treatment; employability and life skills training; and community transition and long-term follow-up. Most youth participants are initially referred to a Project CRAFT site by their state departments of juvenile justice or by juvenile judges or probation officers. Once accepted, student-participants engage in 840 hours of pre-apprenticeship training and industry-approved curriculum over a six-month period. About 75 percent of this time is spent engaged in hands-on construction projects, many of which involve service to the community, while the remaining time is spent receiving classroom instruction in the use of tools, safety, work habits, and trades-related mathematics in addition to field-specific education on topics such as electrical wiring, carpentry, plumbing, and landscaping. Before they are eligible for graduation, participants must demonstrate a mastery of several skills related to the building industry. Upon completion of the program, participants are given an industry-recognized certificate and a personal set of hand tools. Program staff additionally work with participants to connect them with steady employment or additional training or career advancement opportunities following graduation.

Thus far, the program has shown remarkable success in reducing juvenile recidivism and providing at-risk youth with the opportunity for economic mobility and career success.

Project CRAFT currently serves around 400 youth annually and operates at 9 sites in Florida, Tennessee, New Jersey, and Mississippi funded in large part by state departments of juvenile justice.

Project Lead the Way

Project Lead the Way (PLTW) is an educational nonprofit that disseminates STEM-based K-12 curriculum to public, private, and charter schools with the goal of better preparing students to thrive in the modern global economy. The curriculum is rooted in the activity, project, problem-based (APB) instructional method and is designed to encourage students to develop and apply in-demand, transportable skills—such as problem solving, critical and creative thinking, collaboration, and communication—by engaging in real-world challenges. Instructors who use the PLTW curriculum are required to participate in an intensive training program designed to immerse teachers in the PLTW approach, so they are prepared to coach students and facilitate progress as students guide their own learning through the curriculum.

As they work their way through the K-12 curriculum, PLTW students are empowered to explore different career paths. PLTW Launch is designed to allow students from kindergarten to fifth grade to engage in hands-on activities in computer science, engineering, and biomedical science. The next stage of the curriculum, PLTW Gateway, encourages sixth to eighth graders to engage in more in-depth collaborative activities in computer science, engineering, and biomedical science. The final stage aims to help ninth through twelve graders develop knowledge and real-world skills, while they engage in and explore particular career paths in each of the three fields.

A review of research on PLTW found that use of the curriculum has a positive impact on mathematics and science achievement and drastically increases students' interest in science and engineering and the likelihood that they pursue postsecondary education in STEM fields (Tai 2012).

PLTW is funded in part by fees from participating schools and in part by state governments and private foundations.

Project Quest

Project Quest is a workforce training program founded in San Antonio in 1992 in response to the acute skills mismatch that developed as the city's economic base began to shift from manufacturing to service and technology-driven fields. At the same time that several thousand manufacturing jobs were eliminated, nearly 20,000 new high-paying jobs were created in other fields. Yet, the skills and expertise required for the newly available positions were in short supply among San Antonio's low-income residents. Project Quest thus grew out of a grass-roots effort to implement training programs that would enable San Antonio residents to acquire the skills necessary for the professional, high-paying jobs available in growing sectors of the local economy.

Project Quest provides comprehensive support and resources—including financial assistance, remedial instruction, counseling, life skills courses, and job placement assistance—to help individuals complete occupational training programs at local community colleges, pass certification exams, and obtain jobs in targeted industries. Project Quest training programs, which are funded in large part by the Casey Foundation and are conducted primarily through local community colleges, are based on four principles: the program is jobs driven, the program focuses on training and careers that offer family wages and advancement opportunities, the program incorporates intensive support services to help participants overcome financial aid and personal barriers to skill acquisition, and the program leverages the training resources already operational in the community. Since its inception, Project Quest has helped more than 6,000 job seekers complete training. A six-year evaluation of the program conducted by the Economic Mobility Corporation revealed that program strategies and services have been successful at lifting low-income workers out of poverty (Elliot and Roder 2017). The evaluation found that Quest participants work more consistently, earn higher hourly wages, and experience larger increases in their pay overtime than people in the control group. In fact, average annual earnings of graduates grew from $11,400 when they first entered the program to more than $38,000 by the final year of the controlled trial. According to the Economic Mobility Corporation study, few workforce development programs have created this kind of mobility. Furthermore, 96 percent of Quest participants were still living in Texas and 85 percent remained in the San Antonio area six years after enrollment.

Over the years, Project Quest's workforce development model has been replicated by other organizations in cities throughout Texas and outside of Texas in Monroe, Louisiana; Tucson and Phoenix, Arizona; and Des Moines, Iowa, to meet the employment needs of their particular communities.

This Way Ahead

In 2007, Gap Inc. launched This Way Ahead, a life skills and paid internship program, to help teens and young adults from low-income communities gain access to life-changing first job experiences at Gap Inc. stores—Old Navy, Gap, and Banana Republic.

This Way Ahead participants are first recruited by urban nonprofits and are then enrolled in two months of in-person and online job training and coaching. After this initial training period, participants are eligible to apply for paid internships at one of the Gap Inc. stores. During the internship period, participants receive ongoing support from nonprofit job coaches, store managers, and fellow employees.

To date, nearly 4,000 youth have participated in and graduated from the This Way Ahead program, and GAP Inc. reports that they eventually hire nearly 75 percent of program interns. This Way Ahead participants also tend to stay with the company and more engaged than young employees who did not participate in the program. Gap Inc. expects that 10,000 young people will participate in the program by 2020, and the company aims to hire 5 percent of its entry-level store employees from the program by 2025.

Urban Alliance

Urban Alliance, a national youth development nonprofit, was founded in 1996 in Washington, D.C., to provide students at risk of disconnection with the opportunity, support, and training to transition to higher education or employment after high school and, ultimately, to place them on the path to self-sustaining careers and lifelong economic self-sufficiency.

Urban Alliance's core program, the High School Internship Program, matches underserved high school seniors with paid, professional internships, job skills training, one-on-one mentoring, and ongoing post-program support. The program now serves over 500 interns annually and has expanded to new locations in Baltimore, Chicago, and Northern Virginia.

In 2017, the Urban Institute released the results of a six-year evaluation of the Urban Alliance High School Internship Program in Washington, D.C., and Baltimore. The study revealed that the programs have a significant positive impact on their participants (Theodos 2017). All program alumni have graduate high school on time. Within one year of graduation, 80 percent of program alumni are connected through employment, college, a vocational training program, or the military. Participating in the program increased the likelihood that young men would attend college by 23 percentage points, and the likelihood that middle-tier students (those with a 2.0 to 3.0 high school GPA) would enroll in a four-year college by 18 percentage points. The study additionally concluded that participation in the program increased students' retention of critical professional skills.

Urban Institute

The Urban institute, a Washington-based think tank, was established as an independent research organization in 1968 by the Johnson Administration to study the problems in urban communities and to evaluate the impact of Great Society initiatives. Over the past 50 years, institute experts have immersed themselves in urban communities to collect data on whether government efforts to strengthen families, cities, and neighborhoods are effective. The institute has additionally expanded the scope of its research to include topics such as the challenges of short- and long-term unemployment, the effectiveness of crime prevention efforts, and the need for education reform. Since its inception, the organization's research into urban communities and its policy recommendations for tackling complex social and economic barriers to opportunity in such communities has been funded by a variety of entities including the federal government, state and local governments, private foundations, corporations, individuals, and international organizations.

U.S. FIRST

U.S. FIRST (For Inspiration and Recognition of Science and Technology) was cofounded in 1989 by Dean Kamen, a prolific inventor and entrepreneur, in order to spur excitement for science and technology and to inspire students to become innovators and pursue education and careers in STEM-related fields. Since its inception, FIRST has worked to engage children and teens from kindergarten through high school in exciting, mentor-based research and robotics programs that encourage them to grow in their knowledge, appreciation, and enthusiasm for science and technologies and to prepare them to become future industry leaders.

Among FIRST's most high-profile programs are its annual regional and national Robotics Competitions. Every year, thousands of teams of high school students from around the world work with adult mentors to assemble robots based on kits and guidelines provided by FIRST. These teams then take the finished robots to compete against rival teams at FIRST-sponsored contests. Thousands of corporate sponsors and professional volunteers now help facilitate the 48 regional and district competitions, which take place in March, and the National Championship, which takes place in April.

FIRST additionally hosts a LEGO League competition for 9- to 14-year-old students and operates an invention challenge summer day camp that invites students and teachers to think like scientists and engineers as they design, build, and program autonomous robots using LEGO Mindstorms sets and robotic software.

FIRST is universally recognized as the leading, nonprofit STEM engagement program for primary and secondary school students worldwide, and its participants are three times more likely to pursue advanced degrees in engineering than nonparticipants.

William E. Simon Foundation

The William E. Simon foundation is named after its principal benefactor, a former deputy secretary of the Treasury and catholic entrepreneur, who was committed to helping those in need experience the blessings of American opportunity and liberty by realizing the full promise of their own talent and drive.

In line with its founder's vision, the foundation's primary aim is to strengthen the free-enterprise system by helping inner-city youth and families gain access to education and community-based services that promote their character development and help them become independent, contributing members of society. The foundation works to achieve this goal by funding direct services in Jersey City and South Bronx and engaging in public policy research and advocacy. The foundation's direct service and policy research efforts focus largely on the themes of education, faith, and family. In the realm of education, the foundation supports research on school reform, accountability, and transparency and the promotion of ideas with the potential to improve school governance, teaching, and learning. The foundation funds private scholarship programs and supports the start-up and maintenance of public charter, independent, and parochial schools that feature academic rigor, respectful learning environments, attention to students as unique individuals, and an unwavering belief that their students can succeed. In the realm of faith, the foundation funds research on the positive impact of faith in the lives of young people and supports programs and churches that provide youth mentoring, after-school and summer enrichment, literacy and tutoring, sports and recreation, and community service. In the realm of family, the foundation supports research on the negative impact of increasing family fragmentation on the lives of children and their capacity for economic and educational success. The foundation additionally supports programs designed to strengthen the family, such as parenting courses and emergency support, as well as programs that provide mentoring, advocacy, and educational and career guidance for young people who lack a strong family support system.

Work Colleges

Work Colleges are accredited institutions of higher education that help low-income students—many of whom are first-generation college students—obtain a quality liberal arts college education and developing transferable real-world professional skills without being burdened by debt. Work Colleges award bachelor degrees based on a model that incorporates traditional learning with work responsibilities and service. Most students are required to work an average of 10 to 15 hours a week and participate in community service in a way that enhances their academic learning.

The work programs have a proven track record of enabling students of limited means to earn a college degree, while cultivating career-ready qualities and skills. Graduates also leave with considerably less debt than their peers at traditional colleges. There are currently eight geographically and academically diverse Work Colleges in the United States that run distinctive work programs designed to meet campus need and complement relevant coursework.

Alice Lloyd College, located in Pippa Passes, Kentucky, is the only liberal arts college in the nation to exclusively recruit its students from Appalachia. Full-time qualifying students from this region do not have to pay out-of-pocket tuition, which helps generate its *U.S. News and World Report* ranking as the Top College in America for graduating students with the least amount of debt. A large majority of the college's graduates return post-graduation to Appalacia to serve and work in their former communities.

Berea College, located in Berea, Kentucky, was named the top liberal arts college in the nation in 2011 by *Washington Monthly* based on the school's record of promoting social mobility, excellence in education, and community service. Founded in 1855, the college was the first interracial and coeducational college in the South. It recruits students who could not otherwise afford a high-quality liberal arts education and is the only top college in America that awards four-year full tuition scholarships to all of its students.

Blackburn College, located in Carlinville, Illinois, was established more than 175 years ago and is currently ranked as the #2 Best Value College by *U.S. News and World Report*. Blackburn's ten campus buildings were constructed in part by students. Students are required to hold work positions that support campus operations in the bookstore, administration, academic tutoring, informational technology, and maintenance. The work program is run by student managers.

College of the Ozarks, located in Point Lookout, Missouri, is consistently ranked by a variety of national publications as "a best buy" and one of the best colleges in the nation. The college, also known as "Hard Work U," is a Christian school where students are able to cover their tuition through student work, grants, and scholarships offered by the college. Students are assigned to one of 80 diverse work assignments that are selected to complement their career path. Work performance grades are included along with academic grades on students' transcripts.

Ecclesia College, located in Springdale, Arkansas, has been awarded a place on the President's Higher Education Community Service Honor Role. The Christian college, which serves students regardless of their family resources, focuses on developing good work ethic and character among its students, while allowing them to offset educational expenses through work. Students also participate in a wide variety of community service projects in the local community and around the world.

Sterling College, located in Craftsbury Common, Vermont, is a small progressive liberal arts college with a focus on environmental protection and grassroots sustainability. Students can design their own environmentally focused major or choose from a variety of established majors, such as Conservation Ecology, Sustainable Agriculture, and Outdoor leadership. Students put their coursework to practice by monitoring campus energy use and food production, teaching classes on sustainability in the local public school system, participating in wildlife mapping projects, and engaging in environmental activism.

Warren Wilson College, located just outside of Asheville, North Carolina, is known for its international and environmental emphasis. It was named one of the "25 Best Buys" among private colleges and universities in the *Fiske Guide to Colleges* and was referred to as "one of the most earth-friendly colleges on the planet" by *Outside Magazine*. The college offers full tuition scholarships to every incoming student from North Carolina who qualifies for state or federal need-based aid. The school is also introducing 25 full-tuition scholarships for middle-income or out-of-state students. The campus contains a working farm, gardens, and forests that are tilled and harvested by students.

YearUp

YearUp is an innovative program—founded in response to the hundreds of thousands of jobs unfilled every year because of the skills gap—that works with employers to help prepare low-income 18- to 24-year-old high school graduates for successful careers in fields like IT and financial services.

The YearUp program begins with six months of intensive technical, academic, and professional skills training. This initial training period is followed by a six-month internship with a corporate employer in which participants are paid an average of $30,000 a year.

The program, which began in Boston, now operates in more than 15 U.S. cities and has more than 250 corporate partners. The program has also developed a strong track record of success. An evaluation of programs in Boston, Providence, and New York found that YearUp participants were more likely to be working full time and earned wages 30 percent higher than the control group, and these earning gains continued three years after the program ended (Elliot and Roder 2017).

Young Invincibles

Young Invincibles (YI) is a Washington-based youth advocacy group working to expand opportunity for young adults aged 18 to 34 and to amplify the voice of youth in the national political conversation. YI was founded in the summer of 2009 by a group of students who contended that young people's voices were being ignored in the debate over health care reform. YI thus began as a movement to share young people's stories, to provide facts and information on the barriers they face in acquiring affordable, quality health insurance, and to propose solutions.

YI has since grown into a national organization—with offices across the country—and is a leading voice for young people on issues including health care, higher education, and employment. The organization aims to continue working to expand economic security for young adults and to make sure that the voices of young people are heard whenever policy decisions about their collective future are made.

References

Bettinger, Eric, and Rachel Baker. 2011. *The Effects of Student Coaching in College: An Evaluation of Randomized Experiment in Student Mentoring.* Working Paper 16881. Cambridge, MA: National Bureau of Economic Research. March. Accessed June 22, 2018. http://www.nber.org/papers/w16881.pdf

Boteach, Melissa, Joy Moses, and Shirley Sagawa. 2009. *National Service and Youth Unemployment: Strategies for Job Creation amid Economic Recovery.* Center for American Progress. November 16. Accessed June 10, 2018. https://cdn.americanprogress.org/wp-content/uploads/issues/2009/11/pdf/nation_service.pdf

Bowen, Scott. 2016. "Why One Company Is Giving Youth a Leg Up in the World of Work." *Forbes.* September 12. Accessed June 28, 2018. https://www.forbes.com/sites/gapincthiswayahead/2016/09/12/why-one-company-is-giving-youth-a-leg-up-in-the-world-of-work/#6816dd0c3f8e

Coffee & Company. 2015. "Top US Based Companies Launch 100,000 Opportunities Initiative." *Starbucks Newsroom.* July 13. Accessed June 26, 2018. https://news.starbucks.com/news/top-us-based-companies-launch-100k-opportunities-initiative

Collins, Benjamin. 2016. *Apprenticeship in the United States: Frequently Asked Questions.* Congressional Research Service. January 29. Accessed June 15, 2018. https://fas.org/sgp/crs/misc/R44174.pdf

Conrad N. Hilton Foundation. 2017. "2017–2022 Foster Youth Strategic Initiative Strategy: Executive Summary."

Accessed June 30, 2018. https://hilton-production
.s3.amazonaws.com/documents/271/attachments/FY_
Phase_II_Strategy_Paper.pdf?1500072849

Corps Network. 2018. "Fact Sheet." Accessed June 25, 2018.
https://www.corpsnetwork.org/sites/default/images/pdfs/
TCN%20Fact%20Sheet_Jan2018_v2.pdf

Elliot, Mark, and Anne Roder. 2017. *Escalating Gains: Project
Quest's Sectoral Strategy Pays Off.* Economic Mobility
Corporation. April. Accessed July 1, 2018. https://
economicmobilitycorp.org/wp-content/uploads/2018/01/
Escalating-Gains_WEB.pdf

Fain, Paul. 2013. "Coach Knows Best." *Inside Higher Ed.*
May 24. Accessed June 1, 2018. https://www.inside
highered.com/news/2013/05/24/insidetracks-student-
coaching-proves-completion-payoff

Fernandes-Alcantara, Adrienne L. 2017. *Vulnerable Youth:
Employment and Job Training Programs.* Congressional
Research Service. January 23. Accessed March 12, 2018.
https://fas.org/sgp/crs/misc/R40929.pdf

Hamilton, Robert, and Kay McKinney. 1999. *Job Training
for Juveniles: Project Craft.* Fact Sheet. US Department
of Justice Office of Juvenile Justice and Delinquency
Prevention. August. Accessed July 3, 2018. https://www
.ncjrs.gov/pdffiles1/ojjdp/fs99116.pdf

Johnson, Byron, William Wubbenhorst, and Curtis Schroeder.
2013. *Recidivism Reduction and Return on Investment: An
Empirical Assessment of the Prison Entrepreneurship Program.*
Baylor Institute for Studies on Religion. Accessed July 2,
2018. https://www.pep.org/wp-content/uploads/2018/02/
Baylor-2013-Study-of-PEP.pdf

Kemple, James J. 2008. *Career Academies: Long-Term Impacts on
Work, Education, and Transitions to Adulthood.* MDRC. June.
Accessed June 27, 2018. https://www.mdrc.org/publication/
career-academies-long-term-impacts-work-education-and-
transitions-adulthood

MENTOR. "Expanding Quality Youth Mentoring." Fact Sheet. Accessed July 3, 2018. https://www.mentoring.org/ new-site/wp-content/uploads/2017/11/Brochure-FINAL-Print.pdf

Millenky, Megan, Dan Bloom, Sarah Muller-Ravett, and Joseph Broadus. 2011. *Staying on Course: Three-Year Results of the National Guard Youth ChalleNGE Evaluation.* MDRC. Accessed June 18, 2018. https://www.mdrc.org/ sites/default/files/full_510.pdf

Price, Christofer, et al. 2011. *National Evaluation of Youth Corps: Findings and Follow-Up.* Washington, DC: Prepared for the Corporation for National and Community Service. Cambridge, MA: Abt Associates Inc. Accessed June 10, 2018. https://www.nationalservice.gov/pdf/nat_eval_ youthcorps_impactreport.pdf

Ross, Tracey, Shirley Sagawa, and Melissa Boteach. 2016. *Utilizing National Service as a 21st Century Workforce Strategy for Opportunity Youth.* Center for American Progress. March. Accessed June 10, 2018. https://cdn.americanprogress.org/wp-content/ uploads/2016/02/29105313/NatlServiceReport.pdf

Rusch, Emilie. 2016. "$9.5 Million in Grants Back Apprenticeship Program for Colorado High School Students." *The Denver Post.* September 15. Accessed June 16, 2018. https://www.denverpost.com/2016/09/ 15/9-5-million-grants-apprenticeship-program-for-colorado-high-school-students-careerwise/

Spera, Christopher, et al. 2013. *Volunteering as a Pathway to Employment: Does Volunteering Increase Odds of Finding a Job for the Out of Work?* Washington, DC: Corporation for National and Community Service. Accessed June 10, 2018. https://www.nationalservice.gov/sites/default/files/upload/ employment_research_report.pdf

Symonds, William C., Robert B. Schwartz, and Ronald Ferguson. 2011. *Pathways to Prosperity: Meeting the*

Challenge of Preparing Young Americans for the 21st Century.
Pathways to Prosperity Project, Harvard Graduate School
of Education. February. Accessed May 15, 2018. https://
www.gse.harvard.edu/sites/default/files/documents/
Pathways_to_Prosperity_Feb2011-1.pdf

Tai, Robert H. 2012. *An Examination of Research Literature
on PLTW.* University of Virginia. Project Lead the Way.
Accessed July 3, 2015. http://www.socialimpactexchange
.org/sites/www.socialimpactexchange.org/files/PLTW%20
DR%20TAI%20-%20brochure.pdf

Theodos, Brett, et al. 2017. *Pathways after High School:
Evaluation of the Urban Alliance High School Internship
Program.* Urban Institute. August. Accessed July 2,
2018. https://www.urban.org/sites/default/files/
publication/91661/urban_alliance_finalized_0.pdf

Wenger, Jennie W., et al. 2017. *National Guard Youth
ChalleNGe: Program Progress in 2015–2016.* Santa Monica,
CA: Rand Corporation. Accessed June 20, 2018. https://
www.rand.org/pubs/research_reports/RR1848.html

Work Colleges Consortium. 2012. *Understanding and
Measure Success of Work College Graduates.* Accessed
June 1, 2018. http://workcolleges.org/sites/default/files/
attachments/WCC%202012%20Brochure.pdf

Wyman, Nicholas. 2015. *Job U: How to Find Wealth and
Success by Developing the Skills Companies Actually Need.*
New York: Crown Business.

Websites

http://about.att.com/content/csr/home/possibilities/at-t-
aspire.html.

http://nyec.org/.

http://opportunityamericaonline.org/.

http://workcolleges.org/.

http://www1.cuny.edu/sites/bmi/.

http://www.aei.org/.

http://www.apprenticeshipcarolina.com/about.html.

http://www.gapincsustainability.com/people/way-ahead.

http://www.jag.org/.

http://www.ncwd-youth.info/solutions/innovative-strategies/
home-builders-institute/.

http://www.nfte.com/.

http://www.questsa.org/.

http://www.usaconservation.org/programs/
conservation-corps/.

http://www.wesimonfoundation.org/.

http://younginvincibles.org/.

https://advancingopportunity.org/.

https://apprenticeshipusa.workforcegps.org/
resources/2017/02/02/10/56/Apprenticeship-Youth.

https://dwd.wisconsin.gov/youthapprenticeship/.

https://education.ky.gov/CTE/cter/Pages/TRACK.aspx.

https://naf.org/.

https://theurbanalliance.org/.

https://www2.ed.gov/programs/fws/index.html.

https://www.100kopportunities.org/.

https://www.afterschoolmatters.org/.

https://www.brookings.edu/.

https://www.careerwisecolorado.org/.

https://www.corpsnetwork.org/about.

https://www.cristoreynetwork.org/about.

https://www.dol.gov/general/topic/training/apprenticeship.

https://www.epi.org.

https://www.epionline.org/.

https://www.firstinspires.org/.

https://www.insidetrack.com/.

https://www.jff.org/.

https://www.jointservicesupport.org/NGYCP/.

https://www.juniorachievement.org/web/ja-usa/home.

https://www.manhattan-institute.org.

https://www.mentoring.org/.

https://www.nationalservice.gov/programs/americorps.

https://www.ncacinc.com/nsop/academies.

https://www.pep.org/.

https://www.pltw.org/.

https://www.rockefellerfoundation.org/our-work/initiatives/
impact-hiring/.

https://www.urban.org/.

https://www.yearup.org/.

Introduction

This chapter contains figures and primary resources for further research on the topic of youth employment in the United States. The first section presents data on trends in youth employment, and the second section provides excerpts from federal legislative actions, presidential speeches, and other government documents pertaining to youth employment organized in chronological order.

Data

Figure 5.1 at the top of the next page presents data on the youth unemployment rate in July each year from 2000 to 2016. July is a peak month for youth participation in the labor force as large numbers of high school and college students seek summer employment or long-term employment following graduation. The data indicates that by July 2016, the rate of youth unemployment had receded to pre-recession levels but was still higher than the youth unemployment rate in July 2000.

A Career and Technical Education Specialist with the Alabama Department of Education gives information to students at a career fair at Selma High School in Alabama on February 13, 2015. The past couple of decades have witnessed increased experimentation with Career and Technical Education, which has demonstrated strong potential to improve the labor market outcomes of young people. (Ann Hermes/The Christian Science Monitor via Getty Images)

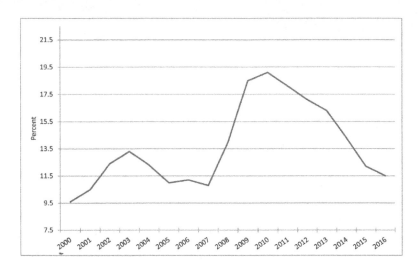

Figure 5.1   Youth Unemployment Rate (2000–2016)

Source: Bureau of Labor Statistics, U.S. Department of Labor, *The Economics Daily*, Youth unemployment rate, 11.5 percent; employment–population ratio, 53.2 percent in July 2016 on the Internet at https://www.bls.gov/opub/ted/2016/youth-unemploy ment-rate-11-point-5-percent-employment-population-ratio-53-point-2-percent-in-july-2016.htm.

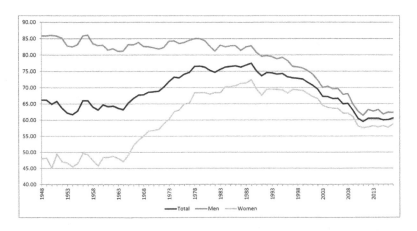

Figure 5.2   Historical Youth Labor Force Participation Rates (1948–2017)

Figure 5.2 demonstrates the dramatic rise of female youth partici-pation in the labor force in the decades following World War II and the steady decline of the participation rate for both genders that has taken place over the past several decades.

Source: Bureau of Labor Statistics, U.S. Department of Labor, *The Economics Daily*, Summer youth labor force in July 2017 on the Internet at https://www.bls.gov/opub/ted/2017/summer-youth-labor-force-in-july-2017.htm.

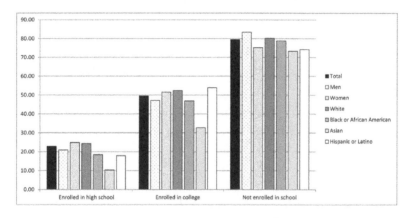

Figure 5.3   Demographics of Labor Force Participation Rates (2017)

Figure 5.3 reveals the differences in school enrollment rates and participation in the labor force by race, ethnicity, and gender.

Source: Bureau of Labor Statistics, U.S. Department of Labor, *The Economics Daily*, Female students more likely than male students to participate in labor force in October 2017 on the In-ternet at https://www.bls.gov/opub/ted/2018/female-students-more-likely-than-male-students-to-participate-in-labor-force-in-october-2017.htm.

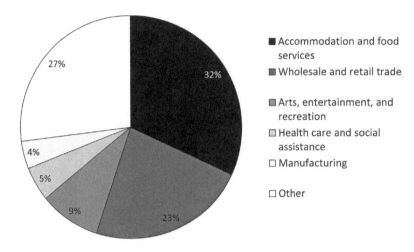

Figure 5.4   Where Teens Work (2015)

Figure 5.4 reveals which industries are providing the largest percentage of summer employment opportunities for 16- to 19-year-olds.

Source: Drew DeSilver, "The Fading of the Teen Summer Job," Pew Research Center, June 23, 2015. http://www.pewresearch .org/fact-tank/2015/06/23/the-fading-of-the-teen-summer-job/.

Although earnings and employment are affected by several factors including industry, geographic location, and level of experience, figure 5.5 on the facing page demonstrates the overall correlation between individuals' educational attainment and their earning and employment prospects.

Source: Dennis Vilorio, "Education Matters," U.S. Bureau of Labor Statistics, March 2016. https://www.bls.gov/careerout-look/2016/data-on-display/education-matters.htm.

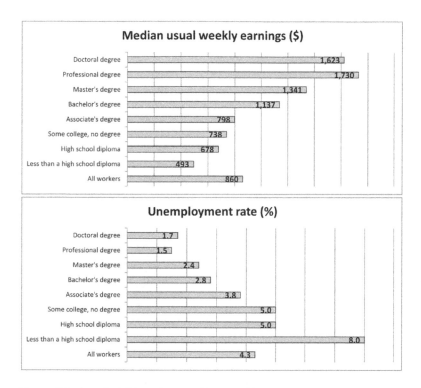

Figure 5.5   Level of Education and Earnings/Employment (2015)

Documents

Fair Labor Standards Act (1938)

The Fair Labor Standards Act of 1938 is a federal law that applies to employees engaged in any activity affecting interstate commerce. It established a federal minimum-wage and overtime pay require-ments and imposed several provisions regulating age, hour, and occupational standards for youth. For example, aside from certain parental exemptions, youth under 18 cannot be employed in haz-ardous occupations, and youth between the ages of 14 and 16 can-not be employed during school hours. Subsequent amendments to the law have raised the federal minimum-wage and extended the law's coverage to additional employees. The law continues to be the chief federal statute for defining the conditions under which youth, below the age of 18, may be employed.

An Act

To provide for the establishment of fair labor standards in employments in and affecting interstate commerce, and for other purposes.

Be it enacted by the Senate and House of Representatives of the United States of America in Congress assembled, That this Act may be cited as the "Fair Labor Standards Act of 1938."

. . .

(1) "Oppressive child labor" means a condition of employment under which (1) any employee under the age of sixteen years is employed by an employer (other than a parent or a person standing in place of a parent employing his own child or a child in his custody under the age of sixteen years in an occupation other than manufacturing or mining) in any occupation, or (2) any employee between the ages of sixteen and eighteen years is employed by an employer in any occupation which the Chief of the Children's Bureau in the Department of Labor shall find and by order declare to be particularly hazardous for the employment of children between such ages or detrimental to their health or well-being ; but oppressive child labor shall not be deemed to exist by virtue of the employment in any occupation of any person with respect to whom the employer shall have on file an unexpired certificate issued and held pursuant to regulations of the Chief of the Children's Bureau certifying that such person is above the oppressive child-labor age. The Chief of the Children's Bureau shall provide by regulation or by order that the employment of employees between the ages of fourteen and sixteen years in occupations other than manufacturing and mining shall not be deemed to constitute oppressive child labor if and to the extent that the Chief of the Children's Bureau determines that such employment is confined to periods which will not interfere with their schooling

and to conditions which will not interfere with their health and well-being.

. . .

Child Labor Provisions

SEC. 12. (a) After the expiration of one hundred and twenty days from the date of enactment of this Act, no producer, manufacturer, or dealer shall ship or deliver for shipment in commerce any goods produced in an establishment situated in the United States in or about which within thirty days prior to the removal of such goods therefrom any oppressive child labor has been employed: Provided, That a prosecution and conviction of a defendant for the shipment or delivery for shipment of any goods under the conditions herein prohibited shall be a bar to any further prosecution against the same defendant for shipments or deliveries for shipment of any such goods before the beginning of said prosecution.

(b) The Chief of the Children's Bureau in the Department of Labor, or any of his authorized representatives, shall make all investigations and inspections under section 11 (a) with respect to the employment of minors, and subject to the direction and control of the Attorney General, shall bring all actions under section 17 to enjoin any act or practice which is unlawful by reason of the existence of oppressive child labor, and shall administer all other provisions of this Act relating to oppressive child labor.

. . .

Learners, Apprentices, and Handicapped Workers

SEC. 14. The Administrator, to the extent necessary in order to prevent curtailment of opportunities for employment, shall by regulations or by orders provide for (1) the employment of learners, of apprentices, and of messengers employed exclusively in delivering letters and messages, under special certificates issued pursuant to regulations of the Administrator, at such wages lower than the minimum-wage applicable under section 6 and subject to such limitations as to time, number, proportion, and length of service as the Administrator shall prescribe, and (2) the employment of individuals whose earning capacity is impaired by age or physical or mental deficiency or injury, under special certificates issued by the Administrator, at such wages lower than the minimum-wage applicable under section 6 and for such period as shall be fixed in such certificates.

. . .

Source: Public Law 75–718, Ch. 676, 52 Stat. 1060, June 25, 1938.

John F. Kennedy's Message on the Nation's Youth (1963)

In response to high unemployment and sluggish recovery following the economic recession of 1958, John F. Kennedy campaigned on the promise of "getting America moving again" through the implementation of his "New Frontier" plan for social and economic reforms. Although his first two years in office were largely consumed by a focus on foreign policy, Kennedy began to implement a bold domestic program in 1962 that included tax cuts and enhanced spending on employment and training opportunities, particularly for those whose jobs were affected by the growth of automation. One of these programs, the Manpower Development and Training Act of 1962, empowered the Department of Labor to fund training opportunities for the unemployed and underemployed. In early 1963, Kennedy shifted focus to the problem of youth unemployment in particular, calling on Congress to increase employment opportunities for the nation's youth. Because Kennedy's life was cut short by assassination that same year, the implementation of much of what he envisioned was postponed until the passage of the Economic Opportunity Act under the Johnson administration.

To the Congress of the United States:

"The youth of a nation," said Disraeli, "are the trustees of posterity." The future promise of any nation can be directly measured by the present prospects of its youth. This Nation facing increasingly complex economic, social and international challenges—is increasingly dependent on the opportunities, capabilities and vitality of those who are soon to bear its chief responsibilities. Such attributes as energy, a readiness to question, imagination and creativity are all attributes of youth that are also essential to our total national character. To the extent that the Nation is called upon to promote and protect the interests of our younger citizens, it is an investment certain to bring a high return, not only in basic human values but in social and economic terms. A few basic statistics will indicate the nature and proportion of our need to make this investment.

. . .

Unemployment among young workers today is two and one-half times the national average, and even higher among minority groups and those unable to complete their high school education. During the 1960's seven and one-half million students will drop out of school without a high school education, at present rates, thereby entering the labor market unprepared for anything except the diminishing number of unskilled labor openings. In total, some 26 million young persons will enter the job market for the first time during this period, 40 percent more than in the previous decade. Already out-of-school youth, age 16–21, comprise only 7 percent of the labor force but 18 percent of the unemployed. During the school months of 1962 there were on the average 700,000 young persons in this age category out of school and out of work.

. . .

The employment prospects of youth depend on the general level of economic activity in the Nation, as well as on specific efforts to increase opportunities for young persons. The high level of unemployment which the Nation has experienced for the past 5 years has had sharply aggravated effects in this age group, as shown by the statistics earlier cited.

I have already proposed tax and other measures designed to quicken the pace of economic activity to increase the prospects for full employment, and thereby to diminish the incidence of youth unemployment. But the rate of youth unemployment will still remain disproportionately high for some time unless other, more direct measures are adopted. Our young persons are caught in cross-currents of population growth and technological change which hold great danger as well as great promise.

While the number of young persons entering the labor force will increase sharply in this decade, augmented by an excessive number of school drop-outs, many of the traditional occupational opportunities for young and relatively unskilled workers are declining. For example, as a result of the technological economic changes of the last decade and more, it is not likely that more than 1 out of every 10 boys now living on farms will find full-time work in agriculture.

New programs recently begun by the Federal Government and by public and private organizations throughout the Nation are devoted to stimulating employment of youth. Under the Manpower Development and Training Act of last year, the Federal Government is assisting State and local officials to provide additional training for out-of-school youth at the community level. The 1,900 local public employment offices provide counseling, testing, and placement services for young workers, including the use of demonstration projects to assist school dropouts to obtain employment.

My Committee on Youth Employment, consisting of Cabinet officers and distinguished public members, having studied these efforts and problems, has reported to me that the immediate need for additional youth employment opportunities is critical. The Administration's Youth Employment bill, which received wide endorsement when introduced in the Congress, is designed to meet this need.

Early enactment of this measure would spur Federal leadership and support to programs which would provide useful jobs and training for young persons who need them. The 1964 budget recommendations include $100 million in authorizations for the first year of this program, consisting of two distinct activities. First, a Youth Conservation Corps would be established, putting young men to work improving our forests and recreation areas. This would initially provide useful training and work for 15,000 youth. Second, the Federal Government will provide half the wages and related costs for young persons employed on local projects that offer useful work experience in nonprofit community services—such as hospitals, schools, parks and settlement houses. Forty thousand youths can be employed in the first year in this part of the program.

This bill is a measure of the first priority. The effects of unemployment are nowhere more depressing and disheartening than among the young. Common sense and justice compel establishment of this program, which will give many thousands of currently unemployed young persons a chance to find employment, to be paid for their services, and to acquire skills and work experience that will give them a solid start in their working lives.

I urge the Congress to enact at the earliest opportunity the Youth Employment Act which is so vital to the welfare of our young people and our Nation. . . .

Source: John F. Kennedy, "Special Message to the Congress on the Nation's Youth," February 14, 1963. Online by Gerhard Peters and John T. Woolley, *The American Presidency Project.* http://www.presidency.ucsb.edu/ws/?pid=9561.

Ronald Reagan's Message on Proposed Employment Legislation (1983)

Early on his administration, President Ronald Reagan began to emphasize the detrimental effects that increases in the minimum-wage had on the employment opportunities of unskilled teenagers and minorities. He correspondingly advocated the establishment of a "subminimum" wage for teenagers to incentivize firms to hire young, inexperienced workers. Various proposals to create a lower minimum-wage for teenage workers were introduced into Congress during the *first couple years of Reagan's presidency, but these proposals faced significant blowback from Democrats and labor representatives who argued that allowing employers to hire younger workers at less than the minimum-wage would encourage employers to replace older workers with less-expensive teenage employees. In response, Reagan scaled back on earlier proposals. In a message to Congress in early 1983, Reagan highlighted efforts already undertaken to combat the negative consequences of youth unemployment and called for Congress to cut the current minimum-wage of $3.50 an hour to $2.50 during the summer months of May to September for youth under the age of 22. It was not for some time, however, that Congress passed a provision for a youth minimum-wage. In 1996, President Clinton signed into law amendments to the Fair Labor Standards Act that permitted employers to pay a youth minimum-wage not less than $4.25 an hour to employees who are under the age of 20 for the first 90 days of employment. This federal allowance for a temporary youth minimum-wage has had a minimal effect, however, because most states and localities have failed to adopt a similar provision in their labor codes, which means that state and local adult minimum-wages supersede the federal law.*

. . . Young people are a third group suffering from structural unemployment. Unemployment among youth constitutes over 30 percent of our overall unemployment. The rate among the 16–21 age group is an unacceptable 23 percent, over twice the national average, and among minority youth, the unemployment rate of 44 percent represents the single most important social labor market problem.

The consequences of youth unemployment are different from those of adult unemployment. Among adults, unemployment is primarily a matter of financial loss and temporary economic hardship. Most of our nation's youth, on the other hand, live in families in which they are the second or third breadwinner. Unemployment among the majority of youth, therefore, does not usually create severe financial hardship. In 1981, the annual income of families with unemployed youth averaged almost $25,000.

Prolonged periods of unemployment among many youths, however, often lead to serious long-term consequences. First, sustained unemployment can tempt some to channel their energies and ambitions into antisocial or criminal activities. Second, long-term unemployment undermines a young person's potential for success. Recent studies show that those who have prolonged unemployment during their formative years also have less stable employment and diminished earning capacity during their adult years.

Prolonged unemployment among youth is partially due to a lack of initial labor market skills. The problem of skill deficiencies is exacerbated by a lack of career-oriented job opportunities. To combat the problem of skill deficiencies, the Administration worked with Congress to enact the landmark Job Training Partnership Act (JTPA) of 1982. Under the Act, in FY 1984, $724 million in resources are targeted at economically disadvantaged youth in need of training. These resources will provide young people with a fresh chance to develop fully their potential for a productive career.

As a second step toward improving the job skills of our nation's youth, the Administration worked with Congress to extend the Targeted Jobs Tax Credit (TJTC) Program. As part of the extension, the program was modified to target resources more tightly on economically disadvantaged youth. The tax credits provided by the program will encourage employers to aid in the process of developing the skills of many of our young people.

Enactment of enterprise zone legislation would be a third step in this process of improving employment opportunities for youth, particularly disadvantaged youth in our inner cities and rural areas. However, the problem of youth unemployment is too large and too severe for the Federal government alone to provide the sole remedy. The private sector must also help open up career-oriented job opportunities.

One of the most important causes of the lack of career-oriented jobs in which young people can start their careers is the minimum-wage. When many young people first enter the labor market their job skills are well below those of older, experienced workers. In a free market, unhampered by government restrictions, young people could compensate for their relative lack of experience and skills by offering to work for a lower wage. Then, as they gain experience on the job, their growing skills would make them more valuable to employers and they would progress up the pay scale. The minimum-wage destroys this opportunity: young people are prevented from offering their services at less than a government mandated wage. Faced with the prospect of hiring an unskilled youth at a wage in excess of the current value of his labor, many firms not surprisingly turn young people away. Unable to get an initial job, many young workers never learn the job skills that are needed to earn more than the minimum-wage.

Evidence of the effects of the minimum-wage is abundant. For nearly a century and a half, this nation experienced no significant youth unemployment problem. Then, just after the turn of the century, state legislatures began enacting minimum-wage laws. At first, these mandated wages were not far from market wages and there was little impact. In 1938, however, the Federal government imposed a Federal minimum-wage applicable to firms engaged in interstate commerce. Initially this meant that the Federal minimum-wage was largely confined to manufacturing. The Federal minimum-wage contributed to declining youth employment in manufacturing. But other industries such as retail trade and the service sector still provided an outlet for the energies of youth who wished to work.

During the 1960s and 1970s the minimum-wage was increased and its coverage was expanded. At the same time, the youth unemployment problem continued to worsen, especially among minorities.

Youth Employment Opportunity Wage

To help those young people who want to work find jobs, I am proposing a youth employment opportunity wage for youngsters under the age of 22. This youth opportunity wage will be $2.50 per hour, 25 percent below the regular minimum-wage of $3.35 per hour. Young people will not, of course, be forced to accept the lower wage, and many will receive more than $2.50 an hour. But all will have the opportunity to offer their services at $2.50 if lack of job skills or other factors make this appropriate.

I am not the first to propose a youth differential minimum-wage; indeed, the government more than once has come close to implementing such a proposal. Each time it failed, however, due to concerns that adults would be displaced by younger workers. I am unconvinced by such arguments but I appreciate the concern behind them. Therefore, I am proposing that the youth employment opportunity wage only be effective during the summer—specifically from May 1 to September 30. This is the period when the greatest number of youth are in the labor market and, therefore, the period in which this proposal will generate the most employment opportunities. By restricting the youth opportunity wage to the summer months, the jobs of older workers will be protected. An employer will not wish to disrupt his or her work force by attempting to use youth during the summer and adults the rest of the year.

To ensure that existing jobs are protected, the Employment Act of 1983 prohibits displacement of current workers by those hired at the youth employment opportunity wage. It also protects the wages of youth employed at the current minimum-wage by prohibiting employers from reducing their rate of pay. Thus it expands youth employment opportunities, but net at the expense of older workers.

Some may try to use this proposed legislation as an opportunity to raise the level of the Federal minimum-wage above the current $3.35 per hour. I will vigorously oppose any such attempt. Raising the level of the minimum-wage would cause many adult workers to lose their jobs. At a time of 10.4 percent unemployment, it would simply create further job loss and more unemployment. . . .

Source: Ronald Reagan, "Message to the Congress Transmitting Proposed Employment Legislation," March 11, 1983. Online by Gerhard Peters and John T. Woolley, *The American Presidency Project.* http://www.presidency.ucsb.edu/ws/ ?pid=41038.

Ensuring Economic Opportunities for Young Americans (2009)

Because large numbers of high school and college students begin between April to June to search for summer employment or long-term employment following graduation, July is the peak month for youth participation in the labor force. In July 2009, the number of youth participating in the labor force reached its lowest rate since July 1955, and the number of young people employed reached the lowest July rate on record since data recording began in 1948. According to records from the U.S. Bureau of Labor Statistics, nearly a million more youth were unemployed in July 2009 than the number of unemployed the previous summer. The sharp decline of the youth employment-to-population ratio rate between July 2008 and July 2009 was a result, in part, of the weak labor market conditions caused by the recession, but the numbers additionally reflected a long-term downward trend in the summer youth labor force participation and employment rate. In fact, youth seasonal employment began to steadily decline in 2001, long before the 2007–2008 recession. In response, the House Committee on Education and Labor held a hearing in October 2009 to consider the extent to which American youth have access to part-time summer jobs, long considered a foundation stone for character development and future gainful employment. The hearing additionally considered various programs that might be expanded and various strategies that might be implemented to improve youth employment opportunities.

The Education and Labor Committee meets this morning to examine strategies for ensuring better economic opportunities for young Americans.

A summer or part-time job has traditionally been the gateway to future success for generations of Americans.

In fact, every member on this committee can probably look back fondly on that first job at the corner grocery during high school that may have put a little gas money in your pocket every week.

In my case, working a back-breaking summer job at the local refinery helped me pay for college and escape debt free.

These job opportunities not only provide needed cash to help pay for school or save for a first car; but, they also give young workers an introduction to what it means to work with others on a shift and try to make a living.

Unfortunately, these opportunities are scarcer for today's young workers than ever before.

One reason may be that workers are retiring later because of shrinking pension benefits and 410(k) accounts. This means fewer new opportunities for younger workers because older workers may stay on longer in order to rebuild their retirement security.

The dramatic fall in youth employment over the last decade is startling. Sixty percent of 16 to 24 year-olds were employed in 1999.

Today, fewer than 48 percent have a job; the lowest level since World War II.

This situation is grim, especially when you take into account under-employment.

During the first quarter of 2009, workers younger than 25 had an under-employment rate of 32 percent. That is nearly 20 points higher than workers ages 35 to 54.

The financial crisis has had a severe impact on the employment prospects of millions of Americans, not just the young.

Indeed, because of the horrible economy, younger workers are now competing with more experienced workers for positions traditionally the domain of the young and less experienced.

Until the economy as a whole turns around, younger workers will continue to be hit the hardest.

But the recession has only made a bad situation worse for younger workers.

The falling overall employment rate among young workers 16 to 24 began more than a decade ago and has declined nearly every year.

Even in periods of economic stability, fewer young people do not make the transition to the workforce. They face challenges completing high school and obtaining the skills they need to succeed.

For these young people, alternative education and job training models provide a critical link to the workplace. Today, we will hear about some of these programs and how they are trying to meet the needs of our nation's most vulnerable youth.

Teens looking for a summer job have been especially hard-hit. The unemployment rate among 16 to 19 year-olds during the summer has increased by 113 percent compared to ten years ago.

By looking at this data, it is clear that the drop in employment is not just the result of a sudden shock to the system, but a part of a larger trend.

You cannot ignore the fact that 20 percent fewer younger workers are participating in the labor market today than in 1999.

This tells me that more needs to be done or perhaps we need to rethink strategies to help young workers find meaningful employment, in any economy.

The consequences of reduced work opportunities among young Americans mean fewer long-term employment prospects, less earnings, and decreased productivity.

Fewer work opportunities also result in higher debts—more student loans, credit card debts, and so on.

If these dramatic trends are not reversed, our nation faces the potential of a generation of youth disconnected from the employment market.

That's why as a part of the American Recovery and Reinvestment Act, we invested an additional $1.2 billion to beef up youth jobs programs, including summer employment opportunities, under the Workforce Investment Act.

The additional funding for summer jobs have proved successful.

In fact, the Government Accountability Office found that most states they reviewed either met or exceeded the state's goals with nearly a quarter million summer jobs created.

The House also just approved legislation to make an unprecedented $10 billion investment to make community colleges part of our economy's recovery.

The Student Aid and Fiscal Responsibility Act will help prepare young workers for the jobs of the future and build a 21st century workforce by strengthening partnerships among community colleges, businesses and job training programs that will align community college curricula with the needs of high-wage, high-demand industries.

Today's hearing will also give us an opportunity to look at other programs that serve young workers and look at ways we can expand programs that are making a real difference.

We will also explore new strategies, some developed by young people themselves, to ensure that younger workers can compete in this job market.

Source: Statement of Hon. George Miller, Chairman, Committee on Education and Labor, "Ensuring Economic Opportunities for Young Americans." Hearing before the Committee on Education and Labor, House of Representatives, 111th Congress, 1st Session, October 1, 2009. Serial No. 111–34. Washington, DC: Government Printing Office, 2009. https://www.govinfo.gov/content/pkg/CHRG-111hhrg52413/html/CHRG-111hhrg52413.htm.

Barack Obama's Message on a New College Scorecard (2015)

In his 2013 State of the Union Address, President Obama announced his intention to encourage college affordability and raise awareness concerning the costs and benefits of attending different institutions of higher learning. He additionally suggested cutting government financial aid to institutions that did not provide a good return on student investment—a proposal strongly resisted by industry leaders.

In late 2015, as the academic year commenced, the president announced the launch of a White House–sponsored College Scorecard that would publish information on individual colleges based on a range of variables, including the number of low-income students enrolled, student debt levels, graduation rates, and average graduate earnings. The goal of the Scorecard was to provide federal data to parents and other third parties so they might evaluate institutions of higher learning based on their contributions to student economic success. The Scorecard, however, restricted data collection only to institutions that grant more degrees than certificates and to students within those institutions who receive federal aid. The Whitehouse College Scorecard thus excluded analysis of schools with low rates of federal aid, community colleges that offer a large number of certificate programs in addition to associate degrees, and non-federal aid recipients.

. . . Next week marks seven years since a financial crisis on Wall Street that would usher in some hard years for working families on Main Street. Soon after that, I took office. And we set out to rebuild our economy on a new foundation for growth and prosperity by investing in things that grow our middle class—things like jobs, health care, and education.

Today, our businesses have created more than 13 million new jobs over the last five and a half years. The unemployment rate is the lowest it's been in more than seven years. Another 16 million Americans have gained health insurance. Our high school graduate rate is the highest it's ever been, and more people are graduating from college than ever before. We are coming back—and stronger.

Still, in an economy that's increasingly based on knowledge and innovation, some higher education is the surest ticket to the middle class. By the end of this decade, two in three job openings will require some higher education. That's one reason why a degree from a two-year college will earn you $10,000 more each year than someone who only finished high school. One study showed that a degree from a four-year university earns you $1 million more over the course of a lifetime.

The country with the best-educated workforce in the world is going to win the 21st century economy. I want that to be America. But as college costs and student debt keep rising, the choices that Americans make when searching for and selecting a college have never been more important. That's why everyone should be able to find clear, reliable, open data on college affordability and value—like whether they're likely to graduate, find good jobs, and pay off their loans. Right now, however, many existing college rankings reward schools for spending more money and rejecting more students—at a time when America needs our colleges to focus on affordability and supporting all students who enroll. That doesn't make sense, and it has to change.

So, today, my Administration is launching a new College Scorecard, designed with input from those who will use it the most—students, families, and counselors. Americans will now have access to reliable data on every institution of higher education. You'll be able to see how much each school's graduates earn, how much debt they graduate with, and what percentage of a school's students can pay back their loans—which will help all of us see which schools do the best job of preparing America for success. And to reach more folks, we're working with partners in the academic, nonprofit, and private sectors that will help families use this new data to navigate the complicated college process and make informed decisions.

The status quo serves some colleges and the companies that rank them just fine. But it doesn't serve our students well—and that doesn't serve any of us well. There are colleges dedicated to helping students of all backgrounds learn without saddling them with debt. We should hold everybody to that standard. Our economic future depends on it.

This work is just beginning. In the coming weeks and months, we'll continue to improve the Scorecard based on what we learn from students, parents, counselors, and colleges themselves. The goal is to help everybody who's willing to work for a higher education search for and select a college that fits their goals. Together, we can make sure that every student has the chance to get a great education and achieve their full potential. . .

Source: Barack Obama, "Weekly Address," September 12, 2015. The Whitehouse Office of the Press Secretary. https://obamawhitehouse.archives.gov/the-press-office/2015/09/12/weekly-address-new-college-scorecard.

Student Safety in the Job Corps Program (2017)

Job Corps is the largest federal residential, employment training, and career development program for disadvantaged youth in the nation. It is specifically designed to enable vulnerable, low-income youth to escape gangs and insecure homes and communities, while they pursue education and career goals. In recent years, however, widespread reports of systemic serious criminal misconduct, drug use, and a lack of adequate security within the program have been a cause of growing concern. Testimony by government auditors at a hearing sponsored by the House Education and Workforce Committee confirmed these concerns making the program vulnerable to millions of dollars in proposed budget cuts by the Trump administration.

Ms. Barnes. Chairwoman Foxx, Ranking Member Scott and members of the committee, I am pleased to be here today to discuss GAO's preliminary observations on the safety and security of students in the Job Corps program. This work is part of our recently started effort to examine this issue.

Job Corps is the Nation's largest residential, educational and career development program for low-income youth between the ages of 16 and 24. The program is administered by the

Department of Labor and currently serves about 50,000 students each year at 125 Job Corps centers nationwide.

My remarks today will cover one, the number and types of reported safety and security incidents. And two, student perceptions of safety at Job Corps centers.

For this testimony we analyze the Department of Labor's incident data from January 2007 through June 2016. Due to concerns about the completeness of the data, we report the minimum number of incidents in the aggregate for those 9 years, but the actual numbers are likely higher. We also analyzed national student survey data from March 2007 through March 2017. Overall, we found that Job Corps centers reported nearly 50,000 safety and security incidents of various types that occurred both on site and off site from January 2007 through June 2016.

During this time period, over 500,00 students were enrolled in the program. We found that 76 percent or about 38,000 of the reported incidents occurred on site and 24 percent occurred off site. In addition, about 21 percent of reported incidents involved violence.

As you can see, with the figure on the monitor, three types of incidents represent 60 percent of all reported on site and off site incidents. Serious illnesses or injuries are 28 percent, assaults at 19 percent, and drug related incidents at 13 percent. The remaining 40 percent of reported incidents included theft, or damage to property, and breaches of security or safety, and other incidents.

During this time, Job Corps centers reported 265 deaths captured in the other and assault categories in the figure on the screen. And the majority of these deaths occurred off site. Most of these deaths were due to homicides, medical causes and accidental causes.

As shown in the table on the screen, Job Corps centers reported over 10,000 violent incidents, which include homicides, assaults and sexual assaults. Students were the majority of the victims in 72 percent of these reported violent incidents and perpetrators in 85 percent of these incidents. Staff were victims in 8 percent of these incidents and perpetrators in 1 percent of these incidents.

As for the student survey data, we found that students generally reported feeling safe, but reported feeling less safe with respect to certain safety issues. The student survey asked 49 questions about students' experiences in the Job Corp program, including 12 questions related to safety. Across these 12 survey questions an average of 72 percent of students reported feeling safe.

However, the average percentage of students who reported feeling safe on each individual survey question ranged from 44 percent to 91 percent. For example, an average of 44 percent of students reported that they had never heard students threaten each other or had not heard such threats within the last month. The remaining 56 percent of students on average reported hearing such threats at least once in the last month.

In conclusion, Job Corps students should be provided with a safe learning environment. However, as our preliminary analysis demonstrates, too many safety and security incidents are occurring at Job Corps centers and this is a cause for concern. And it is likely that the actual number of safety and security incidences is greater than the number we report in this statement. Our ongoing work will present opportunities for us to further examine these issues.

Source: Testimony of Cindy Brown Barnes, Director of Education Workforce and Income Security, Government Accountability Office, "Student Safety in the Job Corps Program." Hearings before the Committee on Education and the Workforce, House of Representatives, 115th Congress, 1st Session. June 22, 2017. Serial No. 115–20. Washington, DC: Government Printing Office, 2017. https://www.govinfo.gov/content/pkg/CHRG-115hhrg25922/html/CHRG-115 hhrg25922.htm.

Teen Labor Force Participation and the Great Recession (2017)

After reaching a peak in 1979, the youth labor force participation rate has undergone a steady decline. Since 2000, the decline has been especially sharp and has consistently remained at levels lower than what the nation has experienced since the post–World War II era. The following report produced by the Bureau of Labor Statistics examines the extent to which the decline over the past two decades correlates to higher levels of youth participation in education-related activities and a growing level of competition from older workers who are remaining in the workforce at higher levels than in previous generations and increasingly working in fields that have traditionally employed high numbers of youth.

Teen labor force participation has been on a long-term downward trend. Since reaching a peak of 57.9 percent in 1979, the rate fell to 52.0 percent in 2000, just prior to the 2001 recession. The rate then dropped rapidly during and after the 2007–09 recession to reach 34.1 percent in 2011, and since then, it has stayed within a narrow range. The latest projection of labor force participation from the U.S. Bureau of Labor Statistics (BLS) points toward an even lower teen participation rate by 2024.

Current and historical data on labor force participation are available from the BLS Current Population Survey (CPS), which is a monthly survey of about 60,000 households. The Employment Projections program at BLS produces projections of labor force participation and other economic data. BLS releases the projections every 2 years, and they cover 10-year periods; the most recent projections are for the 2014–24 decade. BLS data include the civilian noninstitutional population. The labor force consists of employed people and those people without a job who are actively searching for work and are available for work. The labor force participation rate is the percentage of the population who participates in the labor force.

Why has teen labor force participation declined and remained low? A growing proportion of people ages 16 and 19 years old are in school, and school enrollment has an impact on labor force participation. Other factors besides education affect the participation rate as well. This study will concentrate on labor force participation rates for the 16-to-19 age group, using not seasonally adjusted historical data from BLS, along with projected data. The historical participation rate data are annual averages, except for an analysis of the July rate that is used for evaluating teen labor force participation during the summer.

Trends in Teen Labor Force Participation

Labor force participation for teens trended down from 52.5 percent in 1948 (the start of the data) to 44.5 percent in 1964. The rate moved upward until it reached its high point of 57.9 percent in 1979. Several recessions occurred since 1979, including those of 1981–82, 1990–91, 2001, and the most recent recession, often called the "Great Recession" of 2007–09. Over the past several decades, the rate exhibited a similar pattern; it fell just before, during, and for a short time after recessions ended, followed by little change during most of the recovery. The overall drop in the rate was especially steep, however, during the two most recent recessions. In 2000, just before the 2001 recession, a little more than one-half of teenagers (52.0 percent) were in the labor force. By 2003, the rate had fallen to 44.5 percent. In 2006 (just before the 2007–09 recession), the rate was 43.7 percent. The participation rate declined during that recession and immediately after, falling to 34.1 percent in 2011. It has changed little since 2011.

Traditionally, teens held summer jobs even if they did not work during the school year, and labor force participation is higher during the summer than during the school year. Even though some teens still have summer jobs, the proportion of teens who participate in the labor force during the summer has dropped dramatically. The summer break typically includes

July. In July 2016, the teen labor force participation rate was 43.2 percent, down almost 30 percentage points from the high point of 71.8 percent in July 1978.

Education Impacts

Educators, parents, policymakers, and other stakeholders are paying more attention to the value of education. Workers with more education tend to have higher pay and lower unemployment. Indeed, data from BLS illustrate this relationship. As stakeholders pay more attention to the value of education, teen school enrollment has continued to grow and labor force participation to decline.

Teen School Enrollment

In 2015, about 3 out of 4 teens were enrolled in school. Despite dipping in 2013, this proportion trended up from 58.7 percent in 1985, which is the first year of data. These annual averages include all months during the year.

More teens attend school during the summer now than in previous years. The proportion of teenagers enrolled in July 2016 was more than 4 times higher than it was in July 1985—42.1 percent versus 10.4 percent.

According to the Annual Social and Economic Supplement of the CPS, the major reason teens give for not being in the labor force is that they are attending school. The supplement includes a question for those who did not work at all in the previous year: "What was the main reason (you/he/she) did not work in [year]?" In 2014, 92 percent of 16-to-19-year-olds who did not participate in the labor force cited "going to school" as the main reason. In 2004, this percentage was 89 percent. The percentage of teens who did not work at all during the year because they were going to school was 59.5 percent in 2014 versus 46.1 percent 10 years earlier.

Labor force participation rates are available by enrollment status. The participation for enrolled teens is much lower than for nonenrolled teens. Both rates were at their highest points in 1989. Both rates began to decline sharply before the 2001 recession and continued to descend until 2011; since then, both have stayed within a narrow range. The decline for enrolled teens has been sharper than the decline for teens not in school. About one-quarter of enrolled teens participated in the labor force in 2015, whereas the rate was 42.8 percent in 2000. The rate for teens who are not enrolled fell from 71.6 percent in 2000 to 58.9 percent in 2015.

Reasons for the dip in teen enrollment in 2013 are not clear. A corresponding increase in labor force participation for this age group did not occur in 2013. Many researchers point toward cyclical trends in school enrollment; that is, people tend to return to school during recessionary periods and to the labor force during recoveries. This factor likely affects young adults more than teenagers, however. Other researchers point toward the high cost of college and concerns about debt. Indeed, tuition costs and college debt have been rising (see the later section on paying for college). Despite the dip in enrollment in 2013, the proportion enrolled still remains high by historical standards.

High School Coursework

Pressures to increase achievement and to better prepare high school students for college have grown, as shown by changes in coursework. High schoolers are taking tougher and more advanced courses, including those specifically designed for college preparation and credit—Advanced Placement (AP) courses. Dedicating more time to studies may leave less time for participation in the labor force.

The National Commission on Excellence in Education recommended in 1983 that all college-bound students take the following as a minimum during 4 years of high school: 4 years of English; 3 years each of social studies, science, and mathematics; 2 years of a foreign language; and one-half year of computer science. The National Center for Education

Statistics (NCES) has data on combinations of courses taken by high school graduates, including the combination recommended by the Commission, minus computer science. The proportion of high school graduates completing the previous combination of years, at a minimum, was 9.5 percent in 1982. It grew to 61.8 percent of 2009 high school graduates, or more than 6 times higher than the proportion for 1982 high school graduates.

NCES also has data on selected courses taken by high school graduates by area of study for selected years from 1982 to 2009. As for mathematics, the proportion of graduates who have taken advanced math courses in high school has grown. Notably, the proportion taking algebra II grew from 39.9 percent in 1982 to 75.5 percent in 2009. The proportion with a semester in analysis/precalculus was just 6.2 percent of graduates in 1982, and it climbed to a little more than 35 percent of graduates in 2009. Coursework in statistics/probability and calculus also rose over the period.

More high school graduates have been taking science, including multiple science courses. Nearly all 2009 graduates earned at least 1 year in biology (95.6 percent), 70.4 percent earned 1 year in chemistry, and 36.1 percent earned at least 1 year in physics. The proportion of graduates earning multiple years in the sciences has grown. In 2009, 68.3 percent of graduates earned years in both biology and chemistry, and 30.1 percent earned years in biology, chemistry, and physics. By comparison, 29.3 percent of 1989 graduates earned years in biology and chemistry and 11.2 percent in biology, chemistry, and physics.

As for foreign languages, 86.4 percent of 2009 graduates had taken a foreign language, compared with 54.4 percent in 1982. The proportion of graduates taking 1 year or less of a foreign language declined since 1982. Those having taken a minimum of 2 years in foreign languages was 19.5 percent in 1982 and 35.3 percent in 2009, having dipped from 2005. The proportion earning 3 or more years has more than doubled since 1982. In 2009, nearly 40 percent of graduates had 3 or more years of a foreign language.

The proportion of graduates with credits in AP courses has increased as well. AP courses allow students to take college-level courses in high school, and they can earn college credit for the courses if they achieve a minimum score on an AP examination. In 2009, 36.3 percent of public high school graduates had taken an AP course, compared with 26.9 percent in 2000.

College After High School

BLS data show that the proportion of high school graduates who go to college immediately following graduation has trended up, despite dipping slightly in recent years. In October 2015, the proportion of 2015 high school graduates enrolled in college was 69.2 percent, close to the high point of 70.1 percent in October 2009. Although this proportion dipped from 2009 through 2013 (from 70.1 percent to 65.9 percent), it has trended up since. By comparison, less than half of recent high school graduates were enrolled in college in October 1959. As noted earlier, students are less likely to participate in the labor force.

Time Spent on School Activities

The time that teens spend on school-related activities can take away from any hours left in the day for a job. According to the BLS American Time Use Survey (ATUS), participation in educational activities consumes a large amount of time in a young person's day. Educational activities in ATUS include attending class, doing homework and research, and other activities, including related travel. Estimates are available for youth who are ages 15 to 19 years old and enrolled in high school. According to ATUS, enrolled youth who participated in educational activities spent 7.72 hours a day on the activities for the combined years 2010–14. This measure is up slightly from 2003–07, when it was 7.59 hours. Only sleeping, at 8.63 hours in 2003–07 and 8.68 hours in 2010–14, accounted for more time in a 24-hour period than educational activities.

Some high schools require prospective graduates to spend time volunteering to graduate. The CPS has a supplementary survey on volunteering. The data show that the proportion of the 16-to-19-year-old population who volunteer has been a little more than one-quarter of the teenage population. This proportion has moved little since the CPS supplement started in 2002. Teenagers do volunteer at higher rates than several other age groups, including 20-to-24-year-olds. Data from ATUS on time use also indicate that among teens who volunteer, the time spent on volunteering has not risen. According to ATUS, 15-to-19-year-old volunteers enrolled in high school spent 1.65 hours volunteering during school weekdays in 2010–14 versus 2.1 hours in 2003–07. Still, hours spent during the day on volunteering take time from other activities, including working.

Earlier School Start Dates

School terms have become less likely to start after Labor Day. The school starting dates for many school districts have moved earlier into the summer, oftentimes to extend the school year so that students have more time to prepare for standardized tests. For example, schools in Cleveland, Ohio, have moved their starting dates up about 1 week for the past two summers and moved up another week in 2016 to a start date of August 8, 2016. In Texas, many school districts want to change the state law on when school starts (which is currently late August) to allow more time for test preparation and to better balance school days with school breaks. Last school year, just three states (Virginia, Minnesota, and Michigan) had state laws that prohibited schools from starting before Labor Day unless they received a waiver; some school systems, such as those in Hawaii, started at the end of July. With a shorter summer off from school, students may be less inclined to get a summer job, and employers may be less inclined to hire them.

Paying for College

The price of college tuition has continued to rise. The average cost for undergraduate tuition, fees, room, and board for school year 2014–15 (in constant 2014–15 dollars) was nearly $22,000, more than double the amount experienced 30 years earlier. Tuition for both public and private colleges has risen. The average public school tuition was about $16,000 in 2014–15, compared with about $7,600 for the 1984–85 school year. The increase in private (both for-profit and nonprofit) tuition was even greater, from approximately $18,000 to about $37,000 over the same period.

As tuition costs have risen, so has the proportion of students receiving financial aid. During the 2011–12 school year, 84.4 percent of full-time, full-year undergraduates received financial aid (grants, loans, and workstudy), up from 58.2 percent in 1992–93. The proportion receiving grants grew from nearly one-half to close to three-fourths, and the share with loans from about 3 in 10 to almost 6 in 10. In addition, parents are borrowing more, through Parent Plus loans. The average per borrower of a Parent Plus loan for an undergraduate was $11,999 for the 2015–16 school year, up from $3,231 (in constant 2015 dollars) for the 1995–96 school year.

Taxpayers also can take advantage of tax credits or deductions to assist with tuition costs. As of tax year 2009, the American Opportunity Credit replaced the former Hope Scholarship Credit. The American Opportunity Credit is for students in their first 4 years of school who are attending school at least half time. It allows taxpayers to qualify for a credit for education expenses when they file their taxes, up to $2,500 (depending on income). The amount of education tax credits was $17.8 billion in 2014, up from 4.3 billion in 1998 (in 2014 dollars)

Since college is so costly, teen earnings may not make much of a dent in the tuition bill. Moreover, with available financial aid and tax credits, teens still in school may not have to work as much to pay for college. In fact, teens' buying power has declined in recent years. In 2014, median hourly earnings for teens paid hourly rates was $8.43 (in constant 2014 dollars), down from $9.09 in 2002.

Parental Emphasis on School-Related Activities

Anecdotal evidence points toward parents preferring that their children do not work and that they instead use their time for school-related activities. This preference is more apparent among highly educated families and those with the highest incomes according to analyses using CPS and ATUS data. Shirley L. Porterfield and Anne E. Winkler analyzed teen employment rates using CPS data and found that declines in employment from 1995–96 to 2003–04 were greatest for teens in the most educated families. The same study analyzed ATUS data, and results showed that teens in families with the highest incomes spent more time on the "traditional activities" of extracurricular pursuits, plus hobbies, reading, and writing.

Another study of time use data found a large increase in time that parents with college education spend in "childcare," meaning time spent with children. Garey Ramey and Valerie A. Ramey studied time use data from 1965 to 2007 and found that the increase in time spent with children was twice as great for college-educated parents, and the increase was mainly time spent on activities of older children. The authors state, ". . . the increase in time spent in childcare, particularly among the college educated, may be a response to an increase in the perceived return to attending a good college, coupled with an increase in competition in college admissions."

Competition for Jobs

Are teens competing with other workers for jobs? Older workers looking for jobs, perhaps after retiring from their careers;

young, underemployed college graduates; and immigrants are among those who may compete with teens for low-wage jobs. Competition with other workers could affect the labor force participation of all teens, whether enrolled or not.

Older Workers and Young College Graduates

While teens have seen reductions in their labor force participation rates, participation among the 55-and-over age group has been growing. The labor force participation rate for people ages 55 and over surpassed the rate for teens in 2009. By 2015, the participation rate for the older age group was 39.9 percent versus 34.3 percent for teenagers. In 2015, the number of employed people ages 55 and over was about 7 times greater than the number of employed 16-to-19-year-olds. Older people are staying in the labor force longer than ever before. In addition, even though older workers may officially "retire" from their career jobs, many do not officially exit the labor force; instead, they increasingly take on "bridge" jobs, usually part-time or part-year and lower wage jobs.

Data from the CPS show that fewer teens are employed in the occupational groups in which they are concentrated and that greater shares of older workers are employed in these groups, particularly workers ages 55 and over. The three occupational groups that employ the most teenagers are food preparation and serving, sales and related occupations, and office and administrative occupations. Although the share of food preparation employment held by teenagers fell between 2005 and 2015, it grew among those ages 20–24, 25–34, and ages 55 and over. As for sales and related occupations, older people increased their share to more than 1 in 5 workers in 2015, while the share of sales jobs held by teens dropped to 7 percent. In office and administrative support occupations, the only age group to increase in share was the 55-and-older set. In 2015, nearly one-quarter of workers in office and administrative support were ages 55 and up.

Other researchers noted that college graduates may be working in jobs that do not require a college degree, particularly after the most recent recession. Neeta P. Fogg and Paul E. Harrington at the Center for Labor Markets and Policy, Drexel University, noted, "That is, young college graduates increasingly will choose to work in occupations that do not use much of the knowledge, skills, and abilities usually developed by earning a college degree rather than accept the alternative of joblessness." In a study from the Federal Reserve Bank of New York, Jaison R. Abel, Richard Deitz, and Yaqin Su estimated that about 20 percent of young, recent college graduates were employed in low-wage jobs in 2009, such as cashiers or food servers, compared with 15 percent in 1990.

Foreign-Born Workers

Overall, the percentage of the total labor force held by the foreign born was 16.7 percent in 2015, whereas it was 14.8 percent in 2005 (the first year of CPS published foreign-born data). These foreign-born workers may compete directly with teens for the types of jobs teens would typically hold, which would be those with low educational requirements. The educational attainment of foreign-born workers is lower than that of native-born workers. According to the CPS, about one-quarter of the foreign-born labor force ages 25 and over had less than a high school diploma as their highest level of educational attainment in 2015, while that proportion was about 5 percent for the native-born labor force ages 25 and over. An analysis by Christopher L. Smith of the Federal Reserve Board found that immigrant employment has a greater effect on employment of native-born 16-to-17-year-olds than it does on native-adult employment. According to Smith, ". . . a 10-percent increase in the number of immigrants with a high school degree or less is estimated to reduce the average total number of hours worked in a year by 3 to 3 1/2 percent for native teens and by less than 1 percent for less educated adults."

Fewer Teens Not in the Labor Force Actually "Want a Job"

Do those teens who are not in the labor force want to be working? According to the CPS, in 2015, just 8.8 percent of 16-to-19-year-olds not in the labor force wanted a job. In 1994, this proportion was 20.0 percent. It declined to 9.8 percent in 2007 and has ranged from about 9 to 10 percent since then.

What About 2024?

BLS projects declining teen labor force participation in the next decade—the rate is projected to drop from 34.0 percent in 2014 to 26.4 percent in 2024. BLS links the projected decline to increased school enrollment. Overall labor force participation (for all ages) is projected to fall. This projection for the overall rate is partly due to declines among youth, but mainly, it is due to the baby-boom generation moving into the older age groups who have lower labor force participation rates. At the same time, the participation rates for cohorts ages 55 and over are projected to increase over the projection period. In fact, the projected participation rate for the ages 65-to-74 cohort, at 29.9 percent in 2024, is greater than the rate projected for teenagers.

Conclusion

Overall, labor force participation of teens has been declining since 1979, and their low rates of labor force participation continued into the recovery period following the latest recession. In particular, teen participation during the summer has dropped dramatically. School enrollment has increased, especially during the summer months, and enrollment affects the participation of teenagers in the labor force. Along with the increased emphasis toward college, coursework has also become more strenuous in high school. In addition, teens spend much of their time on school activities—only sleeping accounts for more time in a teenager's day. Teens who do want jobs may face competition from others for the types of jobs they typically hold. As for the future, the labor force participation rate for teens is projected to decline further in 2024, according to the latest BLS projections.

Source: Teresa L. Morisi, "Teen Labor Force Participation before and after the Great Recession and Beyond," *Monthly Labor Review,* U.S. Bureau of Labor Statistics, February 2017. https://doi.org/10.21916/mlr.2017.5.

Donald Trump's Executive Order Expanding Apprenticeships (2017)

A few months into the Trump administration in 2017, job vacancies in the United States had reached a record high in spite of high rates of non-employment, due in part to employers' inability to find employees with job-ready skills, particularly in manufacturing. In response, President Trump issued an executive order designed to expand apprenticeship opportunities nationwide with the goal of increasing the number of job-ready candidates. Based on the argument that federal regulations had prevented different industries from creating occupation-specific apprenticeship programs, Trump's executive order shifted the role of developing government-funded apprenticeship programs from the Department of Labor to private entities—such as companies, labor unions, and industry groups. The Department of Labor would still be responsible for approving such programs but would no longer be the sole entity in charge of developing and establishing guidelines for them.

The order also sought to significantly increase the number of apprenticeships available by doubling the amount of money allocated to fund them, presumably by reducing funding to other job-training programs deemed ineffective under the order's increased auditing and program evaluation requirements.

By the authority vested in me as President by the Constitution and the laws of the United States of America, and to promote affordable education and rewarding jobs for American workers, it is hereby ordered as follows:

Section 1. Purpose. America's education systems and workforce development programs are in need of reform. In today's rapidly changing economy, it is more important than ever to prepare workers to fill both existing and newly created jobs and to prepare workers for the jobs of the future. Higher education, however, is becoming increasingly unaffordable. Furthermore, many colleges and universities fail to help students graduate with the skills necessary to secure high paying jobs in today's workforce. Far too many individuals today find themselves with crushing student debt and no direct connection to jobs.

Against this background, federally funded education and workforce development programs are not effectively serving American workers. Despite the billions of taxpayer dollars invested in these programs each year, many Americans are struggling to find full-time work. These Federal programs must do a better job matching unemployed American workers with open jobs, including the 350,000 manufacturing jobs currently available.

Expanding apprenticeships and reforming ineffective education and workforce development programs will help address these issues, enabling more Americans to obtain relevant skills and high-paying jobs. Apprenticeships provide paid, relevant workplace experiences and opportunities to develop skills that employers value. Additionally, they provide affordable paths to good jobs and, ultimately, careers.

Finally, federally funded education and workforce development programs that do not work must be improved or eliminated so that taxpayer dollars can be channeled to more effective uses.

Sec. 2. Policy. It shall be the policy of the Federal Government to provide more affordable pathways to secure, high paying jobs by promoting apprenticeships and effective workforce development programs, while easing the regulatory burden on such programs and reducing or eliminating taxpayer support for ineffective workforce development programs.

Sec. 3. Definitions. For purposes of this order:

(a) the term "apprenticeship" means an arrangement that includes a paid-work component and an educational or instructional component, wherein an individual obtains workplace-relevant knowledge and skills; and

(b) the term "job training programs" means Federal programs designed to promote skills development or workplace readiness and increase the earnings or employability of workers, but does not include Federal student aid or student loan programs.

Sec. 4. Establishing Industry-Recognized Apprenticeships.

(a) The Secretary of Labor (Secretary), in consultation with the Secretaries of Education and Commerce, shall consider proposing regulations, consistent with applicable law, including 29 U.S.C. 50, that promote the development of apprenticeship programs by third parties. These third parties may include trade and industry groups, companies, nonprofit organizations, unions, and joint labor-management organizations. To the extent permitted by law and supported by sound policy, any such proposed regulations shall reflect an assessment of whether to:

(i) determine how qualified third parties may provide recognition to high-quality apprenticeship programs (industry-recognized apprenticeship programs);

(ii) establish guidelines or requirements that qualified third parties should or must follow to ensure that apprenticeship programs they recognize meet quality standards;

(iii) provide that any industry-recognized apprenticeship program may be considered for expedited and streamlined registration under the registered apprenticeship program the Department of Labor administers;

(iv) retain the existing processes for registering apprenticeship programs for employers who continue using this system; and

(v) establish review processes, consistent with applicable law, for considering whether to:

(A) deny the expedited and streamlined registration under the Department of Labor's registered apprenticeship program, referred to in subsection (a)(iii) of this section, in any sector in which Department of Labor registered apprenticeship programs are already effective and substantially widespread; and

(B) terminate the registration of an industry-recognized apprenticeship program recognized by a qualified third party, as appropriate.

(b) The Secretary shall consider and evaluate public comments on any regulations proposed under subsection (a) of this section before issuing any final regulations.

Sec. 5. Funding to Promote Apprenticeships. Subject to available appropriations and consistent with applicable law, including 29 U.S.C. 3224a, the Secretary shall use available funding to promote apprenticeships, focusing in particular on expanding access to and participation in apprenticeships among students at accredited secondary and postsecondary educational institutions, including community colleges; expanding the number of apprenticeships in sectors that do not currently have sufficient apprenticeship opportunities; and expanding youth participation in apprenticeships.

Sec. 6. Expanding Access to Apprenticeships. The Secretaries of Defense, Labor, and Education, and the Attorney General, shall, in consultation with each other and consistent with applicable law, promote apprenticeships and pre apprenticeships for America's high school students and Job Corps participants, for persons currently or formerly incarcerated, for persons not currently attending high school or an accredited postsecondary educational institution, and for members of America's armed services and veterans. The Secretaries of Commerce and Labor shall promote apprenticeships to business leaders across critical industry sectors, including manufacturing, infrastructure, cybersecurity, and health care.

Sec. 7. Promoting Apprenticeship Programs at Colleges and Universities. The Secretary of Education shall, consistent with applicable law, support the efforts of community colleges and 2 year and 4 year institutions of higher education to incorporate apprenticeship programs into their courses of study.

Sec. 8. Establishment of the Task Force on Apprenticeship Expansion.

(a) The Secretary shall establish in the Department of Labor a Task Force on Apprenticeship Expansion.

(b) The mission of the Task Force shall be to identify strategies and proposals to promote apprenticeships, especially in sectors where apprenticeship programs are insufficient. The Task Force shall submit to the President a report on these strategies and proposals, including:

 (i) Federal initiatives to promote apprenticeships;

 (ii) administrative and legislative reforms that would facilitate the formation and success of apprenticeship programs;

(iii) the most effective strategies for creating industry-recognized apprenticeships; and

(iv) the most effective strategies for amplifying and encouraging private-sector initiatives to promote apprenticeships.

(c) The Department of Labor shall provide administrative support and funding for the Task Force, to the extent permitted by law and subject to availability of appropriations.

(d) The Secretary shall serve as Chair of the Task Force. The Secretaries of Education and Commerce shall serve as Vice-Chairs of the Task Force. The Secretary shall appoint the other members of the Task Force, which shall consist of no more than twenty individuals who work for or represent the perspectives of American companies, trade or industry groups, educational institutions, and labor unions, and such other persons as the Secretary may from time to time designate.

(e) Insofar as the Federal Advisory Committee Act, as amended (5 U.S.C. App.), may apply to the Task Force, any functions of the President under that Act, except for those of reporting to the Congress, shall be performed by the Chair, in accordance with guidelines issued by the Administrator of General Services.

(f) Members of the Task Force shall serve without additional compensation for their work on the Task Force, but shall be allowed travel expenses, including per diem in lieu of subsistence, to the extent permitted by law for persons serving intermittently in the Government service (5 U.S.C. 5701–5707), consistent with the availability of funds.

(g) A member of the Task Force may designate a senior member of his or her organization to attend any Task Force meeting.

(h) The Task Force shall terminate 30 days after it submits its report to the President.

Sec. 9. Excellence in Apprenticeships. Not later than 2 years after the date of this order, the Secretary shall, consistent with applicable law, and in consultation with the Secretaries of Education and Commerce, establish an Excellence in Apprenticeship Program to solicit voluntary information for purposes of recognizing, by means of a commendation, efforts by employers, trade or industry associations, unions, or joint labor-management organizations to implement apprenticeship programs.

Sec. 10. Improving the Effectiveness of Workforce Development Programs.

(a) Concurrent with its budget submission to the Director of the Office of Management and Budget (OMB), the head of each agency shall submit a list of programs, if any, administered by their agency that are designed to promote skills development and workplace readiness. For such programs, agencies shall provide information on:

   (i) evaluations of any relevant data pertaining to their effectiveness (including their employment outcomes);

   (ii) recommendations for administrative and legislative reforms that would improve their outcomes and effectiveness for American workers and employers; and

   (iii) recommendations to eliminate those programs that are ineffective, redundant, or unnecessary.

(b) The Director of OMB shall consider the information provided by agencies in subsection (a) of this section in developing the President's Fiscal Year 2019 Budget.

(c) The head of each agency administering one or more job training programs shall order, subject to available appropriations and consistent with applicable law, an empirically rigorous evaluation of the effectiveness of such programs, unless such an analysis has been recently conducted. When feasible, these evaluations shall be conducted by third party evaluators using the most rigorous methods appropriate and feasible for the program, with preference given to multi-site randomized controlled trials.

(d) The Director of OMB shall provide guidance to agencies on how to fulfill their obligations under this section.

Sec. 11. General Provisions.

(a) Nothing in this order shall be construed to impair or otherwise affect:

   (i) the authority granted by law to an executive department or agency, or the head thereof; or

   (ii) the functions of the Director of OMB relating to budgetary, administrative, or legislative proposals.

(b) This order shall be implemented consistent with applicable law and subject to the availability of appropriations.

(c) This order is not intended to, and does not, create any right or benefit, substantive or procedural, enforceable at law or in equity by any party against the United States, its departments, agencies, or entities, its officers, employees, or agents, or any other person.

Source: Donald J. Trump, "Presidential Executive Order Expanding Apprenticeships in America," June 15, 2017. The Whitehouse. https://www.whitehouse.gov/presidential-actions/3245/.

NOW HIRING
FULL TIME & PART TIME POSITIONS

Apply Online at
www.lowes.com/
careers

Scarborough, ME
Store 2407
207-883-1309

LIKE TO WEAR
A SMILE?

Rewarding Opportunities Will Include:
Drivers, Cashiers, Product Handlers, Customer Service Associates
Part Time & Full Time Benefits!

LOWE'S NEVER STOP IMPROVING

Lowe's is an Equal Opportunity Employer committed to diversity and inclusion. Lowe's maintains a drug-free workplace.

DOLLA

Karen

Spectrum
Heather Devereaux
Recruiter

people ready
A TRUEBLUE COMPANY
Anne Ballard
Market Recruiter
74 Elm Street
Portland, ME 04101
207.774.1500 | 207.245.4859 | 207.774.1061
aballard@peopleready.com
PeopleReady.com

five BELOW
just go!
198 maine mall rd
south portland, me 04106

home office 215-546-7909
fax 215-546-8099
www.fivebelow.com

LOWE'S
1000 Gallery Blvd
Scarborough, ME 04074
Phone 207-883-1309
Fax 207-883-1310
mary.l.brockman@store.lowes.com
Mary Brockman - Support Manager

Resi
Residence
Inn
Marriott

★ macy's
Customer engagement and selling skills are top priorities at Macy's,
and I think that you have what it takes to be a part of our team.

Discover the magic online at www.macysJOBS.com

MANAGER'S NAME & PHONE NUMBER

Macy's is an equal opportunity employer,
committed to a diverse and inclusive work environment.

Join our growing team

Spectrum
Our Missi...

grow with us.
careers.burlingtoncoatfactory.com

I like to
BRAG ABOUT
where I work...

Hannaford

Susan Graves
HR & Hiring Manager
Scarborough Hannaford

work somewhere
work somewhere you ♥

Introduction

This chapter provides an annotated list of selected books, articles, and reports on a variety of topics related to youth employment and unemployment, which offers readers a starting point for further research. A few nonprint sources are listed and annotated as well.

Books

Alsop, Ron. 2008. *The Trophy Kids Grow Up: How the Millennial Generation Is Shaking Up the Workplace.* San Francisco: Jossey-Bass.

Ron Alsop, a former writer and editor at the *Wall Street Journal*, observes that as the first wave of millennials—those born between 1980 and 2001—enter the workforce, they present new challenges and opportunities for employers. Compared to previous generations, millennials have drastically different expectations, skills, and attitudes in the workplace. Through surveys and interviews with millennials, their parents, admissions counselors,

Business cards from local companies looking to hire employees from the recently closed Toys R' Us store in South Portland on March 22, 2018. Companies often prefer to hire workers with previous work experience and a demonstrated record of reliability. (Derek Davis/Portland Press Herald via Getty Images)

and recruiters, Alsop seeks to provide colleges, companies, and other organizations with the information they need to recruit millennials and to capitalize on their strengths, while managing their weaknesses.

Anders, George. 2017. *You Can Do Anything: The Surprising Power of a "Useless" Liberal Arts Education*. New York: Little, Brown and Company.

In contrast to the commonly promulgated claim that science and engineering degrees are most likely to lead to a successful postgraduate career, George Anders makes the case for the utility of a liberal arts education in our rapidly evolving high-tech economy. According to Anders, students of the liberal arts develop valuable soft skills—including judgment, curiosity, creativity, and empathy—that can open the door to thousands of cutting-edge jobs.

The book is a valuable resource for anyone considering how a liberal arts education can be used to meet society's needs.

Arum, Richard, and Joseph Roksa. 2014. *Aspiring Adults Adrift: Tentative Transitions of College Graduates*. Chicago: University of Chicago Press.

In a follow-up to their landmark study of how undergraduate education fails to result in significant learning, Richard Arum and Joseph Roksa examine the relationship between college experience and the transition between graduation and adulthood. Through a series of interviews and surveys of more than 2,000 current students and recent graduates from a diverse range of colleges and universities, Arum and Roksa reveal the difficulties recent graduates—including those with high GPAs from prestigious schools—face as they attempt to transition into successful adulthood. Although remarkably optimistic about their future prospects, recent graduates report high levels of difficulty in finding employment, becoming financially independent, assuming civic responsibility, and developing stable long-term relationships. Through an examination of how college experiences and academic performance coincide with graduates' ability to successfully transition into adulthood, Arum and Roksa encourage readers to re-examine the contemporary aims and approaches of institutions of higher learning. They conclude that colleges could improve student outcomes by paying more attention to improving academic rigor and promoting critical thinking, complex reasoning, and writing skills.

Anderson, Elijah, ed. 2008. *Against the Wall: Poor, Young, Black, and Male*. Philadelphia: University of Pennsylvania Press.
This edited collection of essays addresses the alienation and marginalization experienced by many urban, young black males, who are frequently trapped in a cycle of discrimination, unemployment, violence, crime, and incarceration. Several essays focus specifically on the joblessness and economic plight of inner-city black males and provide suggestions for how to re-engage urban youth through programs such as youth entrepreneurship training.

Besharov, Douglas A., ed. 1999. *America's Disconnected Youth: Toward a Preventative Strategy*. Washington, DC: Child Welfare League of America and American Enterprise Institute.
The essays in this collection provide an in-depth examination of some of the reasons why large numbers of youth fail to transition from adolescence into productive adulthood. They also explore the importance of strategies, such as mentoring and school-to-work programs, which serve as effective preventative means of assisting vulnerable youth before they become disconnected.

Coates, Ken S., and Bill Morrison. 2016. *Dream Factories: Why the Universities Won't Solve the Youth Jobs Crisis.* Toronto: TAP Books.

> While university enrollment numbers continue to increase, more and more graduates are failing to find good jobs, based on their college major or acquired skill set. In contrast to prominent politicians, who emphasize the importance of increasing access to college education, Ken Coates and Bill Morrison challenge what they call the *Learning = Earning* formula (the idea that the number of years spent in postsecondary education correspondingly increases the guarantee of a higher income or long-term career success). Instead, they argue that, in a world of rapid technological change, the traditional university setting is producing graduates with the wrong skills and is therefore contributing to the problem of youth unemployment.

Eberstadt, Nicholas. 2016. *America's Invisible Crisis: Men without Work.* West Conshohocken, PA: Templeton Press.

> Nicholas Eberstadt, a political economist at the American Enterprise Institute, draws attention to a growing crisis lurking below the surface of positive employment numbers. Although overall employment rates continue to improve following recovery from the Great Recession, Eberstadt points out that the workforce participation rate among men of prime-working age (25 to 54) has been on a path of decline for the past half century and has now reached Depression-era levels. One in six men of prime-working age is without work and one in eight has stopped looking for work altogether. This widespread detachment from the workforce, Eberstadt warns, will have significant, long-term negative economic, social, and political consequences.
>
> The largely invisible socioeconomic crisis plaguing American men is similar to the employment crisis of

America's youth, who are likewise increasingly living lives alienated from civil society.

Edelman, Peter, Harry Holzer, and Paul Offner. 2006. *Reconnecting Disadvantaged Young Men*. Washington, DC: Urban Institute Press. The authors of this study maintain that while the trends for less-educated young women in school enrollment and employment have been relatively positive, this has not been the case for young men—particularly African American, Hispanic, and low-income young men. The authors thus analyze the growing crisis of youth disconnectedness, particularly among low-income urban young men, and offer clear policy prescriptions for improving the educational and employment opportunities available to them. The authors argue that a full strategy to combat youth disconnectedness would include systemic attention to the children's well-being from the time they are conceived, but here they focus on a few policy areas that they believe will contribute to lasting change: enhancing education and training through broad community initiatives, increasing financial incentives to work, and removing barriers for young offenders and noncustodial parents.

Furchtgott-Roth, Diana, and Jared Meyer. 2015. *Disinherited: How Washington Is Betraying America's Youth*. New York: Encounter Books.
As members of the millennial generation enter the workforce, they will have a harder time succeeding than those born in previous generations. Diana Furchtgott-Roth and Jared Meyer argue that this is not due to inherent character flaws in millennials themselves, rather it is the result of ballooning entitlement spending, ineffective education systems, and workplace constraints imposed by Washington policy makers. Furchtgott-Roth and Meyer, thus, call for political change to ensure that young people have the opportunity to achieve the future they deserve.

Holzer, Harry J., and Sandy Baum. 2017. *Making College Work: Pathways to Success for Disadvantaged Students.* Washington, DC: Brookings Institution Press.

    In this practical manual for improving higher education outcomes for disadvantaged students, Harry Holzer and Sandy Baum draw attention to the problem that many low-income and minority college students in America experience low completion rates, while others concentrate in fields with low labor market value. As a result, they lose valuable time, while not measurably improving their employment prospects. Meanwhile, many of these students struggle to pay for their schooling and those who do not complete their degree or are unable to find remunerative employment acquire debts that they will have a hard time repaying. In response, Holzer and Baum review the causes of poor college outcomes for disadvantaged students and offer suggestions for how to reform postsecondary education and create stronger connections between education and the labor market as early as high school.

Peck, Don. 2011. *Pinched: How the Great Recession Has Narrowed Our Futures and What We Can Do about It.* New York: Crown Publishers.

    In spite of continued recovery from the economic crises caused by the Great Recession, Don Peck argues that the Great Recession is likely to have an enduring and transformative effect on the character of American society. In the fourth chapter, he specifically focuses on future ramifications of the recession on youth and concludes that many millennials will emerge from the recession "with their earning power permanently reduced, their confidence dimmed, and their ideals profoundly challenged" (11).

Putnam, Robert D. 2016. *Our Kids: The American Dream in Crisis.* New York: Simon and Schuster.

    Robert D. Putnam, a professor of public policy at Harvard, explores the disturbing trend of a growing class-based opportunity gap among America's youth. He provides evidence that youth born into poverty-stricken backgrounds today are far less likely than their counterparts in previous generations to experience upward mobility. In fact, Putnam demonstrates that although gender and racial bias are less of a barrier to upward mobility in modern America than they were in the 1950s, class origin has become a greater barrier. He explores how changes in neighborhoods, education, family structure, parenting styles, community, and religion have contributed to diminished opportunities for America's poverty-stricken youth.

Selingo, Jeffrey J. 2016. *There Is Life after College: What Parents and Students Should Know about Navigating School to Prepare for the Jobs of Tomorrow*. New York: Harper Collins.

In this practical guide for prospective college students and their parents, journalist and former editor for *The Chronicle of Higher Education*, Jeffrey Selingo highlights how changes in training and hiring have left many questioning whether the time and money they have invested in a college degree was useful for preparing them for the world of work. Today, employers provide less on-the-job training and expect experienced workers capable of doing the job from day one. While employers sometimes require a degree as a screening device for applicants, Selingo maintains that rarely do college courses help develop the skills employers are looking for. In response, Selingo discusses the skills today's employers are seeking and offers advice for how prospective students and young jobseekers can better utilize the years leading up to, during, and directly following college to jumpstart their career and prepare themselves for productive employment following graduation. His suggestions include choosing the right colleges in the right locations, taking a gap year prior to college in order to acquire real-world work experience, registering for the right courses, and participating in internships.

Sullivan, Mercer. 1989. *"Getting Paid": Youth Crime and Work in the Inner City.* Ithaca, NY: Cornell University Press.

A dated, but still relevant, study of the attitudes and behaviors of inner-city youth who engage in crime and the common social factors affecting those who have been able to move from a lifestyle of youth crime into one of legitimate work.

Twenge, Jean. 2006. *Generation Me.* Revised and updated edition. New York: Free Press.

In this revised and expanded edition of a previous work, psychologist Dr. Jean Twenge uses data from dozens of studies with over 11 million respondents to examine the unique characteristics of the generation of young people born in the 1980s and 1990s, whom she collectively terms "Generation Me." According to Twenge, young people belonging to this generation are more tolerant, confident, and ambitious, but they are also more disengaged, narcissistic, and anxious.

In Chapter 8 of the book, titled "Generation Me at Work," Twenge reflects on how the typical attitudes and traits of "Generation Me" employees impact the workplace. She gives advice for "Generation Me" employees seeking employment or promotion and for employers seeking to recruit, retain, and motivate them.

Vogel, Peter Michael. 2015. *Generation Jobless? Turning the Youth Unemployment Crisis into Opportunity.* New York: Palgrave Macmillan.

Peter Vogel, an entrepreneur and researcher, examines the characteristics of today's youth and the underlying causes of youth unemployment. He then explores existing opportunities and argues that in a digital world of rapid technological change, it is becoming increasingly possible for young people to make their own work through the establishment of new business ventures. He highlights importance of turning job seekers into job creators and maintains that parents, educators, industry leaders, and society as a whole have a duty to help young people develop the skills and mind-set necessary to become a successful entrepreneur.

Wyman, Nicholas. 2015. *Job U: How to Find Wealth and Success by Developing the Skills Companies Actually Need.* New York: Crown Business.

Although the youth unemployment rate in the United States remains high, millions of jobs go unfilled every year because companies can't find employees whose skills match their needs. In this handbook for individuals in search of a career, Nicholas Wyman explores how alternatives to traditional education—such as professional certification courses, associates degrees, apprenticeships, and occupational learning—can help bridge the skills gap and lead young people into rewarding occupations.

Articles and Reports

Abel, Jaison R., Richard Dietz, and Yaqin Su. 2014. "Are Recent College Graduates Finding Good Jobs?" *Current Issues in Economics and Finance*, 20(1): 1–8. Federal Reserve Bank of New York. https://www.newyorkfed.org/medialibrary/media/research/current_issues/ci20-1.pdf.

The authors of this Federal Reserve report analyze more than two decades of data to determine the degree to which recent college graduates are having trouble finding jobs suited to their level of education in comparison to earlier periods. The authors determine that fairly high unemployment and underemployment rates were common for recent graduates even prior to the Great Recession, in large part due to the time required for graduates to transition into the labor market. They did, however, find that the quality of jobs held by recent underemployed graduates had deteriorated and that post-recession graduates were more likely to be working in low-wage or part-time jobs than graduates of earlier periods. In comparing the outcomes based on college major, however, the authors found that unemployment and underemployment rates vary based on major and that students majoring in engineering or math or growing fields such as education and health have better labor market outcomes than their peers in other majors.

Aguiar, Mark, Mark Bils, Kerwin Kofi Charles, and Erik Hurst. 2017. *Leisure Luxuries and the Labor Supply of Young Men.* Cambridge, MA: National Bureau of Economic Research. http://www.nber.org/papers/w23552.

A study by the National Bureau of Economic Research revealing that the percentage of young men, aged 21 to 30, not working has increased since 2000 and that such young men are increasingly living with their parents and allocating a greater amount of their free time to playing video games and other computer-related activities.

Allison, Tom. 2017. *Financial Health of Young America: Measuring Generational Declines between Baby Boomers and Millennials.* Washington, DC: Young Invincibles. http://younginvincibles.org/wp-content/uploads/2017/04/FHYA-Final2017-1-1.pdf.

This report is the first in a series examining the financial challenges facing millennials—the most educated, most diverse, and most indebted generation in America's history. In this first installation that focuses on the financial security of millennials compared to their parents, Tom Allison presents new evidence that the current generation of workers earn lower incomes, have a lower net worth, and are less likely to own a home than their parents at the same stage of life. Allison concludes by making high priority recommendations for policy makers.

Belfield, Clive R., Henry M. Levin, and Rachel Rosen. 2012. *The Economic Value of Opportunity Youth*. Washington, DC: Civic Enterprises. http://www.civicenterprises.net/MediaLibrary/Docs/econ_value_opportunity_youth.pdf.

> The authors of this report analyze the size, demographics, and common activities of the cohort termed "opportunity youth"—youth who are not developing into productive, independent adults because they are neither accumulating human capital through education or accumulating labor market skills by working. The authors then calculate the immediate and long-term fiscal and social costs associated "opportunity youth" both for the youths themselves and for society as a whole. They advocate cost-effective, targeted investments to help "opportunity youth" become productive members of society—such as investment in educational and training programs that are well-integrated with transitions into the labor market.

Boteach, Melissa, Joy Moses, and Shirley Sagawa. 2009. *National Service and Youth Unemployment*. Washington, DC: Center for American Progress. https://cdn.americanprogress.org/wp-content/uploads/issues/2009/11/pdf/nation_service.pdf.

> The authors of this policy memo advocate increased federal investment in National Service programs—such as YouthBuild, AmeriCorps, Volunteers in Service to America (VISTA)—as part of a broad strategy to reduce youth unemployment and poverty by preparing low income youth for long-term employment in the public and private sector.

Burd-Sharps, Sarah, and Kirsten Lewis. 2012. *One in Seven: Ranking Youth Disconnection in the 25 Largest Metro Areas*. Brooklyn, NY: Measure of America, of the Social Science

Research Council Measure of America. http://ssrc-static
.s3.amazonaws.com/moa/MOA-One_in_Seven09-14.pdf.

This paper ranks the 25 most populous metropolitan
areas in terms of youth disconnection and the disconnection rates based on gender, race, and ethnicity within
those areas. The paper explores the risk factors and
consequences of disconnection and concludes with an
analysis of strategies and programs for helping vulnerable youth successfully transition into adulthood and
employment.

Burd-Sharps, Sarah, and Kirsten Lewis. 2017. *Promising Gains,
Persistent Gaps: Youth Disconnection in America*. Brooklyn, NY:
Measure of America, of the Social Science Research Council.
https://ssrc-static.s3.amazonaws.com/moa/Promising%20
Gains%20Final.pdf.

The authors of this report celebrate the five-year decline
in youth disconnection from the peak of 14.7 percent
in 2010 to 12.3 percent in 2015. They emphasize, however, that nearly 4.9 million youth remain detached from
school and the workforce. Moreover, those who remain
disconnected—following the nationwide decline in
unemployment resulting from the economic recovery—
are more likely to have higher barriers to reconnection.
These barriers are more likely to exist for certain groups of
young adults. Thus, the numbers demonstrating an overall reduction in youth disconnection mask the great variation of that decline in terms of demographic groups and
geographic regions.

The report examines the youth disconnection data in
terms of race, ethnicity, gender, and geographic location.
It also compares the different rates and characteristics of
disconnection in rural suburban, and urban communities
in an effort to understand the particular challenges different groups of disconnected youth face, where they live,
and what kind of support they require to make successful
transitions to adulthood.

Cooper, Preston. August 9, 2016. *Reforming the U.S. Minimum-Wage.* New York: Manhattan Institute. https://www
.manhattan-institute.org/html/reforming-us-youth-minimum-
wage-9134.html.

> Preston Cooper, a policy analyst at the Manhattan Institute, responds to those advocating for minimum-wage increases by presenting evidence that such policies will only worsen the already high rates of teen unemployment. Cooper alternatively makes the case for a lower "youth minimum-wage" or YMW, which he contends would contribute to the creation of a substantial number of new jobs for young workers. Cooper highlights the fact that the federal government has already adopted a YMW under which workers up to the age of 20 may earn a wage of $4.25 an hour for their first 90 days on the job on the grounds that a YMW will incentivize employers to hire young people who lack experience and relevant skill. The federal YMW has had a minimal effect, however, both because it only applies to a teen's first 90 days on the job and because many states have failed to adopt a YMW in their state labor code, which means that the adult minimum-wage imposed by the states applies across the board. Cooper contends that if all 50 states and the federal government adopted a YMW with no 90-day limit for individuals aged 16 to 19, the teen employment rate would improve by nearly 9 percent and employers would generate almost half a million jobs in the first year following enactment.

Fernandes-Alcantara, Adrienne L. 2012a. *Youth and the Labor Force: Background and Trends.* Washington, DC: Congressional Research Service.

> In this report, compiled for policy makers in Congress, Adrienne Fernandes-Alacantara provides a context for youth employment prospects in the wake of the Great Recession. Beginning with the post–World War II period, but focusing specifically on trends since 2000,

Fernandes-Alacantara provides data on youth employment and analyzes factors affecting youth participation in
the workforce.

Fernandes-Alcantara, Adrienne L. 2012b. *Vulnerable Youth:
Employment and Job Training Programs.* Washington, DC:
Congressional Research Service.
    Adrienne Fernandes-Alcantara, a specialist in social
    policy, highlights the increasing concern among policy
    makers that young people, particularly among vulner-
    able populations, may lack the educational attainment
    and employment experience to become highly skilled
    workers, contributing taxpayers, and successful par-
    ticipants in civic life. In this report, she provides an
    overview of the current challenges in preparing youth
    for the workforce and a history of federal efforts to
    connect at-risk youth to education and employment
    pathways. She specifically details and compares four
    programs authorized by the Workforce Investment
    Act of 1998 and administered by the Department of
    Labor's Employment and Training Administration:
    Youth Activities, Job Corps, YouthBuild, and Reentry
    Employment Opportunities.

Fernandes-Alcantara, Adrienne L., and Thomas Gabe. 2015.
*Disconnected Youth: A Look at 16 to 24 Year Olds Who Are Not
Working or in School.* Washington, DC: Congressional Research
Service. https://fas.org/sgp/crs/misc/R40535.pdf.
    This report was compiled in response to growing congres-
    sional interest in enacting policies to assist youth who are
    not working or in school. The authors provide an overview
    of the research on disconnected youth, identify common
    causes and characteristics of disconnection, and discuss
    implications of the research for developing an effective
    policy response.

Fischer, Karin. March 4, 2013. "The Employment Mismatch." *The Chronicle of Higher Education.* https://www.chronicle .com/article/The-Employment-Mismatch/137625.

This article summarizes the results of a survey based on responses from over 700 employers conducted by *The Chronicle of Higher Education* and America's Public Media *Marketplace.* The survey asked employers a series of questions pertaining to their perception of how well colleges and universities were preparing their graduates for the workplace, what skills the college graduates should possess, what types of institutions and credentials are most desired, which majors are the most useful, and so on. Although most of the employers surveyed require applicants to possess a college degree—viewing it as an indicator that an individual can work towards achieving a goal—half of those surveyed reported trouble finding qualified graduates. A third of those surveyed lamented that a large percentage of bachelor's-degree holders lack basic workplace proficiencies, such as adaptability, written and oral communication skills, and the ability to problem solve, make decisions, analyze data, and construct cogent arguments. Although college major was mentioned as the most important academic credential in evaluating a recent graduate for employment, employers additionally testified that they give more weight to the applicant's previous work experience, including internships and employment, than to their academic credentials including their GPA and college major.

Furchtgott-Roth, Diana. 2012. *The Unemployment Crisis for Younger Workers.* New York: Manhattan Institute. https://www .manhattan-institute.org/html/unemployment-crisis-younger- workers-5740.html

Economist Diana Furchtgott-Roth highlights Congress's various attempts to insulate older workers from the effects of the Great Recession. She argues that this concern for older workers is somewhat misplaced because, in actuality, the unemployment losses and other negative effects of the recession have fallen disproportionately on younger workers, whose labor force participation rate continued to decline even as overall employment numbers improved. Furthermore, in terms of net worth, older generations of Americans are better off than their predecessors, whereas younger Americans are worse off than their parents' generation.

Furchtgott-Roth contends that efforts to combat unemployment through increased employment regulation—such as a proposal to make it easier for the unemployed to sue employers for discrimination—would actually make the problem worse by raising the cost of hiring in America. She, instead, proposes a series of alternative policies that she maintains will encourage domestic job creation and help improve the employment prospects for American workers of all ages.

Gallup, Inc. 2018. *The State of Opportunity in America*. Washington, DC: Center for Advancing Opportunity. http://www.advancingopportunity.org/wp-content/uploads/2018/01/The-State-of-Opportunity-in-America-Report-Center-for-Advancing-Opportunity.pdf.

This report is based on the initial phases of a project to understand the perceived barriers to opportunity in fragile communities—areas in which a high percentage of residents experience daily financial struggles and have limited opportunity for social mobility—with the goal of serving such communities through evidence-based solutions. The report identifies three interrelated factors that create a barrier to social mobility in fragile communities: low education levels, lack of employment opportunities, and high crime rates.

Gelber, Alexander, Adam Isen, and Judd B. Kessler. 2016. "The Effects of Youth Employment: Evidence from New York City Lotteries." *The Quarterly Journal of Economics*, 131: 423–460. doi:10.1093/qje/qjv034.

Across the United States, a large number of cities sponsor programs that provide youth with summer jobs. These programs are supported by the federal Work Opportunity Tax Credit, which subsidizes the employment of summer youth employees. The authors of this report study randomized lotteries for access to the New York City Summer Youth Employment Program (NYC SYEP), the largest summer youth employment program in the United States, to determine the degree to which summer youth employment programs improve future employment and educational outcomes and reduce risky or delinquent behavior among participants. The authors found that the program had little impact on the future earning, employment prospects, and college enrollment rates of participants. Nevertheless, the program did achieve the goal of reducing risky or delinquent behavior. Participants had significantly lower rates of incarceration and mortality than applicants who did not win access to the program through the city lottery.

Harrington, Paul, and Ishwar Khatiwada. 2016. *U.S. Teens Want to Work*. Federal Reserve Bank of Boston. https://www.bostonfed.org/publications/communities-and-banking/2016/spring/us-teens-want-to-work.aspx.

Paul Harrington and Ishwar Khatiwada, economists at Drexel University, challenge the conventional wisdom that an aging population leaving the workforce has led to the decline in the nation's overall employment rate. On the contrary, they point out that the economic turbulence that has characterized the U.S. economy since 2000 is historically unique in that it has most significantly impacted the employment prospects of teens (aged 16 to 19). Furthermore, in spite of improvements in the labor market since 2011, teens are continuing to experience extraordinary difficulty finding part-time work during the school year and full-time work during the summer. The authors conclude that evidence of underutilization among teens—measured by unemployment, hidden unemployment, and underemployment—reveals that the drop in teen employment does not stem from a lower desire among teens to work, but rather from a deterioration in their ability to find work.

Houle, Jason N., and Cody Warner. 2017. "Into the Red and Back to the Nest? Student Debt, College Completion and Returning to the Parental Home among Young Adults." *Sociology of Education*, 90(1): 89–108.

In response to growing concern that rising levels of student debt are delaying the transition to adulthood for a large percentage of American youth, sociologists Jason Houle and Cody Warner examine the claim that student debt is leading to a rise in students who "boomerang" or return to their parents' home after they have initially left. Houle and Warner discovered that among those who acquire student debt, those with lower levels of debt have a significantly higher risk of returning home than those with higher levels of debt. The reason for this seeming anomaly is that those with lower levels of student debt are more likely to have attended nonselective colleges or to have failed to complete their degree. Thus, degree completion is a stronger predictor than acquiring student loans of whether students will return home. Those who fail to complete their degree have a higher risk of "boomeranging." Individuals carrying student debt, without the economic benefits of a degree, are more vulnerable to a variety of socioeconomic ills and face greater challenges in their attempt to transition in to self-sufficient adulthood.

Jones, Janelle, and John Schmitt. 2014. *A College Degree Is No Guarantee*. Washington, DC: Center for Economic and Policy Research. http://cepr.net/documents/black-coll-grads-2014-05.pdf.
This report examines the labor-market experience of blacks who graduated college during and directly after the Great Recession. The authors conclude that while a college degree blunts the disproportionate negative effect of the economic downturn on young workers and ongoing racial discrimination in the labor market, it is not a guarantee of protection against either. Black graduates consistently have higher unemployment and underemployment rates than their white counterparts. The authors conclude that this fact reinforces concerns that racial discrimination remains an important factor in the contemporary labor market and that economic solutions to black youth unemployment focused solely on improving skills and education of the workforce may be inadequate.

Kalenkoski, Charlene Marie. 2016. *The Effects of Minimum-Wages on Youth Employment and Income*. Texas Tech University: IZA World of Labor. https://wol.iza.org/uploads/articles/243/pdfs/effects-of-minimum-wages-on-youth-employment-and-income.pdf?v=1.
In this report written for the IZA World of Labor project, finance professor Charlene M. Kalenkoski summarizes empirical evidence from a substantial body of research demonstrating that minimum-wages reduce employment among young, unskilled workers. Kalenkoski, hence, maintains that minimum-wage increases are not an effective way to improve the labor market situation of unskilled youth. While some working youth will benefit from higher minimum-wages in the form of a temporary increase to their current earnings, higher minimum-wages have the overall effect of reducing employment opportunities for unskilled youth, consequently, reducing their

lifetime earnings. Kalenkoski advises policy makers to implement policies that improve labor market opportunities for unskilled youth without increasing the cost to employers of hiring such workers.

Kroger, Teresa, and Elise Gould. 2017. *The Class of 2017.* Washington, DC: Economic Policy Institute. http://www .epi.org/publication/the-class-of-2017/.

Teresa Kroger and Elise Gould analyze the employment and wage trends of recent high school graduates (aged 17 to 20) and college graduates (aged 21 to 24) who are not enrolled in further schooling. Kroger and Gould observe that although youth unemployment levels have largely returned to their pre-recession levels, the economy directly preceding the recession was not a good baseline for determining economic opportunity. The graduating class of 2017 may have better prospects than the class of 2009–2016, but they still face greater economic challenges and higher levels of unemployment, underemployment, and disconnection than those who graduated into the labor market of 2000.

Kroger and Gould conclude their study by proposing a series of regulatory and redistributive measures that they argue would help spur employment and wage growth, including higher minimum-wage mandates, policies that strengthen collective bargaining rights, increased sick leave and paid family leave.

Lerman, Robert I. 2010. *Expanding Apprenticeship: A Way to Enhance Skills and Careers.* Washington, DC: The Urban Institute. https://www.urban.org/sites/default/files/publication/29691/ 901384-Expanding-Apprenticeship-A-Way-to-Enhance-Skills-and-Careers.PDF.

In this policy brief, economist Robert Lerman outlines the nature and scope of current apprenticeship opportunities in the United States and advocates expanding the scale of such training. He demonstrates that apprenticeships have proven more effective in smoothing the transition from school to work than school-based preparation programs alone, and that apprenticeships are particularly useful for integrating minorities, especially minority men, into rewarding careers.

While policy makers tend to view community colleges, for-profit career colleges, and apprenticeships as separate approaches to improving youth employment prospects. Lerman maintains that the in-class instruction at community or career colleges can serve as a valuable complement to the work-based instruction of apprenticeships and that joint initiatives between the various systems will better bridge the gap between skills learned and skills needed. He, thus, recommends public support for programs that promote a direct link between course-based learning and on-the-job apprenticeship training.

Manyika, James, et al. 2013. *Disruptive Technologies: Advances That Will Transform Life, Business, and the Global Economy.* McKinsey Global Institute. https://www .mckinsey.com/~/media/McKinsey/Business%20Functions/ McKinsey%20Digital/Our%20Insights/Disruptive%20 technologies/MGI_Disruptive_technologies_Full_report_ May2013.ashx.

In this report, McKinsey Global Institute director James Manyika and several fellow researchers examine the potential impact of 12 emerging technologies on the way we live and work. Manyika et al. maintain that these technologies—among which are advanced robotics, the mobile Internet, autonomous vehicles, 3D printing, and renewable energy—have tremendous potential benefit for society. They will likely lead to better products, lower prices, a cleaner environment, and better health. At the same time, however, these emerging technologies present tremendous consequences. Manyika et al. contend that if governmental and business leaders are not proactive in preparing to adapt the changes caused by evolving technology, they will be unable to capture the benefits or adequately respond to the consequences. They call in particular for innovative education and training programs to minimize the negative impact that these technologies will have on the future of employment.

Mroz, Thomas A., and Timothy H. Savage. 2006. "The Long Term Effects of Youth Unemployment." *The Journal of Human Resources*, 41(2): 259–293. http://jhr.uwpress.org/content/XLI/2/259.

In this study, economists Thomas Mroz and Timothy Savage analyze policy-relevant effects of youth unemployment on labor market outcomes. They find that young men who experience early bouts of involuntary unemployment are more likely to engage in short-term human capital development such as work-related training to mitigate possible setbacks. Despite this catch up response to unemployment, however, unemployment experienced early in a youth's employment cycle has a long-term negative impact on earnings that can last up to ten years.

Oreopolous, Philip, Till Von Wachter, and Andrew Heisz. 2013. "Short- and Long-Term Career Effects of Graduating in a Recession." *American Economic Journal: Applied Economics*, 4(1): 1–29. http://www.nber.org/papers/w12159.pdf.

The authors of this study track the earnings, employers, and career outcomes of a large sample of Canadian graduates who left college and entered the labor market during a recession compared to those who graduated during an economic boom. They found that downturns in the labor market affect some graduates more than others. Graduates who have previous labor market experience or who graduate from more prestigious schools and academic programs face persistent, but not permanent, earning losses. On the other hand, college graduates at the bottom of the wage and ability distribution experience larger and more persistent losses in annual earnings and are more liable to be permanently down-ranked to lower wage firms. The study, thus, suggests a large degree of heterogeneity in the costs of recessions.

O'Sullivan, Rory, Konrad Mugglestone, and Tom Allison. 2014. *In This Together: The Hidden Cost of Young Adult Unemployment.* Washington, DC: Young Invincibles. http://younginvincibles.org/wp-content/uploads/2017/04/In-This-Together-The-Hidden-Cost-of-Young-Adult-Unemployment .pdf.

The authors of this report compare the historic impact the Great Recession and sluggish economic recovery had on young people's employment prospects in comparison with previous economic downturns. They warn that the missed work opportunities caused by the Great Recession will lead to dismal economic outcomes for America's youth in terms of future employment, wages, and productivity. Furthermore, historic levels of youth unemployment will eventually affect not only the individuals who are directly suffering from bouts of unemployment but also the nation as a whole in terms of lower tax revenue and higher safety net expenditures for federal and state governments. The authors conclude with several policy recommendations including the expansion of the Department of Labor's Registered Apprenticeship program and of paid service programs such as AmeriCorps.

Pager, Devah, Bruce Western, and Naomi Sugie. 2009. "Sequencing Disadvantage: Barriers to Employment Facing Young Black and White Men with Criminal Records." *The Annals of the American Academy of Political and Social*

Science, 623: 195–213. https://www.ncbi.nlm.nih.gov/pmc/articles/PMC3583356/pdf/nihms-439026.pdf.

The authors of this study, sociologists at Princeton and Harvard, report results from a large-scale field experiment tracking the effects of race and prison record on employment. The experiment consisted in teams of black and white men who were sent to apply for low-wage jobs throughout New York City. Participants were furnished with equivalent resumes and differed only in their race and criminal background. The experiment revealed that while employers exhibited a strong reluctance to hire applicants with criminal records, especially black ex-offenders, the employment prospects of ex-offender applicants improve significantly if they are able to interact with hiring manager. Personal contact can help alleviate fears a prospective hiring manager might have concerning the worker reliability and performance of ex-offenders. Unfortunately, however, black ex-offenders were much less likely to be invited to interview, giving them fewer opportunities to establish the good rapport with a prospective employer necessary to combat negative stereotypes.

Ross, Martha, and Nicole Prchal Svajlenka. 2016. "Employment and Disconnection among Teens and Young Adults: The Role of Place, Race, and Education." Washington, DC: Brookings Institution. https://www.brookings.edu/research/employment-and-disconnection-among-teens-and-young-adults-the-role-of-place-race-and-education/.

This report examines disparities of employment and unemployment among teens and young adults compared to prime working age adults based on age, race, educational attainment, and geographic location. The report also analyzes the demographics of disconnected teens and young adults who live below the poverty line, have less than an associate's degree, and are neither working nor in school.

Schwartz, Amy, Jacob Leos-Urbel, and Matthew Wiswall. 2015. *Making Summer Matter: The Impact of Youth Employment on Academic Performance.* Cambridge, MA: National Bureau of Economic Research. http://www.nber.org/papers/w21470.pdf.

> The New York Summer Youth Employment Program (SYEP) allocates slots for high demand summer jobs to youth aged 14 to 24 through a random lottery system. While prior research has indicated that adolescent summer employment decreases violence and crime, improves financial well-being later in life, and fosters noncognitive skills, such as time-management and confidence, this paper narrowly examines the correlation between participation in SYEP and improved academic achievement. The authors find a strong correlation between participation in SYEP and improved academic outcomes, particularly for students who have participated in SYEP multiple times.

Steuerle, Eugene, Signe-Mary McKernan, Caroline Ratcliffe, and Sisi Zhang. 2013. *Lost Generations? Wealth Building among Young Americans.* Washington, DC: Urban Institute. https://www.urban.org/sites/default/files/publication/23401/412766-lost-generations-wealth-building-among-young-americans.pdf.

> As a society accumulates wealth, each generation of children is typically wealthier than their parents' generation at any given age. This is no longer the case. Today, young Americans—based on their share of private wealth and the student and government debt with which they are being saddled—are less likely to be wealthier than older generations. If this trend continues, today's young people will be more dependent, especially as they retire, on government safety net programs that are becoming less capable of providing support.

Sum, Andrew, et al. 2010. *Vanishing Work among U.S. Teens, 2000–2010: What a Difference a Decade Makes!* Boston: Center for Labor Market Studies, Northeastern University. https://repository.library.northeastern.edu/downloads/neu:376342?datastream_id=content.

This paper describes the changing labor market fate of teens by analyzing the percentage of teens employed each year from 2000 to 2010 in the early summer month of June, the month that the teen labor force would normally expand substantially as the nation's high schools and colleges let students out for summer. Based on the data, Andrew Sum concludes that the ability of teens (aged 16 to 19) to obtain employment during the summer considerably deteriorated over the decade—especially for younger, lower income, and minority teens. By June 2010, the teen employment rate had fallen to 28.6 percent, nearly 23 percentage points below the teen employment rate in 2000 and the first time in post–World War II history that the June rate had fallen below 30 percent. Sum maintains that comparing these numbers to the labor market fate of older adults during this same time period reveals a massive shift in the age structure of the nation's employment rates. He concludes by identifying the long-term negative consequences of this rise in teen joblessness not only for the youth themselves but also for their families, communities, and the nation as a whole.

Sum, Andrew, et al. 2014. *The Plummeting Labor Market Fortune of Teens and Young Adults.* Washington, DC: Metropolitan Policy Program Brookings Institution. https://www.brookings.edu/wp-content/uploads/2014/03/Youth_Workforce_Report_FINAL-2.pdf.

Andrew Sum et al. find that while American workers in general fared poorly during the first decade of the 20th century, which included the Great Recession and its aftermath, teens and young adults were among those most adversely affected in terms of unemployment, labor force underutilization, and year-round joblessness. Sum et al. examine the demographics behind different outcomes in the labor market and conclude that education and previous work experience were strongly correlated with better employment prospects. They contend that policy and program efforts to reduce youth unemployment and labor force underutilization should focus on the following priorities: incorporating more work-based learning into education and training, creating tighter linkages between secondary and postsecondary education, ensuring that training meets regional market needs; expanding the Earned Income Tax Credit; and facilitating the transition of young people into the labor market through enhanced career counseling, mentoring, occupational and work-readiness skills development, and the creation of short-term subsidized jobs.

Symonds, William C., Robert Schwartz, and Ronald F. Ferguson. 2011. *Pathways to Prosperity: Meeting the Challenge of Preparing Young Americans for the 21st Century.* Cambridge, MA: Pathways to Prosperity Project, Harvard University Graduate School of Education. https://www.gse.harvard .edu/sites/default/files//documents/Pathways_to_Prosperity_ Feb2011-1.pdf.

According to the authors of this study, the American education system, once effective at equipping youth to transition into prosperous and productive adulthood, is now badly broken. Growing evidence suggests that many young people are entering adulthood lacking the market-able skills and work ethic necessary to achieve the American Dream, which rests on the promise of economic opportunity and a middle-class lifestyle for those willing to work for it.

This skills gap, according to the authors, is largely attributable to the fact that in the 21st century—due in part to a decrease in manufacturing—job growth in America has been generated by positions that require at least some postsecondary education. Consequently, those who have dropped out of high school or have only a high school degree have fallen out of the middle class, while those with advanced degrees have moved up the income scale.

Although it is clear that in the 21st century, education beyond high school is often necessary to achieve middle-class status, the authors point out that it is a mistake to view a four-year degree—which continues to be unattainable by many disadvantaged youth—as the only pathway to a rewarding and lucrative career. On the contrary, the authors draw attention to several burgeoning and expanding industries in which young people who earn an associate's degree or complete an occupational certificate program may actually earn more than those who complete a college degree.

As traditional employment opportunities for young people continue to evaporate, the authors emphasize the need to refocus secondary education to equip a larger percentage of young people with occupationally relevant skills and credentials. One of the best ways to achieve this goal, they contend, would be to develop an American strategy of vocational training based on the European model of engaging educators and employers in a collaborative approach to work and learning so that learning is contextual and applied.

United States Government Accountability Office (GAO). 2008. "Disconnected Youth: Federal Action Could Address Some of the Challenges Faced by Local Programs That Reconnect Youth to Education and Employment." Report to the Chairman, Committee on Education and Labor,

House of Representatives. https://www.gao.gov/new.items/
d08313.pdf.

This report summarizes a GAO review of federal programs
and grants designed to help community-based organizations, charter schools, and residential facilities serve disconnected youth at the local level with the goal of putting
them on the path to self-sufficiency through education
and/or employment. The report summarizes the key elements of success and the core challenges organizations
experience in achieving this goal.

Veddar, Richard, Christopher Denhart, and Jonathan
Robe. 2013. *Why Are Recent College Graduates Under-
employed?: University Enrollments and Labor-Market Realities.*
Washington, DC: Center for College Affordability and
Productivity. https://files.eric.ed.gov/fulltext/ED539373
.pdf.

With common frequency, political leaders, educators, and industry leaders emphasize the importance of
increasing the proportion of American adults with a college degree based on the belief that expanding access to
college education is the most reliable way to ensure a
growing, competitive economy and high levels of intergenerational income mobility. Such advocates of higher
education point to a plethora of studies and data from
the Bureau of Labor demonstrating significant earning
premiums and greater job security associated with the
attainment of a college degree. Thus, the argument is
that the financial gains resulting from acquisition of a
college degree far outweigh the large sums of money
used to finance that degree.

The authors of this study, in contrast, challenge the effi-
cacy of encouraging more and more students to attend
college. They argue that while claims of increased earning and employment potential associated with a college
degree do have some merit, they do not tell the full story.

The data associating higher levels of income and employment opportunity with a college degree is problematic in that it is based on an examination of the entire college graduate population, many of whom graduated 30 or more years ago. Furthermore, such data fails to distinguish between earning potential based on the prestige of the degree program and university and does not account for how the cognitive skills of individuals may contribute to better employment and earning rates. Although many graduates over time have reaped substantial economic benefits from higher education, a large percentage of recent college graduates do not receive a good financial return on their investment and end up unemployed, underemployed, or in jobs unrelated to their skills or education level. The authors conclude that a flawed perception of the economic value of a college education is leading to an overinvestment in higher education and a growing disconnect between employer needs and the volume and nature of college training of students. Consequently, the growth of supply of college-educated labor is exceeding the growth of demand for such labor in the marketplace.

Wald, Michael, and Tia Martinez. 2003. *Connected by 25: Improving the Life Chances of the Country's Most Vulnerable 14–24 Year Olds*. William and Flora Hewlett Foundation Working Paper. https://www-cdn.law.stanford.edu/wp-content/uploads/2015/07/Wald-and-Martinez-Connected-by-251.pdf.

In this report, Michael Wald and Tia Martinez contend that the process of adult disconnection from the labor force begins in the early teens. While a majority of youth have support networks—in the form of family, friends, and community—that provide guidance and support, most disconnected youth, in contrast, experience extremely limited support as they attempt to navigate the difficult transition into adulthood. Instead of designing programs to serve the general population of adolescents or unemployed youth, Wald and Martinez argue that alternative support systems should be developed for teens (aged 14 to 17) and young adults (aged 18 to 24) who are at the highest risk of long-term disconnection and are least likely to transition successfully into adulthood by age 25. Such youth tend to fall into one or more of the following groups: youth who have not completed high school, youth who are deeply involved in the juvenile justice system, young unmarried mothers, and adolescents who experience foster placement.

Zweig, Janine M. 2003. *Vulnerable Youth: Identifying Their Need for Alternative Educational Settings.* Washington, DC: Urban Institute. https://www.urban.org/sites/default /files/publication/59366/410828-Vulnerable-Youth- Identifying-their-Need-for-Alternative-Educational-Settings .PDF.

Traditionally, alternative education options were used to remove youth who presented disciplinary problems or who were unable to meet standards set by testing environments. This paper examines the extent to which alternative education schools and programs can meet the needs of and reconnect those youth who fail to achieve developmental goals during adolescence and who eventually become disconnected from mainstream institutions and systems—including education and the marketplace. Author Janine Zweig specifically examines the characteristics and risks factors of youth facing disconnection and estimates the number of students who are currently being served or who could potentially benefit from alternative education schools and programs.

Nonprint Sources

Generation Jobless. 2017. Directed by Sharon Bartlett. Santa Monica, CA: Kinonation. DVD.

> This documentary film set in Canada presents evidence that the days are over in which a university degree provided a sure path to a good job, good pay, and a comfortable life. Instead, the film contends that institutions of higher learning are failing to keep up with the transitioning job market of the 21st century and are inadequately preparing young graduates for the world of work. Consequently, many graduates leave college mired in debt only to end up overeducated and underemployed. The film further explores how the failure of the current generation to gain a strong toehold in the economy has widespread economic implications that will affect older generations as well.

Herold, Cameron. 2010. *Let's Raise Kids to Be Entrepreneurs*. TED Video, 21:24. https://www.ted.com/talks/cameron_herold_let_s_raise_kids_to_be_entrepreneurs.

> In this TED talk, Cameron Herold—himself an entrepreneur since childhood—highlights entrepreneurs' invaluable contribution to society and makes the case for parenting and education that promote an entrepreneurial spirit and help young, would-be entrepreneurs flourish.

Langer, Arthur. July 23, 2014. Creating Employment Opportunities for Underserved Youth. TEDxTeachersCollege. https://www.youtube.com/watch?v=2DwJFY34_yY.

> This independently produced TEDx talk features Dr. Arthur Langer, founder and chairman of Workforce Opportunity Services (WOS), an organization that seeks to improve opportunities for inner-city and rural low-income individuals to climb the ladder of success. In this talk, Dr. Langer explores the question of how corporations, social organizations, and universities can

collaborate to create systemic, lasting change for under-served populations.

Lemonade Stories. 2004. Directed by Mary Mazzio. Babson Park, MA: 50 Eggs Films. DVD.

This documentary film examines the question of whether entrepreneurs are born or made by focusing on the relationship between extraordinary entrepreneurs and their mothers. Featuring the stories of Richard Branson (founder of the Virgin Group), Russell Simmons (founder of Def Jam), Arthur Blank (founder of Home Depot), Kay Koplovitz (founder of USA Network) and others, the film chronicles how mothers contribute to the entrepreneurial spirit of their sons and daughters.

Locked Out: A Mississippi Success Story. 2014. Directed by Sean W. Malone. Honest Enterprise.

This documentary film chronicles the struggles of Melony Armstrong, who fought to become the first professional African hair braider in Mississippi and to remove arbitrary regulations that stood in the way of other aspiring entrepreneurs seeking to enter the profession. After learning how to braid hair, Armstrong sought to start using her skills to earn a living, but when she tried to open the first professional hair-braiding salon in Mississippi, she was blocked by the Mississippi State Board of Cosmetology (MSBC). The MSBC demanded that Armstrong first obtain a cosmetology license costing nearly $10,000 and attend years of board-approved training, none of which had to do with hair braiding. Although Armstrong did not have the means to meet these onerous requirements, she did not give up. Instead she engaged in a legal battle against the state restrictions, which eventually sparked statewide reform and set a precedent for several other states to remove their hair-braiding licensing requirements. Armstrong not only offered new employment opportunities by establishing her own successful business, she also opened the door to hundreds of other aspiring entrepreneurs seeking to enter the hair-braiding business.

Ten9eight: Shoot for the Moon. Directed by Mary Mazzio. Babson Park, MA: 50 Eggs Films. DVD.
This documentary film tells the inspirational stories of several remarkably resilient inner-city teens from all over the country as they compete in an annual business plan competition run by the Network for Teaching Entrepreneurship (NFTE).

7   Chronology

The following is a chronological list of some of the major events impacting youth employment in America and the enactment of key governmental policies and actions intended to help alleviate the crisis of youth unemployment and disconnection in the United States.

1911   Wisconsin institutes the country's first registered apprenticeship system, establishing standards for apprenticeships and safeguards for both the apprentices and employers. Prior to this, law apprenticeships were unregulated in the United States. The law, which placed apprenticeships under the jurisdiction of an industrial commission, became a model for other states and for the federal government to eventually develop their own systems.

1917   The Smith-Hughes Act, formally titled the National Vocational Education Act, authorizes federal aid to the states for the purpose of promoting precollegiate vocational education in agriculture, the industrial trades, and home economics. One of the first federal grant-in-aid programs, the act

New York City high school students attend a HirePower Mock Interview Workshop presented by UBS in partnership with Laureus USA on June 6, 2018. UBS hosted a volunteer day in their offices, holding mock interviews with inner-city high school students to provide them with feedback and guidance. Such guidance is particularly valuable for inner-city youth who are less likely than their peers from more affluent backgrounds to have access to professional advisers. (Jeff Zelevansky/Getty Images for Laureus)

authorizes the creation of the Federal Board of Vocational Education to oversee the distribution of funds and approve states' plans. Critics have pointed out that training programs funded under the law often lagged behind the actual needs of industry. Also, because most vocational education programs were established within existing public schools that had previously provided a common curriculum for all students, they unintentionally led to the practice of sorting students into tracks. This practice tended to reinforce the differential treatment of students based on class and race, with low-income and minority students more frequently relegated to the lesser quality vocational track rather than the college-bound academic track. In the 1980s, as states began increasing the number of courses required for graduation in core academic areas, what is now referred to as career and technical education or CTE began a several decades-long decline. The past decade, however, witnessed a resurgence of interest in CTE and renewed efforts to establish high-quality options both within existing schools and as separate institutions.

1933   President Franklin D. Roosevelt launches the Civilian Conservation Corps, as a temporary work relief program for young men between the ages of 18 and 25. Participants lived in camps administered by the army and worked on construction crews managed by the Department of Interior. Although it was discontinued in 1942, it modeled many of the methods and strategies that were later incorporated in Job Corps and national service programs.

1937   In response to a concerted effort by national employer and labor organizations, educators, and government officials to establish a national, uniform apprenticeship system, Congress passes the National Apprenticeship Act (also known as the Fitzgerald Act). The act established a national advisory committee to issue regulations establishing minimum standards for apprenticeship programs and to certify training under such programs. Initially, federally approved apprenticeships were offered only in manual labor occupations like construction, but following World War II the number of registered programs expanded to include programs for firefighters and medical technicians. Over the past several decades, the number of registered apprenticeship opportunities has significantly increased in a wide variety of professional fields.

1938   President Roosevelt signs the Fair Labor Standards Act of 1938 establishing a federal minimum-wage, overtime pay requirements, and several provisions regulating age, hour, and occupational standards for youth. The law continues to be the chief federal statute for defining the conditions under which youth, below the age of 18, may be employed.

1962   President John F. Kennedy signs the Manpower Development and Training Act empowering the Department of Labor to fund training opportunities for the unemployed and underemployed.

1963   President Kennedy calls on Congress to increase employment opportunities for the nation's youth. In response, Congress amends the Manpower Development and Training Act to provide additional assistance for youth and greatly expands the percentage of funding that can be used to provide job training to youth under the age of 22.

1964   President Lyndon B. Johnson declares a "War on Poverty" in his State of the Union Address, marking the beginning of coordinated federal efforts to improve the labor market prospects of low-income youth.

Congress passes the Economic Opportunity Act that funds a variety of job training and educational service programs, including Job Corps and Volunteers in Service to America (VISTA), for low-income youth.

1973   Congress approves the Comprehensive Employment and Training Act (CETA) that authorizes a sizable investment in employment and training for low-income youth, mainly by subsidizing the wages of young people working for participating employers in the public sector. The act additionally authorizes the Summer Program for Economically Disadvantaged Youth (SPEDY) that provided funds to subsidize employers who hire local low-income youth, ages 14 through 21, during the summer months as assistants in hospitals, libraries, community service organizations, schools, and other settings.

1980s   The upward trajectory of youth participation in the labor force, employment, and wages following World War II begins a several decade decline in the wake of a rapid reduction in manufacturing accompanied by a wave of technological change.

1982   Based on concerns that local governments and nonprofits were using the publicly subsidized employment and training funds under the Comprehensive Employment and Training Act to replace their own efforts at job creation and that public sector jobs were replacing private sector employment opportunities, Congress passes the Job Training Partnership Act of 1982. The act gives states and localities greater oversight and flexibility to design and implement their own employment and training strategies.

1983   President Ronald Reagan calls on Congress to establish a "subminimum" wage for teenagers to incentivize firms to hire young, inexperienced workers. Congress did not act on this proposal until the Clinton administration.

1990   The National and Community Service Act of 1990 creates the Commission on National and Community Service and authorizes the allocation of federal funding to state and local service corps.

1993   The National and Community Service Act of 1993 merges Volunteers in Service to America (VISTA) with the newly created AmeriCorps.

Congress approves legislation authorizing the Department of Defense, National Guard Bureau to establish and oversee the National Guard Youth ChalleNGe Corps, a residential, quasi-military program for 16- to 18-year-olds who have dropped out of high school or not progressing in a traditional high school setting and who are either unemployed or underemployed. Today, the program serves thousands of youth annually at 40 sites in 29 states, the District of Columbia, and Puerto Rico. The program has been recognized as one of the country's most effective and cost-efficient programs for targeting youth who are at a greatest risk for substance abuse, teen pregnancy, delinquency, and criminal activity.

1994   Recognizing the weak career link in U.S. high schools, Congress passes the School to Work Opportunities Act designed to promote stronger ties between secondary and postsecondary learning and the workplace and to increase student engagement and success in school by investing in career-oriented programs in the nation's high schools. The act provides federal grants for activities such as job shadowing, mentoring, internships, apprenticeships, and so on. The act has not been renewed since 2001.

1996   President Clinton signs into law amendments to the Fair Labor Standards Act that permitted employers to pay a youth minimum-wage not less than $4.25 an hour to employees who are under the age of 20 for the first 90 days of employment. This federal allowance for a temporary youth minimum-wage has had a minimal effect, however, because most states and localities have failed to adopt a similar provision in their labor codes that means that state and local adult minimum-wages supersede the federal law.

1998   Congress passes the Workforce Investment Act of 1998 authorizing funding for several major federal youth employment and job-training programs including the Youth Activities program, Job Corps, Youth Build, and Reentry Employment Opportunities Program. The act ends federal funding to stand-alone summer programs in favor of these more comprehensive, year-round services.

2001   The unprecedented period of economic growth in the 1990s comes to an end with the collapse of the speculative dot-com bubble, a decline in business investments, and the September 11 attacks, leading to a brief eight-month recession. In spite of economic growth following the recession, the employment-to-population ratio of teenagers and young adults continues to steadily erode.

2007   Prior to the housing market and financial crash, the youth labor force participation rate falls to 59.4 percent, down from 68.8 percent in 2000.

In response to a shortage of skilled workers, South Carolina adopts a $1,000 business tax credit per apprentice for up to four years to help offset the costs of maintaining apprenticeship opportunities and simultaneously sponsors the creation of Apprenticeship Carolina, one of the largest and fastest-growing apprenticeship programs in the country. The program, which involves a partnership between private and public employers in the state and the 16 technical colleges in the South Carolina Technical College System, provides a model for other states.

The Great Recession begins in December following the subprime mortgage crisis and the collapse of the U.S. housing market.

2008   Falling housing-related assets contribute to a global financial crisis and the failure or collapse of many of the U.S. largest financial institutions, as well as a bankruptcy crisis in the automobile industry. Congress approves an unprecedented $700 billion bank bailout and a nearly $800 billion economic stimulus package that incorporates a combination of government spending and tax cuts. The nation enters into a prolonged economic downturn.

2009   The Great Recession officially ends in June, but the economy continues to struggle as the country undergoes further job losses and anemic growth.

In July, the number of youth participating in the labor force reaches the lowest summer time rate since July 1955, and the number of young people employed reaches the lowest July rate on record since data recording began in 1948.

Congress passes another fiscal stimulus bill, the American Reinvestment and Recovery Act. Although focused mostly on assistance to older workers, the stimulus package directs $1.2 billion to the states for employment and training of youth and strongly encourages the states to use some of the money to support summer jobs programs. The stimulus funds were the first federal funds allocated for summer youth employment since the enactment of Workforce Investment Act of 1998 ended federal funding to stand-alone summer programs in favor of more comprehensive, year-round services.

President Obama signs the Edward M. Kennedy Serve America Act that authorizes more than triple the available national service opportunities in the areas of educational outcomes, conservation, public health, and economic opportunity.

2010 The unemployment rate for youth aged 16 to 24 soars to levels previously unseen, peaking at a record high of 19.6 percent in April.

2011 Recovery from the Great Recession officially begins. Youth unemployment remains elevated around 18 percent.

2013 The Corporation for National and Community Service, which oversees AmericaCorps, announces the launch of the President's Task Force on Expanding National Service. The task force leads to the creation of several collaborative programs between federal agencies and the private sector to provide service opportunities for vulnerable youth. One of these programs, Youth Opportunity AmeriCorps, established in conjunction with the Justice Department's Office of Juvenile Justice and Delinquency Prevention, creates opportunities for formerly incarcerated youth to reconnect to society by enrolling in direct service activities throughout the nation. Another, ServiceWorks, is a collaborative program sponsored by AmeriCorps, the Citi Foundation, and the international nonprofit Points of Light designed to help low-income youth in ten major cities across the United States develop the skills they need to prepare for college and careers while engaging in service. Participants first receive training courses taught by field professionals in 21st-century leadership and workplace skills. Then, under the guidance of a mentor, they participate in and lead volunteer service projects. Additional partnerships were established with the U.S. Forest Service and U.S. Department of Transportation to provide opportunities for youth and veterans to participate in protecting and restoring the nation's forest and grasslands or in improving state and regional transportation.

2014   Congress reauthorizes and expands the Workforce Investment Act. The law is retitled the Workforce Innovation and Opportunity Act (WIOA). Under the act, Congress authorizes and appropriates funds for three job training and employment services for youth: the Youth Workforce Investment Activities Program, Job Corps, and YouthBuild.

2015   President Obama announces the launch of a White House–sponsored College Scorecard, which includes published information on individual colleges based on a range of variables including the number of low-income students enrolled, student debt levels, graduation rates, and average graduate earnings.

The nation begins to experience significant growth in domestic production and in the number of available payroll jobs, yet improvement in the youth unemployment rate continues to lag, remaining twice as high as the national average.

2016   The U.S. Department of Labor grants $21 million worth of funds authorized under the Workforce Innovation and Opportunity Act of 2014 to 11 communities, including Detroit, Indianapolis, and Philadelphia among others, through its "Summer Jobs and Beyond" program.

2017   President Donald Trump signs an executive order calling for the expansion of available apprenticeships under the Department of Labor's Registered Apprenticeship Program.

The order also shifts the role of developing and issuing guidelines for government-funded apprenticeship programs from the Department of Labor to private entities—such as companies, labor unions, and industry groups—pending Department of Labor approval.

The July youth unemployment rate is 9.6 percent, which is 1.9 percentage points lower than the previous July and the lowest summer youth unemployment rate since July 2000.

The U.S. economy completes its eighth year of expansion following the Great Recession, and by the end of the year, the general unemployment rate and the youth unemployment rate hit a 17-year low. The youth labor force participation rate, however, remains at a low of 55 percent.

Glossary

Absolute mobility: A measure of whether the overall standard of living in a society has increased. Occurs when the members of each class in a particular generation are better off and enjoy a higher standard of living, on average, than their counterparts in the previous generation. Absolute mobility generally results from overall economic growth.

Academization: Refers to the growing emphasis on the value of university education and the corresponding societal pressure young people face to pursue "theoretically oriented" academic degrees rather than vocational training.

Active labor market policies: Government intervention in the labor market designed to help the unemployed find work.

Apprenticeships: A method of preparing workers to master occupational skills by allowing them to receive paid training through supervised work-based learning and instruction.

Associate's degree: An undergraduate academic degree generally awarded after a two-year course of study at a community or junior college.

Bachelor's degree: A degree granted to a student from a college or university, usually requiring at least four years (or equivalent) of full-time college-level study.

Career and Technical Education (CTE):   A term applied to schools and educational programs that offer both academic and career-oriented courses and provide students with the opportunity to gain work experience through internships, job shadowing, and other forms of on-the-job training.

Career pathways: Structured sets of credentials attained by taking postsecondary courses while participating in related work experiences that allow progression to high-paying careers over time.

Civilian labor force: The sum of individuals 16 or older among the civilian population who are either employed or unemployed.

Civilian population: The sum of individuals 16 or older who are not in the armed services or other institutions such as prisons, mental hospitals, or nursing homes.

Community colleges: Two-year, generally nonresidential open access government-supported schools, sometimes called junior colleges. Community colleges offer affordable postsecondary education courses to people who live in a particular area that can be utilized to obtain a two-year associate's degree, as a pathway to a four-year degree, or for workforce development and skills training.

Cooperative education programs: An evaluated career education program in which participants alternate between periods of academic coursework and periods of full-time off-campus work.

Disconnected youth: Noninstitutionalized youth, between the ages of 16 to 24, who have been absent from the labor force for a substantial period and are not participating in education or training.

Employment-to-population ratio: The proportion of noninstitutionalized individuals who are currently employed.

Entrepreneurship: The ability to identify an opportunity to create value by developing an innovative product, devising a new business model, or meeting a human need and the willingness to take calculated risks to transform that vision into reality.

Gainful employment: An employment situation in which an individual is steadily employed and receives consistent payment for work.

Generation Z (Gen. Z):   The generation that follows and by some standards overlaps with the millennial generation. Typically includes individuals born between the late 1990s and the early 2000s.

Great Recession: The collapse of housing and financial systems and subsequent economic downturn that occurred during the latter part of the first decade of the 2000s.

Hidden unemployed: Those who want to work but have become discouraged and given up searching for employment.

Intergenerational mobility: The degree to which children move up or down the income spectrum or change social status relative to their parents' generation.

Internship: The position of a student or trainee who works for a limited period of time, sometimes without pay, for a business, nonprofit organization, or government entity with the intention of gaining relevant skills and practical experience in an occupation or profession.

Joblessness: Refers to anyone who is not working. It is not the same as unemployment that includes only those who are not working but who are actively looking for work.

Job-training programs: Programs designed to promote skill development or workplace readiness and to increase individuals' earning and employment potential.

Labor force participation rate (LFPR):   The percentage of those in the civilian noninstitutional population who are working or actively looking for work relative to the population from which they are drawn.

Labor force under-utilization: A measure designed to demonstrate problems in employment that encompasses a broader range of individuals than the unemployment rate alone. It includes the officially unemployed (those who don't have a job but are actively seeking work); the hidden unemployed (those who desire employment but are not actively looking for work);

and the underemployed (those who are working part time but desire and are able to work full time).

Mal-employment rate: A measure of the number of workers who are underemployed or who are working in jobs below their skill capacity or level of training and education.

Marginally attached workers: Those who desire employment but have recently given up searching for work.

Millennials: The generation to reach adulthood in the early 21st century. The term usually includes individuals born after 1980 and before 2000.

Minimum-wage: The minimum amount of compensation an employer is required by law to pay each employee for a defined time period.

National service programs: Federally established programs designed to serve the community, while providing experience and training to youth participants. These programs generally consist in full-time, year-long public service positions—financed by public and private resources—that provide participants a minimal stipend and health care and child care benefits. Several national service programs additionally offer financial awards to participants who complete a term of service that can be used to finance higher education, career training, or student loans.

NEETs (neither employed nor in education or training):   Individuals who are neither working nor in school. They are sometimes referred to as "disconnected" or "detached" youth.

Occupational certificate: A formal award certifying that an individual has satisfactorily completed a postsecondary education program related to a specific field or has demonstrated competent knowledge, experience, and skills to perform a specific job. Sometimes called a professional or technical certificate. Unlike licensing, a system of certification allows anyone to perform a service for pay, but only those who earned certification can claim the certified title.

Occupational licensing: The process by which governments establish qualifications to practice a trade or profession, so that only those who have met the qualifications are legally permitted to receive pay or wages for engaging in work related to the trade or profession.

Opportunity youth: Another term used to describe disconnected youth. It includes individuals between the ages of 16 and 24 who are struggling to develop into productive, independent adults because they are neither accumulating human capital through education nor accumulating market skills by working.

Overeducation/over-skilling: Occurs when an individual's skills or education is not being used to their full potential.

Pre-apprenticeships: Workforce development programs that teach participants of all ages, including low-income high school youth, the skills they need to qualify for and succeed in an apprenticeship program.

Primary education: Also called elementary education. Refers to the first years of compulsory education between kindergarten and eighth grade.

Prime working age: The age of adults considered to be in their prime working years (aged 25 to 54).

Private for-profit college: Higher education institutions operated by private, profit-seeking businesses. Funded primarily by tuition and government-funded student aid, for-profit colleges generally offer more flexible degree programs that allow students to complete programs remotely online or on evenings and weekends.

Private nonprofit college: Privately controlled and operated colleges—including those affiliated with religious organizations—usually governed by a Board of Trustees and supported by endowments, tuition, government funds, and donations. Any income beyond what is required for employee compensation and operational and administrative expenses is reinvested into college operations, such as curriculum, instruction, or other improvements.

Public college or institution: A state-led college or institution primarily funded by public tax revenue that may also rely on tuition or donor support.

Recession: A period of at least six months of negative economic growth as measured by a country's gross domestic product.

Registered apprenticeships: Apprenticeship programs that have been certified by the Department of Labor's Office of Apprenticeship or by a State Apprenticeship Agency as meeting specified standards.

Relative mobility: Refers to a dynamic in which individuals move up or down the social hierarchy in comparison to the socioeconomic position of their parents.

Secondary education: Commonly referred to as high school. Includes 9th through 12th grades in the United States.

Self-employed workers: Workers who work as independent contractors or operate their own businesses rather than working for an employer.

Social capital: An individual's network of relationships and level of social connectedness—includes informal ties to relatives, friends, and neighbors as well as formal ties to civic associations, volunteer or professional organizations, religious institutions, and so on. These connections and relationship networks can help individuals successfully navigate society and its institutions.

Spatial mismatch: A phenomenon that occurs when potential employees live in areas that are geographically isolated from job opportunities.

Undereducated/Under-skilled workers: Workers who do not have sufficient education or skills for the jobs available on the labor market.

Underemployed: Those who are employed part time but desire and are able to work full time.

Unemployed: Refers to individuals who are not employed but who are actively seeking employment by sending out resumes, filling out applications, interviewing for positions, or otherwise engaging in job search activities.

Unemployment rate: The share of those currently in the labor force who are without employment.

Value-added measures: A method of ranking colleges and universities that accounts for student backgrounds and characteristics prior to college—such as family income, academic preparation, and race and ethnicity—in an attempt to predict the distinct contributions of college to short and long-term student employment and income outcomes.

Vocational education and training (VET): Accredited training in job related or technical skills.

Youth: The transition period from the dependence of childhood to the independence of adulthood. In reference to employment in the United States, the term generally encompasses individuals between the ages of 16 and 24.

Youth-to-adult unemployment ratio: The number of unemployed 16- to 24-year-olds divided by the number of unemployed 25- to 74-year-olds. It is meant to show the differential between youth and adult employment.

absolute mobility, 281
academization, 281
Accelerated Learning
    Program (ALP), 64
Affordable Care Act (ACA),
    97, 110, 112, 114
Alaska Airlines, 167
Alice Lloyd College, 179
American Association
    of Colleges and
    Universities, 67
American dream, 28, 125,
    240, 261
American Enterprise
    Institute, 110, 152,
    237, 238
American Recovery and
    Reinvestment Act, 206
American Time Use Survey,
    43, 106, 218
America's Public Media
    Marketplace, 52, 249
Anne E. Casey Foundation,
    159, 173
apprenticeship, 37, 70–74,
    87, 97, 98, 146–147,

148–152, 167, 171,
    195, 225–232, 243,
    254–255, 257, 271,
    272–273, 275–281,
    285, 286
Apprenticeship Carolina,
    74, 148
Armstrong, Melony,
    82–83, 267
associate's degree, 53, 69, 243
AT&T Aspire, 152–153
automation, 21, 160, 196

bachelor's degree, 10, 11, 23,
    48, 52, 67, 76, 77, 86,
    125, 178, 249, 281
Bailey, John P., 152
Baylor University Hankamer
    School of Business, 170
Berea College, 179
Bing Wong Academy, 135
Black Male Initiative, 153
Blackburn College, 179
Blank, Arthur, 267
Bloomberg Philanthropies,
    148